PRAISE FOR 7

MW00679304

"This could be the best
can't be 'dummies.' The biggest part of managing today is dealing
with change, and this book will make you lots smarter."
— Bob Nelson, author
1001 Ways to Reward Employees, and
co-author, *Managing for Dummies*

"*Thriving on Change* presents a variety of terrific ways that
organizations can thrive and prosper on constant change.
— Michael Michalko, author
*Thinkertoys (A Handbook of Business Creativity for the
'90s)* and *ThinkPak(A Brainstorming Card Deck*

"This engaging book is a survival manual for organizational
change. It is filled with spellbinding examples and practical ideas.
Employees, managers, and top executives will learn how to overcome their fears about change, manage transitions creatively, and
ensure their own and their organizations' continued vitality."
— Manuel London, Professor and Director, Center for
Human Resource Management, SUNY at Stony Brook,
author, *Change Agents: New Roles and Innovation
Strategies for Human Resource Professionals*

"A great resource for information necessary to planning your
future....a superb job of bringing things into focus."
— Kevin McGuinness, World Future Society

"Laced with helpful and sometimes humorous insights and
models into a topic we can't know too much about—*change*."
— John Schuster,
co-author, *The Power of Open Book Management*

"Navigating through the challenges of change is not a simple
task. In *Thriving on Change*, a collection of practical readings has
been assembled that provides a wealth of ideas and 'real-world'
applications for not only surviving, but thriving through changes
required to prepare for the 21st Century."
— Richard Y. Chang,
author, *Mastering Change Management*

"The only book that I have seen that addresses change as the
cultural norm of corporate life—which is, indeed, 'the new reality.'
This book provides an invaluable service in showing us how to live
with change, *like it,* and *thrive on it!*"
— Hal W. Hendrick, Past President,
Human Factors and Ergonomics Society

"The various contributors to this enlightening book do a wonderful job of delivering the message that change must be understood and managed from multiple perspectives. It is encouraging to find such an in-depth investigation of change and how it can be dealt with for personal and organizational advantage."
— Andrew J. DuBrin, Professor of Management, Rochester
Institute of Technology, author (most recent book),
10-Minute Guide to Effective Leadership

"*Thriving on Change* is for the young at heart. Our first change-producing message at Avis was "We want to become the fastest-growing company with the highest profit margins in the business of renting and leasing vehicles without drivers." A mouthful: Agreed. But we never wrote it, we all just kept saying it everywhere we went until it happened. To us, change always looked like a gift, not a threat. For an organization to thrive on change, it must learn to love it, not fear it or hate it. It must truly look for change eagerly, not as an obstacle but as an unfailing introduction to the next opportunity. Once an organization learns how to love change, the old geezers seem to leap into early retirement."
— Robert Townsend, author, *Up the Organization* and
The B² Chronicles

"These days, change is more like a cat than a dog. You can't manage or control change any more than you can get your cat to sit, roll over, or fetch the morning paper. But you can stay limber and sleek and flexible, always ready to land on your feet. *Thriving on Change* is one cat-quick book!"
— Louis Patler, president, The B.I.T. Group,
co-author of *If It Ain't Broke-BREAK IT*

"Timely! Just what organizations need today to Thrive on Change."
— Mary Robinson Reynolds, author, *You Are A Success!*

"Successful organizations in the 21st Century will be those which effectively deal with continual and rapid change. *Thriving on Change* is timely and relevant for today's organizations which are creating their vision of excellence for the next century."
— Dr. William H. Hendrix, Professor of Management,
Clemson University; Chairman, The 21st Century
Organizational Excellence Awards

THRIVING on CHANGE

IN ORGANIZATIONS

Featuring chapters from experts—

Phillip P. Andrews • Lance H. Arrington • Eloise Calhoun • Rick Crandall
William R. Daniels • James Feldman • Wayne A. Fogel • Pat Gill
Rick Goldberg • Jerome A. Hahn • Carl E. Huffman, Jr. • John G. Mathers
Charles Milofsky • Don Rapp • James A. Ray • Susan Stephani
William G. Stieber • James A. Tompkins

EDITED BY RICK CRANDALL

INSTITUTE FOR
ORGANIZATIONAL CHANGE

Select Press
Corte Madera, CA

The Institute for Organizational Change
The goal of the Institute is to provide information to help corporations and nonprofit organizations more effectively use change to better fulfill their missions.

Copyright 1997 by Select Press for the Institute for Organizational Change
All rights reserved. No part of this publication my be reproduced, distributed, or transmitted in any form or by any means, including photocopying, recording, or other electronic or mechanical methods, without the prior written permission of the publisher, except in the case of brief quotations embodied in critical reviews and certain other non-commercial uses permitted by copyright law. For permission requests, write to the publisher, addressed "Attention: Permissions Coordinator," at the address below.

Select Press
PO Box 37
Corte Madera, CA 94976-0037
(415) 924-1612

Thriving on Change/Rick Crandall (editor)

ISBN 0-9644294-5-4

Printed in the United States of America
10 9 8 7 6 5 4 3 2 1

Contents

PREFACE

Every change brings tremendous opportunities. You need to use the constant changes around us to your advantage!

You can't wait for change to "be over." You need to learn to *thrive on constant change.*

The chapters in this book cover a variety of approaches to creating change, working with change, and thriving on it. Yet they are only the proverbial tip of the iceberg. As *you* work with change, you'll find your own ways to thrive. The authors would love to hear your success story.

—Rick Crandall, PhD, Editor

Part One
CHANGE: THE NEW REALITY

Chapter 1
HARNESSING THE ENERGY OF CHANGE
James A. Tompkins

Chapter 2
CHANGE—THE NEW COMPETITIVE WEAPON
Rick Goldberg

Chapter 3
MASTERING CHANGE
Corporate Strategies for the New Millennium
James A. Ray

Chapter 1

HARNESSING THE ENERGY OF CHANGE

James A. Tompkins

James A. Tompkins, PhD, is the president and founder of Tompkins Associates, Inc., an internationally recognized, full-service consulting firm specializing in total operations. He has helped hundreds of companies attain peak performance through improvements in workplace leadership, team-building, warehousing, logistics, manufacturing, maintenance, quality, and organizational excellence.

He is the author of 11 books, including *The Genesis Enterprise: Creating Peak-to-Peak Performance* published in 1995 by McGraw-Hill, Inc. He is also the author of more than 300 articles in industry journals. Dr. Tompkins has made more than 3,000 presentations, including keynote addresses, speeches, conference presentations, seminars, short courses, executive forums, and radio and TV interviews throughout the United States and internationally on five continents.

Dr. Tompkins is a Fellow of the Institute of Industrial Engineers and the World Academy of Productivity Science, and has received more than 100 awards including the Outstanding Industrial Engineer Award by Purdue University.

James A. Tompkins, PhD, Tompkins Associates, Inc., 2809 Millbrook Road, Raleigh, NC 27616; phone (919) 876-3667; fax (919) 872-9666.

Chapter 1

HARNESSING THE ENERGY OF CHANGE

James A. Tompkins

"If you always do what you've always done, the future will look a lot like the past."

—Unknown

This quote is true only if everything else (not just what you do) stays the same. Today, the situation is even more challenging. When the environment changes, doing what you've always done will probably result in a future even worse than the past!

ASSUMPTIONS CAN KILL YOU

Extending this thought further, one can see a paradigm that is often an invisible portion of a company's business plan: The past is a good indicator of the future. Unfortunately, for many organizations, this is not true. In most organizations today, the future is not based upon the past but rather upon the present. This radical idea can help us reevaluate our thinking about managing change.

The traditional process of managing change indicates that we used to be (past) at Point A and need to manage the process to get to Point B (future).

Realistically, with today's dynamic environment, if we pursue the management of change as presented in the top half of the figure, reaching Point B will no longer be acceptable performance. Since we are basing the future on the past instead of the present, we will always be behind. In addition, change brings discontinuities that interrupt the smooth flow of a simple line. For instance, when a new technology comes in the market, it makes projecting from the present impossible.

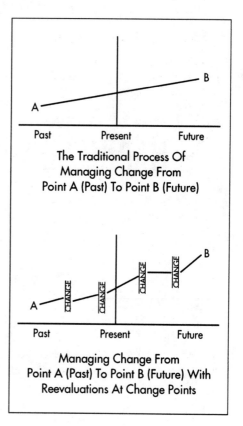

The Traditional Process Of Managing Change From Point A (Past) To Point B (Future)

Managing Change From Point A (Past) To Point B (Future) With Reevaluations At Change Points

Don't Manage Change, Use It

We must realize that the phrase "manage change" is inconsistent. In fact, I believe the phrase is an oxymoron. To manage means to control. In today's dynamic environment, do you believe any person has the ability to control change? None of us can control change, so any attempt to "manage" change will be futile.

What we need to do is not try to manage change, but rather understand how to harness the energy of change. To do this, we must understand the science of change.

Keeping His Eye On Change

What would you call a company that has a 75% market share, and a 58% gross profit margin, with net earnings that make it the most profitable company of its size in the world? The company doubles in size roughly every two years. What would you call such a company?

One label is "hyperaggressive," another is "greedy!" It matters not what label is used, what you are labeling is Intel. At its helm, the leader with his eye on change is Andy Grove.

At a time when Intel was faced with greater competition than ever from the new chip developed jointly by IBM, Motorola, and Apple Computer, how did this leader respond? By spending $1.1 billion on research and development and $2.4 billion on capital investment. At the same time, Intel developed not only the next product, but also the product after, the product after, the product after, and pursued a whole new market—consumer electronics.

When asked if they would be doing what they were doing without the threat poised on the horizon, Grove responds, "Truthfully, no. We are making gutsier moves investment-wise, pricing-wise, every way, because we've got a competitive threat. The next result is we'll get to advance to the next level of competition."

Now *that* is leadership that keeps its eyes on change and sees all that it can see.

THE SCIENCE OF CHANGE

Success today is based upon our ability to harness the energy of change. Unfortunately, many resist change because it often requires pain. By resisting change, we are subconsciously resisting success. Begin understanding the science of change by understanding the relationship between change and pain.

Change And Pain

The creation of pain to accompany change is a natural function. Pain is our body's way of telling us we are harming ourselves. In a similar way, pain is an organization's signal that it is harming itself. This organizational pain may occur in quality problems, competitiveness, customer service, turnover, etc. For your organization to prosper, you will have pain. So, the challenge is not *if* this pain occurs but *how* your organization responds. A relevant quote from W. Clement Stone provides useful insight:

> "Every negative event contains within it the seed of an equal or greater benefit."

The Opportunity In Change

The challenge is not the pain (the negative event). The challenge, and in fact the opportunity, is how we respond to this pain.

We must not resist change and flee from pain. We need to find a process to harness change and eliminate pain. This process of dealing with the causes of pain is known as peak-to-peak performance, and is described later in this chapter.

Resilience And Change

The pain of change is affected by individuals' and organizations' resilience, along with the speed of change. Resilience is an individual's or an organization's ability to absorb change; or the ability to bounce back after setbacks. (See also Chapter 11 on hardiness.)

If the speed of change is less than our resilience, we are able to deal with the pain. As a result, we are able to harness the energy of change and become successful. If the speed of change is greater than our resilience, the pain of change is too much. As a

> ## Fear Of Change, Lost Opportunities
>
> As an illustration of organizations that feared pain and had a corresponding resistance to change, consider the following attitudes that resulted in missed opportunities:
>
> - In 1876,  Western Union said, "The telephone has too many shortcomings to be seriously considered as a means of communication. This device is inherently of no value to us."
> - In 1927, Harry Warner of Warner Brothers Pictures said, "Who the hell wants to hear actors talk?"
> - In 1977, Ken Olson of Digital Equipment Company said, "There is no reason for any individual to have a computer in their home."

result, we feel stress and disorientation, and we gradually grind to a painful halt as we fail. Since we cannot control the speed of change, it is vital that we build up our resilience and the ability to manage our resilience capacity.

Individual resilience depends on our individual perceptions of our certainty and control levels. The higher our certainty of a change and the higher our control over a change, the less energy we need to allocate to a change.

This is why we all respond differently to change. Have you noticed that two individuals faced with the same exact change will react differ-

Principle-centered Leadership And Change

by Stephen R. Covey

There is really no such thing as organizational behavior, only the collective result of individual behavior. Therefore, there is no such thing as organizational change without personal change. Organizational change means collective individual change.

It is cultural change—the change of collective behavior of the individuals personally and interpersonally within the organization—which will ultimately sustain and make effective the structural change at the organization and managerial levels.

This type of change means changing not only the behaviors, but also the paradigms, attitudes, management and leadership styles, and the personal and professional relationships between people throughout the enterprise.

Inside-out Personal Change

Structural change is outside-in: Personal change must be inside-out. Long-term, sustainable organization change (structural and cultural) requires inside-out personal change. And it is changing people from within that is the challenge which makes organizational change so difficult and painful.

Once leaders realize they cannot change other people—they then establish the beginnings of significant cultural change within their organization.

ently? The person with low resilience, a high level of uncertainty, or low perceived control, is going to experience more pain and will resist change. The person with high resilience and a high level of certainty or control will deal with the pain, and harness the energy, of change.ap

The Total System

Interestingly, our personal resilience has to do with our personal lives, our careers, and our social consciousness. Our personal lives often control our resilience capacity. For example, if your personal life occupies all your energy for change, you are under major stress and you have zero capacity to deal with change in your career or on social issues. Obviously, you will not handle new changes well in your personal life, your job, or in dealing with global issues.

When things are going well in your personal life, you have the resilience to deal with political and environmental global concerns while keeping significant capacity to deal with change at work. Thus if one person has car trouble, a parking ticket, a sick child, a sore knee, a big credit card bill, and a broken garage door opener, it is not surprising that he or she resists change. This person is over-capacity and resists change in an attempt to spend as little energy as possible at work.

An interesting conclusion that must be reached here is that an organization has no choice but to be interested in the total person, as resiliency comes from the person's total life. Thus, organizations concerned with their employees' total quality of life, and promoting balance, are on target to better harness the energy of change.

Building Your Capacity

Many people overlook the fact that managing your resilience also involves raising your resilience capacity. Guidelines that will prove useful in managing your resilience capacity include:

1 **Raising your resilience capacity comes from both increased pain management and remedy management.** Pain management is an ability that *pushes* us from the present to the future. Remedy management requires an understanding of the benefits that result from embracing change. This understanding provides the motivation to deal with the pain of change and wholeheartedly embrace the tasks needed to achieve growth. Remedy management *pulls* us from the present to the future. For prolonged change (and thus prolonged success), organizations must excel at both pain management and remedy management.

2 **Lowering the effort needed to harness the energy of change requires an organization to deal with the perceived levels of certainty and control.** Certainty results from clear expectations, no surprises, and continuity of organizational purpose. Control comes from participation, involvement, appropriate empowerment, and the timeliness of information flowing in the organization. When certainty and control are high, individuals require less effort to harness the energy of change. Thus, they are more able to handle an increased speed of change and a corresponding accelerated rate of success.

3 **The energy to deal with change comes from having a balanced life.** Just as tightrope walkers must have everything in balance before they can confidently move forward with a minimal risk of falling, so too must individuals have a balance in their lives so that they may confidently move forward. Organizations must be interested in all aspects of a person's life since things done off the job play a major role in how successful one is on the job.

HARNESSING THE ENERGY OF CHANGE

The need to not *manage* change, but to *harness the energy* of change, and to understand the reality of the science of change is important. A first step in understanding the process of harnessing the energy of change is an awareness that the thought "success breeds success" is false.

> **YOU LEARN MORE FROM FAILURE**
> When you succeed, you usually assume that everything you did was fine. When you fail, you analyze what happened much more closely to discover the problems. Thus success can make you overconfident, and failure can make you wiser.

A Personal Case

Let's take my case as an example. My career can be summarized as having built a successful engineering-based consulting firm while having two major detours, one in diversification and one in real estate. I have been to the peak, to the valley, back to the peak, back to the valley, and once again to the peak. Upon arriving at the peak for the third time, I made a pledge to never again travel to the valley.

Having made this pledge, I began pursuing the science of individual and organizational peak performance. I have learned a lot, and some of what I have learned may shake some of your beliefs. Nevertheless, the natural order of individual and organizational life is clear: Success does not breed success.

The remainder of this chapter presents the science of peak performance. It is this science that defines the process of harnessing the energy of change. It is my hope that you are able to apply this science to stay out of your valleys. Take it from someone who has been there—the peaks are a lot more fun!

ACHIEVING PEAK PERFORMANCE

As I began my understanding of peak performance, I discovered that many before me had wrestled with the issues I was trying to understand. Particularly useful were quotes from Benjamin Franklin and Winston Churchill who said, respectively, "Success has ruined many a man," and "Success is rarely final."

These quotes allowed me to understand that the natural order of life is not "success breeds success." Franklin and Churchill expressed that success is not a permanent state and is often the beginning of failure. But why does this happen? Henry Kissinger lays our groundwork with the quote, "Each success only buys an admission ticket to a more difficult problem."

Success Leads To More Challenges

Let's use a metaphor of life as a series of rooms. Each of us, individually and collectively as organizations, needs an admission ticket to travel from room to room. At any given point, you and your organization may find yourselves in a room full of challenges. You work hard, you overcome these challenges, and you achieve peak performance.

While you're basking in your success in the first room, you receive an admission ticket to the next room with a new set of challenges (see diagram at right). In fact, these challenges could be major problems that will send you to a valley, instead of a peak, if not conquered. These new problems are difficult because they are different from the problems in the previous rooms. Albert Einstein referred to this when he said, "We cannot solve today's problems with the same level of thinking that created

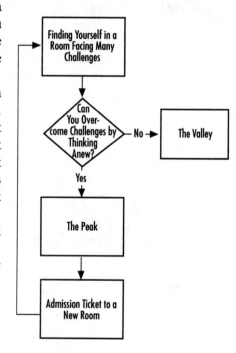

The Natural Order Of Life

the problem in the first place."

We obtain admission to a new room because of our success, but if we think like we did in the old rooms, we will never maintain peak performance.

HOW TO TRAVEL PEAK-TO-PEAK

For individuals, understanding the natural order of life is the foundation in building peak-to-peak performance and harnessing the energy of change. To use this understanding, you must:

1. Accept the continuously accelerated rate of change occurring in today's world.

2. Develop a process that allows you to continuously develop and use new ideas.

To deal with continuous change, an organization needs to undertake the following four major organization shifts:

- from management to leadership
- from individuals to teams
- from customer service to partnerships
- from traditional compensation to performance-based rewards and recognition

You must be careful to pursue all four shifts. Any one deficiency will result in your organization falling into a valley.

FROM MANAGEMENT TO LEADERSHIP

Traditional management is passé. What is required today is *both* good management and good leadership. To create the necessary balance, a shift from management to leadership is required. The three elements required to make this shift are:

> "The best moments [of flow] usually occur when a person's body or mind is stretched to its limits in a voluntary effort to accomplish something difficult and worthwhile."
> —Mihaly Csikszentmihalyi, *Beyond Boredom and Anxiety*

1 **Moving from a traditional culture to a culture of continuous renewal.** Culture is the foundation upon which organizations are built. A peak-to-peak leader will fail if the culture he/she is working in doesn't embrace peak-to-peak performance. Therefore, the first task for a leader is to shift an organization's culture from control to growth, from analysis to vision, from slow decision-making to progressive action, from optimization to peak-to-peak, from fighting change to harnessing change, and from bureaucracy to learning.

2 **Moving from wandering priorities to focus.** The most important task of a leader is defining an organization's model of success and obtaining alignment with it. The five elements of this model are vision, mission, requirements of success, guiding principles, and evidence of success. An organization's focus, and thus peak-to-peak performance, will result when alignment occurs with the model of success.

The Model Of Success

1 **Vision**: a description of where you are headed.

2 **Mission**: how to accomplish your vision.

3 **Requirements of success**: the science of your business.

4 **Guiding principles**: the values you practice as you pursue your vision.

5 **Evidence of success**: measurable results that demonstrate when you're moving toward the vision.

3 **Redefining work from "doing a job" to "making a difference."** It is the leader's job to assure motivation within an organization so that a peak-to-peak enterprise can overcome obstacles along its path. Leaders define motivation for their organizations by how they think, how they communicate, how they work, and how they treat people.

These three changes in the way organizations work are the foundation upon which a peak-to-peak enterprise is built. Without this first shift, organizations fail because there is nothing to hold them up if they begin to fall. From here, peak-to-peak leaders must move forward and shift the organization's structure from being individually motivated to one that relies on the teaming process for success.

FROM INDIVIDUALS TO TEAMS

AT&T Teams Drive Change. AT&T's Global Business Communications System business was going nowhere by 1989. Several teams were created to redesign the core processes. In their assessment phase, they found that there was no accountability or coordination between how phone systems were sold and installed. And the process from sale to installation required 16 handoffs! Customer willingness to repurchase was a strikingly low 53%, and profits were unacceptable.

After nine months of assessment and planning, the teams redesigned the process. They minimized the time between sales and installation by minimizing handoffs and improving coordination within the company. After several trials, the new process was finally installed. Profits reached record highs and customer willingness to repurchase soared to 82%.

Professionals in all areas of business agree that successful organizations are team-based. The allure of teams is irresistible. (See also Chapter 6 on teams and change.)

At the same time, many organizations do not achieve success with teams. So, if teams are right, why all the problems? The answer lies in the following three critical areas of teaming that must be improved to become a peak-to-peak enterprise:

The Benefits Of Teams

- Respond more quickly to change.
- Effectively take advantage of opportunities.
- Deliver better quality and customer service.
- Reduce costs and increase profits.
- Have improved employee communications, morale, and satisfaction.

1 **The fad of teams vs. the reality of teams.**
One of the greatest challenges in creating a successful, team-based organization is overcoming all of the existing team paradigms. To move beyond the fad of teams, organizations must understand that a team is defined as a small number of people using synergy to work together for a common end. They must also understand that there are different types of teams as well as different levels of teams, each with different levels of autonomy, accountability, and responsibility. All teams are unique and must be supported by leadership to achieve their potential.

2 **Self-directed teams vs. self-managing teams.** Empowerment has been widely misunderstood. The failure to understand what empowerment really means has led many people to the conclusion that team-based organizations don't work. On the contrary, the peak-to-peak enterprise will be a team-based organization that sees empowerment as the leadership process of building, developing, and increasing an organization's power to perform through the evolution of teams.

3 **Team program vs. team process.** A team program doesn't work and cannot be made to work. A peak-to-peak enterprise will follow a team-based, evolutionary process by having successful teams, and by becoming a learning organization with teams pursuing peak-to-peak performance.

Organizations must understand that teams are not just a tool to implement, but are the essence of how we work.

"We're all team players here, Furgis. Miss Parmenter will break you in."

FROM CUSTOMER SERVICE TO PARTNERSHIPS

For any organization to achieve true success, there must be a major shift in the relationships among the customers and suppliers. An organization must be able to make the shift from traditional customer/supplier relationships to partnerships by:

1 Moving from lip service about customer service to a customer-driven organization. Customer service is more than handling complaints well. This is old customer service. It has little to do with satisfying the customer or being a customer-driven organization. The foundation for a customer-driven organization is leadership's commitment to customer service. From this commitment, an understanding must flow from what the customer wants followed by a process of creating peak-to-peak performance focusing on exceeding customer expectations.

2 Moving from a customer-driven organization to invincible service. To go beyond a customer-driven organization, an organization must understand the motives of its customer. An organization must develop customer loyalty by consistently exceeding expectations, by continuously improving customer service, by being easy to do business with, by presenting no-hassle problem resolution, and by establishing strong relationships between people.

3 Moving from invincible customer service to a cooperative relationship. A cooperative relationship results when organizations begin

---

Simply Delivering *Good* Service Is Not Enough

"*Great* service takes reliability, surprise, recovery, and fairness [customers feeling that you are an ethical company]...Businesses that exceed expectations by surprising customers with unexpected extras, earn immeasurable loyalty and support. This also leads to value creation for the company."

—Leonard L. Berry, *On Great Service*

to pursue projects jointly with customers to improve performance. A cooperative relationship will evolve between the two organizations through the application of the team-based process.

4 **Moving from a cooperative relationship to a true partnership.** As cooperative relationships evolve, so should their level of interaction, participation, and trust. By the time you become partners with your customers, your organizations will enjoy integrated and seamless relationships.

PERFORMANCE-BASED COMPENSATION

Once the previously mentioned shifts begin to take hold, their benefits will be dampened without a further shift in compensation practices. This is because employees will still be driven by the traditional, individual compensation system.

In many firms, decades have passed since the compensation plan was changed. Although there have been numerous studies about compensation, little has changed. Traditional compensation systems consist of a pay scale and little or no recognition. The problems with these systems include lack of fairness, credibility, and accuracy, and the fact that the system is used to evaluate individuals and not

A Broken Pay Plan: Sad Story Number 3268

The 10-year-old company had grown quickly, and hadn't been consistent with its human resource policies. There were pay problems. What people got paid had more to do with when they were hired than with what they did or how well they did it. During its fast growth period, the company had to pay some pretty high wages just to get people in the door. There were no real quantifiable goals or performance criteria. There was a need to implement a new pay plan, and a compensation expert was hired to do this.

Well, after everyone had taken tests, filled out forms, and sat through interviews, the day of the pay raises arrived. Everyone had talked about this for weeks. Everyone had told their spouses about the pay raises, and the whole company was poised for a celebration.

Alas, it was not a happy day. Inconsistency ruled with no explanations. Some people got no raise. Some people were told they were making more money than they should be. Some got very small raises, some got good raises, and some got great raises.

Mary Kay Recognition

Every summer, over 30,000 Mary Kay beauty consultants pay to attend "seminar"—three days of nonstop recognition in Dallas. There are minks, diamonds, sashes, badges, crowns, emblems, flowers, jewelry, kisses, hugs, holding hands, tears, and stories of amazing success.

Emotional compensation is the secret of seminar success and the success of Mary Kay. Beauty consultants can immediately see by inspecting one another what they have accomplished. Salespeople come to seminar for recognition, and it is recognition they get.

Some may think this works for Mary Kay housewives but has little to do with the world of business. Well, think again. Two-thirds of these beauty consultants have full-time jobs in addition to selling Mary Kay. Several are lawyers. There are pediatricians, and even a Harvard MBA.

When considering the issue of when the Mary Kay reward-by-recognition practice will become mainstream, John Kotter, of Harvard Business School, says, "The genius of great leaders is that they understand money is only one of the things that make people light up." Applause, prizes, and peer recognition are very, very powerful. Possibly, Mary Kay is way ahead of the rest of us. Cash is a secondary benefit; *recognition* is the emotional compensation that brings the enthusiasm that creates success.

teams. It also limits earning power, independent of a person's ability to do a job well.

It is important to note that all of the best compensation systems are customized to meet the organization's needs. No two are alike, but all should follow the same basic structure. Performance-based compensation (PBC) is a system based on rewards and recognition that creates a balance for each person's contribution and compensation.

The Power Of Recognition

Emotional recognition. Recognition is an important portion of every leader's job. Some ways a peak-to-peak leader can provide emotional recognition include making a regular habit of saying "thank you," providing specific recognition in a real-time mode, encouraging others to recognize great performance, and expressing spontaneous and genuine excitement for exceptional performance.

Individual goal assessment. The second element in performance-based compensation is individual goal assessment. People need to know what is specifically expected of them. It is important that each person's individual goals and assessments are highly personalized, and that they are done in the context of the organizational goals. These goals should always be objective, observable, and verifiable, but flexibility is important when circumstances change. A rating is the result of the appraisal of each goal. By pursuing emotional recognition and individual goal assessment, the recognition component of a plan can be done properly.

Rewards

Base pay. Base pay should be very straightforward and transparent. In fact, there is just one question a leader must answer when designing a performance-based reward structure: Should base pay be the same for everyone doing a job, or should there be some pay steps based upon seniority? Base pay should be reviewed annually and adjusted in accordance with the market.

Pay-for-skill. Pay-for-skill is a reward and development program designed to increase a non-manager's base pay because of an individual's demonstrated capability to perform a variety of skills. Pay-for-skill programs use a series of base pay increases reflecting increases in skill proficiency. The most significant benefit resulting from pay-for-skill is an increased skill level of the work force. Additional benefits include increased work force flexibility, increased productivity, improved customer service, and reduced turnover and absenteeism.

Individualized bonuses. At the same time individual goals are established, the bonus-for-performance schedule should also be established. The individual bonus should be based upon the

Incentive Programs That Work

"Make sure your incentive program really rewards performance. Don't cheapen it by rewarding everybody. People won't get pumped up if everybody wins.

"Be very specific (to yourself and to the employees) about the kinds of performance you'll be rewarding.

"Establish clear and challenging, but attainable goals. And once you've defined the goal, don't change it. It's really unfair to keep moving the target. You've got to let the old goals be achieved, at least once, before you create new ones."

—Ken Blanchard

performance against individual goals.

Prior to the start of the performance period, the combination of the individual goals and the individual bonus plans should be mutually agreed upon, then signed by the supervisor and the employee to form the "contract" for the performance period. The individual bonus eliminates the problem of a built-in annuity from traditional merit pay plans. This results in a fair overall compensation plan, since individuals are paid based upon their current performance. This allows new employees who are performing at a high level to receive high bonuses. And it requires all employees to continue to perform if they are to continue receiving good bonuses.

Goalsharing. Goalsharing is a program that rewards team performance. Goalsharing is based upon an organization's total performance and not on individual performance. It is up to the Executive Team to decide which levels of employees will participate in the goalsharing program and what factors will define the bonus. Thus, the goals upon which the bonuses will be paid and how the bonuses will be distributed are among the questions the Executive Team must answer when preparing a goalsharing plan.

Difficulties In Changing Compensation Plans

Shifting from a traditional compensation plan to a performance-based plan can be challenging. This is a fundamental area which many organizations are unwilling to change. A key objective of performance-based compensation is to balance each person's contribution with his or her compensation. If this balance does not exist, there will be unhappy people who won't make their maximum contributions to the organization's performance. The balance that must be pursued, however, is not an organizational balance but an individual balance. Individuals must believe that their compensation is balanced with their contribution.

Some key processes

"Beats the heck out of performance reviews."

necessary for making the transition from traditional compensation to performance-based compensation include laying a foundation for shifting through educating leadership, obtaining input on the present compensation plan, and developing an implementation and communication plan. The new performance plan should be communicated during one-on-one meetings with each employee. And a performance-based compensation plan improvement team should be established.

It is only by pursuing this process that a performance-based plan can be implemented to answer the following question for all employees: "What is in it for me?" By answering this question, organizations will fuel their continuous pursuit of peak-to-peak performance.

BOOMERANG PRINCIPLES

In order to become a successful, peak-to-peak enterprise and to truly harness the energy of change, organizations must consider these four "Boomerang Principles":

1) **What comes back is exactly what is put forth.** When you throw a boomerang, you don't get some other boomerang back; you get the same one. As an organization pursues becoming a peak-to-peak enterprise, the reactions, responses, and commitment received will mirror the feelings, thoughts, and commitment you put forth. In both words and actions, your dedication to creating peak-to-peak performance will be mirrored in the words and actions of others.

2) **What comes back is always more than what was put forth.** A boomerang gains momentum and returns at a faster speed. As an organization pursues becoming a peak-to-peak enterprise, the synergy that evolves acts as a multiplier for the evolution of renewal, progress, improvement, growth, and success.

3) **Results are always obtained after the investment is made.** A boomerang never comes back until after it is thrown. How long it takes to return depends upon many complex factors and is very difficult to predict. The same is true with the process of becoming a peak-to-peak enterprise—it takes time.

4 **Benefits will be positive only if the peak-to-peak leader knows the path.** Sometimes a boomerang is thrown and comes back. Sometimes it doesn't. It takes practice to know how to throw a boomerang. The same is true for a peak-to-peak enterprise. The peak-to-peak leader needs to know how to nurture the process and overcome difficulties. To assure success, the leader must have an in-depth understanding of the peak-to-peak enterprise. Only then will peak-to-peak performance result.

Motorola Puts The Boomerang Principles To Work

Motorola is a great success story. Sales and earnings have surged in tough markets.

But guess what? Leadership isn't sitting back basking in their great success. No, leadership understands the success-fail cycle and so it's saying:

"Fame is a fleeting thing. When the alarm clock rings tomorrow morning, you'd better get up and understand that your customers expect more from you than they did the day before. You'd better find a way to be better." (Gary Tooker, CEO)

"Since our inception, Motorola has been managing on the concept of renewal, a willingness to renew our technologies, and to renew the process by which we run the institution." (Christopher Galvin, COO)

"We've met the challenge of the Japanese—our quality is high; demand for our product is strong. Our technical people are bordering on being cocky. That keeps me awake at night. I've got to figure out how to keep these people unhappy." (Hector Ruiz, GM of Paging Products group)

Continuous renewal is being on top but thinking like an underdog. Motorola realizes that what comes back is not what they put in two years ago, but what they put in tomorrow. They understand that they must leverage their expertise, work the global market, and invest in the future. It is clear that Motorola will continue to reap, and reap, and reap. Motorola understands the Boomerang Principles.

CONCLUSION

Unfortunately, there is no seven-step plan to help every organization harness the energy of change.

The key to success is to take action. Starting quickly and continuing to accelerate will create a sense of momentum, which pulls people into the process. This involvement is sustained by the four shifts to leadership, to teams, to partnerships, and to performance-based compensation. Add to these your organization's continuous learning, and the result will be the synergy needed to create peak-to-peak performance.

ACTION SUMMARY

▶ Analyze "pain" symptoms to see what they're telling you.

▶ Balance your life to increase your personal resilience.

▶ Use the energy of changing situations to achieve new goals.

▶ Expect new challenges when you're successful.

▶ Shift from management to leadership.

▶ Recognize support teams as the wave of the future.

▶ Strive for real partnerships with your customers.

▶ Set up a team to institute performance-based rewards.

▶ Develop benchmark and performance measures.

▶ Keep focused on your vision and your organizational mission.

Chapter 2

CHANGE—THE NEW COMPETITIVE WEAPON

Rick Goldberg

Rick Goldberg
is recognized as a leader, educator, entrepreneur, and motivator within the business world. Over the past ten years, he has built his company from zero to $25 million in sales. He is an accomplished public speaker, having appeared both nationally and internationally for companies like Clairol, Revlon, and many others.

Mr. Goldberg's success led to the development of Sigma 6, Inc., which applies the expertise learned in the beauty industry to businesses in general. Sigma 6 provides unique business programs, systems, and solutions to a variety of organizations throughout the world. This is accomplished through personal appearances by Mr. Goldberg, video- and audiotape series, and customized marketing programs based on "Client Direct Mail Retention."

Mr. Goldberg is a great believer in Sigma 6's motto: "Change is good. Change is growth."

Rick Goldberg, Sigma 6, 6811 Flying Cloud Drive, Eden Prairie, MN 55344; phone (612) 946-1992 ext. 368; fax (612) 946-1941; e-mail prbeauty@ix.netcom.com.

Chapter 2

CHANGE—THE NEW COMPETITIVE WEAPON

Rick Goldberg

"Nothing endures but change."
—Heraclitus (c 500 BC)

Change has joined death and taxes as one of the great inevitabilities of our time. We live in a fast-paced, competitive world where every customer is up for grabs and no company can stand still and survive. "Make dust or eat dust" has become the cry of the '90s—and with good reason. Forget the fable of "The Tortoise and the Hare." The tortoise is on the endangered species list and the hares are proliferating.

Unfortunately, most companies fear change. They stand like deer in the headlights of oncoming cars—fearful, frozen and doomed! Of the 100 largest U.S. companies at the beginning of this century only 16 are still here.

Successful companies see change coming and recognize it as a potentially powerful competitive tool. They are hopeful. They are curious. They actively explore the possibilities inherent in change. These are the companies that will survive and prosper while others around them fail.

CRAFTING THE VISION

Change creates opportunity. Whether for riches or ruin depends largely on how prepared you are to handle change and turn it to your advantage. The key to harnessing change is to fully plan for it. The first step is to develop a strategic plan (see box).

Share your strategic plan widely within the firm. It will clearly establish the need for change within your organization, and serve as the platform for crafting the vision that guides your approach to change.

Hold a meeting with the most influential people throughout your company to help define this vision. Ensure that it's a true dialogue with ample time for discussion. The outcome must be a compelling scenario that:

- logically follows from the strategic plan;
- clearly shows the company's future at risk in a com-

Develop Your 5-Point Strategic Plan

Who are you? Paint an image of your firm's values and aspirations that will serve as a touchstone as you move forward in the marketplace.

Where are you today? Identify the business you're in, your markets, your resources, policies and procedures, management characteristics, and how your products and services are different from those of your competitors.

What are you going to be facing? Uncover relevant market trends and make assumptions about the economy, competitors, customers' future needs, etc.

Where do you wish to arrive? When? Set strategic objectives for the company.

How are you going to get there? Outline strategies, based on your distinctive competencies and market opportunities, that will help achieve your objectives.

petitive marketplace (and those of its employees); and

- communicates that you are acting to preserve and protect both your company and your people.

Your vision must promote the idea that change is now the natural order of things and an indicator of competitive vigor and future prosperity.

COMMUNICATING THE VISION

Once you have developed a strategic vision of the role that change will play in your firm, you must fully and effectively communicate that vision to your workforce. A haphazard approach won't do. It will take powerful, strategically designed communication efforts to break through the natural barriers to change and convince your people that change is important, inevitable, and integral to their future work lives.

People dislike uncertainty and helplessness. They would rather be at the tiller against long odds than in the dark in the cargo hold with a better chance for survival. They seek power over their lives. They crave information.

Provide it. Be as open as possible, sharing your strategic vision and as much information as needed to reassure your people. Remember to move quickly, however. You're up against the power of the grapevine: a conduit of facts, fancies and outright fallacies that is legendary for its reach and speed. Given half a chance, rumor will generate resistance to your program, giving detractors a chance to build up defenses and win converts.

You must not only be quicker than your potential opposition but also more vocally persistent. The key to your communication efforts will be to determine a simple and evocative message that conveys your vision. Then communicate it fre-

"No skill is more important than the corporate capacity to change. The company's most urgent task, then, is to learn to welcome —beg for, demand —innovation from everyone."
—Tom Peters

quently and consistently to your people.

A variety of tactics exists for your communication efforts, including:

- **Special face-to-face meetings** between senior management and employees convey the depth of your commitment to change. Be up-front about why change is needed and what role is to be played by the employees. Remember that real communication is a two-way street—encourage dialogue and listen hard.

- **Regular group meetings** allow people to share comments and suggestions, find out what others are up to, and report on what they are doing. Be careful to create an agenda—these should be constructive and informational, *not* social gatherings.

- **Casual get-togethers** provide a forum where fear and mistrust can be more easily spotted and addressed.

- **Celebratory events** offer an opportunity to both recognize people for their successes, and praise them for the efforts and lessons of their failures.

- **Newsletters and plaques** provide low-cost recognition that is appreciated and remembered.

- **Posters, business cards, tapes, mugs, etc.** repeat and reinforce your simple but evocative message.

Multiple and consistent messages using a variety of media reinforce your communication and increase its believability. The success of your communication efforts will help to transform change into an integral force and a bedrock belief within your company.

PREPARING YOUR PEOPLE

The greater your vision for change, the broader is your need for participation from all corners of the company. The more people who are involved, the more quickly change will happen. Avoid making change and innovation the domain of a committee or task force where it will be seen as "special" and "someone else's problem."

Make change endemic, routine, expected. Communicate your assumptions that everyone will contribute to the continual metamorphosis of the company. Your people must do more than see the need for change—they must feel the sense of urgency that necessitates it, envision their role in creating it, and go out and achieve it. Eliciting broad-based commitment and participation will not be an easy task, however. It will involve a great deal of nurturing and require more than a little patience, planning, and perseverance.

Dealing With The Fear

The scent of change in the air is known to cause visible physiological changes in the best of us. Most employees will initially view change as a threat. They will experience anxiety and occasional hostility, and begin to resist change and its myriad implications. For many, the loss of comfort and control is profound. Psychologists identify a five-step "grieving process":

1 **Denial.** In this stage employees fail to see a need for change. They see only the pain of change, and tend to avoid supporting the program.

"The best, most efficient, most profitable way to operate a business is to give everybody in the company a voice in saying how the company is run *and* a stake in the financial outcome, good or bad."
—Jack Stack, Springfield Remanufacturing, *The Great Game of Business*

A typical response is, *"It will blow over."*

2 Hostility. Employees begin to see that the program isn't going to go away. Worse, they see that it's actually going to affect **them**. Morale falls. Management is blamed. Employees are angry. *"It's ill-conceived and unfair."*

3 Negotiation. In this stage, anger subsides and employees get down to the busy work of mapping out their practical strategies. The

"The staff didn't react as favorably as we had hoped."

amount of change they will risk engaging in is directly proportional to the size of the safety net they see provided. They're far from committed, but they'll test the waters. *"I'll give it a try, but for heaven's sake, catch me!"*

4 Depression. The initial try is usually successful but depression sneaks up on employees as they realize that change is truly here to stay. The future looks bleak and they look back with nostalgia on their lost routine. *"OK, but no good will come of this."*

5 Acceptance. At this stage a few more small victories and a persistent push by management convinces people that change is working. Employees adapt their work styles to help make the program a success. *"It's working and it's leaving the station. I'd better jump on board."*

Supplying The Security

Change is a challenge, particularly early on. Dealing with it requires confidence and trust. Actively encourage experimentation and risk taking from your employees. Expect some mistakes and setbacks. Tell your people not to fear failure, for we learn from our mistakes. Tell them to fear *not trying*.

Support Risk Taking

"If you're not failing, you're not trying hard enough." At author and CEO Harvey Mackay's envelope company, employees took five years to create a new service, but the end result was a system that dramatically increased sales. "If I had said no to their first, or second, or even third failure, they never would've continued to work on it. If you stifle people, they clam up or leave. You've got to give yourself and others the power to fail."

The most effective way to encourage risk taking is to provide your people with a safety net, a guarantee that you will make every effort to avoid firings and layoffs. Such a guarantee should be offered after a suitable probationary period and be subject to an acceptable level of individual performance. Let employees know that *security of employment* doesn't mean *permanence of position*.

You will need to retain the flexibility to move people around. It breaks old habits, builds new experiences, and lends new perspective. A job security policy will require that greater care in hiring be taken and more extensive use be made of subcontractors and temporary workers. Design as much flexibility into your program as possible to enable you to minimize layoffs.

Although promising job security may seem risky, you will get a good return on this investment. Security, particularly the knowledge that one's job will continue to exist in one form or another, has been shown to raise the quality of participation, lower resistance to change, and provide an effective means to attract and retain good people.

Furnishing The Tools

Organizations on the cutting edge of change seldom pass up an opportunity to enhance the skills of their people.

A company's workforce is its principle asset and is usually the primary source of its success. Give extensive entry-level training on the skills you most value and allow regular time-off from work for classes. Provide ongoing educational opportunities that will help your people to accept and deal with uncertainty. Make this a critical skill. Reward it. The return on your investment will be a competitive workforce that is knowledgeable, flexible, self-reliant and ready to use change and innovation to their (and your) advantage.

Providing The Incentive

When perched high above even the strongest safety net, people will usually need extra incentives to take that first big leap. One tried-and-true way to encourage risk-taking behavior is to revise your compensation system, basing pay, raises, and bonuses at least in part on the amount of change and innovation people have introduced in the company. Good base pay coupled with incentives for training and productivity offer great encouragement to workers. Low base-pay and high incentive-pay works a similar wonder for managers.

Money is not the only motivator in the workplace, nor is it necessarily the strongest. Recognition is a powerful but underused source of incentive available to you. Create public forums for recognition to reinforce preferred behaviors and to help make them part of the firm's culture. Be sure to publicly applaud challenging failures as well as successes. Praise, plaques, written notes, e-mail, and mentions in the newsletter should all be used to reward the recipient and reinforce the importance of change to the company.

"I've found most employees like frequent, spontaneous forms of recognition, such as being singled out for praise during a staff meeting or being given tickets to a baseball game."

—Bob Nelson,
1001 Ways to Reward Employees

READYING THE ORGANIZATION

It's tragic when a company's people are ready to undertake change but can't find the organizational support to effectively do so. Yet many companies will spend great sums to prepare their workforce for change and innovation and fail to provide them the policies, procedures, command structure and hiring practices needed to truly implement innovation and sustain change in the organization.

Revising Policies And Procedures

No matter how successful a company is initially, it won't continue to successfully deal with change unless it builds flexible and entrepreneurial policies and procedures. You must eliminate the rules, policies, customs, goals, training, rewards, and communications that reinforce the old way of doing things. Replace them with ones that reinforce change and encourage innovation.

Reforming The Bureaucracy

Bureaucracy is the enemy of change. Many-layered hierarchies with rigid chains of command are fortresses against the spread of innovation, and exist largely to enforce control and ensure the continuity of routine. Every layer of management sets up another roadblock to your change effort.

Harold Wilensky has identified a number of groups that tend to restrict the free flow of information and change in a bureaucracy:

- **"Defensive Cliques"**—groups that hoard information, afraid that any change threatens their position;

- **"Time Servers"**—individuals who are physically at their desks but mentally already retired. Already "informational backwaters," they neither receive nor search out information;

- **"Mutual-Aid-and-Comfort Groups"**—people who enjoy a comfortable and routine corporate life and view any sign of ambition or innovation from others as a threat; and
- **"Coalitions of the Ambitious"**—self-aggrandizing individuals who equate information with power and view it as a limited resource to be hoarded, not shared.

These "turf clubs" thrive in tall, hierarchical bureaucracies and restrict the rate of change and innovation in their companies. They need to be identified, understood, and defeated.

Focusing On Solutions And Empowerment

Change comes more easily under freeform management, with its focus on problem solving, than under hierarchical management, with its focus on control. Upper management needs to know when to maintain control and when to delegate it to the troops.

We are operating in an era of trust and shared information. You can't mistrust your people and then ask them to trust you enough to take the risks inherent in creating change and innovation. Whenever possible replace control by bureaucracy and procedures with trust and vision. Become a guide and facilitator rather than a dictator of orders and plans. Fred Brooks, legendary chief designer at IBM, realized early that, "As boss, you must consciously seek out opportunities to help in little ways. You must view yourself as basher-in-chief of small barriers and facilitator-in-chief of trivial aids to action rather than 'the great planner.'"

Change without initiative is rare. Initiative without empowerment is nonexistent. Empower your employees. With power comes initiative. Tell them that they should routinely take whatever initiative is reasonably required to break barriers, move the company forward and provide a legendary level of service to customers. The results will be impressive. That's what change is all about!

> "Powerlessness corrupts. Absolute powerlessness corrupts absolutely."
> —Rosabeth Moss Kanter

Recruiting Carefully

Organizational change must extend to the company's hiring practices to help ensure that change becomes and remains a central part of the firm's culture.

New hires should be chosen from those who reflect the core values of the company. Look at your most productive people, those who are the most flexible and effective in dealing with change. Isolate what common background and traits you can and use these in designing interview questions. Before hiring, never pass up a chance to communicate the importance to the firm of the new hire embracing change.

> "Providing realistic and negative information about a new job reduces resignations and terminations."
> —Ilgen and Seeley, Journal of Applied Psychology

MAKING CHANGE CONTINUOUS

For most companies, change is unfamiliar, a big and wrenching experience forced on them when their backs are against the wall. Change involves anxiety and turnover, a crisis to be weathered and then back to business as usual. For the fortunate few, change is familiar, a small and welcome step toward achieving competitive advantage. It *is* business as usual.

Smart companies have found that change is most successfully accomplished when taken in small but continual steps. Facing sudden, large-scale problems is a daunting task that usually paralyzes rather than motivates employees. Planning for change involves a focus on the future. It helps to catch big problems early and reduce them to manageable proportions that are more actionable and more quickly solved. The victories they engender encourage people and reinforce their belief in the benefits of change.

Constant and successful change creates what Robert Waterman, Jr., co-author of *In Search of Excellence,* calls "stability in motion." It makes change the norm, increasing the comfort level of employees and becoming an integral part of the corporate culture.

> ## Kaizen: Continuous Process Improvement
>
> "Kaizen" is a Japanese term meaning to search unceasingly for ever-higher levels of quality by isolating sources of defects. The goal: zero defects or elimination of waste.

MEASURING AND MONITORING

Change by its very nature is a process in need of constant adjustment. Your first step in measuring the progress of change and innovation in your company is to set specific goals. Don't let your people tell you that you can't measure activities. There isn't one that can't be measured by time, money, or units of some kind.

Remember the old business adage, *"If you can't measure it, you can't manage it."* Even such intangibles as improved teamwork, better communication, and increased customer satisfaction can be measured with the application of a little thought and creativity. Ask the people closest to the activity to come up with new and better measurement criteria. By involving people in setting their own goals and defining their measurement, you are getting a commitment and buy-in from them to tracking and monitoring their performance.

When monitoring change and innovation, keep an eye out for drops in productivity. They can lead you to people in need of additional feedback, training, and motivation.

Likewise, watch for evidence of increased productivity and follow it back to people deserving of recognition and reward. Use them as role models and spread their methods. Tinker. Take risks. Innovate. Watch to see what works and what doesn't.

KNOW WHEN DRASTIC CHANGE IS NEEDED

"Do all your evil at once and then hold the survivors close to you."
—Machiavelli, *The Prince*

Continual incremental change will get you where you need to go more surely and painlessly than drastic change will. Nonetheless, it's important to know when drastic, fundamental change is required.

Large-scale change is a whole new ball game requiring a new set of responses. It involves impact. Drama. Pain. Layoffs. Changes in management.

Drastic change results in high anxiety and resistance and requires greater commitment, communication, and care. It is needed when there is no time to take small steps and the luxury of widespread involvement and participation is denied you. In such cases, particularly if change is not yet an integral part of your policies, procedures and culture, get outside help immediately.

CONCLUSION

Change and innovation are an absolute requirement for continued prosperity in today's marketplace. Encourage, train for, and reward change and innovative behavior.

With the proper planning and communication, your people will be full participants with a stake in successfully molding your evolving organization. They will be both invested and involved. They will be energized and so will your company.

Your competitors won't know what hit them.

ACTION SUMMARY

▶ To create change, first establish the vision of where you're going.

▶ Communicate your vision widely and repeatedly.

▶ Prepare to deal with avoidance and denial of the need for change.

▶ Fight bureaucracy and other entrenched interests against change.

▶ Make small, incremental changes a continuous and expected process.

▶ Monitor and measure every important process and result.

▶ When drastic change is needed, get outside help.

Chapter 3

MASTERING CHANGE
Corporate Strategies for the New Millennium

James A. Ray

James A. Ray
is a professional speaker, author, and business transformation consultant. Mr. Ray has
devoted 17 years to stuyding
success factors. Leaders, managers, and other success-oriented individuals seek
him out for his unbounded enthusiasm and dedication to long-term results.

After achieving top recognition at AT&T in sales and management for
building and leading AT&T's National Telemarketing operation, and a four-year
alliance with the Stephen Covey Leadership Institute, Mr. Ray left to start his own
consulting practice. Since that time, Mr. Ray has worked with such companies
as Bell Canada, Boeing Aircraft, Dow Chemical, IBM, and Tropicana to create
outcomes based on timeless principles that foster creativity, leadership, communication, and teamwork within the organizational culture. He is a master of
motivational techniques to inspire individuals to action.

A National Speakers Association member, Mr. Ray launched his speaking
career after working with corporate leadership for over 15 years. He is committed to balancing his motivational speaking and training with practical applications that participants can immediately use in their own work environments.

James A. Ray, Ray Transformation Technologies, 7319 Brodiaea Way, Suite 100,
La Jolla, CA, 92037; phone (619) 459-6909; fax (619) 459-9186; e-mail
JRaySpeaks@AOL.com; www.JamesRay.com.

Chapter 3

MASTERING CHANGE
Corporate Strategies for the New Millennium

James A. Ray

"A competitive world has two possibilities for you. You can lose. Or, if you want to win, you can change."
—Paul Thurow

CHANGE IS NOT NEW

Many individuals within organizations view change as a new phenomenon. This premise is absolutely untrue! While possibly more rapid or turbulent, change is not new. In fact, change has been the only constant in our world since its inception. Change has always been...and always will be.

If change is constant, why is it such a big issue? Change is a prime concern of managers and executives in today's organizations not because change has just begun...but because the rate of change is accelerating. And the truth is, change will only continue to accelerate.

In response to this acceleration, organizations are using various approaches to deal with change. Some of the most popular approaches are reengineering, downsizing, self-directed teams, and lean manufacturing. Unfortunately, many of these methods are ineffective and, more often than not, counterproductive. The all too typical "program-of-the-month" approach has been the outcome of well-intended leaders not fully understanding the fundamental principle which underlies all change.

UNDERSTAND CAUSES OF CHANGE

To understand and become masters of change, we must recognize that we live in an orderly universe. One of the major laws of the universe, and one that is imperative to understanding organizational change, is the Law of Cause and Effect. While most of us have heard of this law, very few truly understand how it applies to us.

Truth: To change, you must address causes.

We live in a world where individuals and organizations are forever looking for the "quick fix." But the quick fix does not exist. Caught up in a short-term mentality, we invest immeasurable time, energy, and effort addressing effects rather than understanding and addressing causes. This is like taking an antacid and thinking that it will cure your heartburn.

Unfortunately we have become a country of antacid consumers, never changing our eating habits (the cause), but always looking for the quick and easy remedy (treating the effects). Many change efforts do nothing but give us a "Tagamet." The organization may experience a short-term increase in productivity, morale, and effectiveness;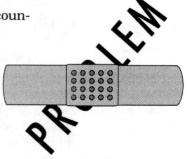

however, the change will never be lasting.

Truth: The only way to guarantee long-term success is to understand and address causes, not effects.

WHAT CREATES CHANGE?

In any organization, culture is the cause. Organizational culture is founded in the collective values, beliefs, identity, attitudes, and expectations—otherwise known as paradigms. While each of us has our own individual paradigms, organizations hold collective paradigms as well. An organization's culture is created by the collective paradigms that are *widely shared* and *deeply held* within that organization. Armed with our collective paradigms, we approach and react within the organizational structure. We interpret what we see and experience according to our shared understandings and culturally determined guidelines. Our paradigms tell us what the game is, and how to play it successfully.

A cultural shift is a change to a new game, or a new set of rules for interaction. The most important truth to understand is that when the game or the rules change, the whole organization will change.

Truth: Organizations don't behave...
people do.

Organizations Are Organic—Not Mechanical—Systems

To successfully change an organization, we must fully understand what constitutes an organization. While this may seem elementary, it is not!

In the study of linguistics, there is a term called a "nomalization." This is the process of turning a verb into a noun. In other words, we turn a process into an object or thing. The verb "organize" evolved into the noun "organization." Thus,

"The limits of my language are the limits of my world."
—Ludwig Wittgenstein

an organization is actually the process of *continually* organizing. Since an organization involves growth and change, it is—in the truest sense—an organism.

Many people still have ties to the mechanistic and industrial paradigms of the past. When people view their organizations as machines, they have a tendency to facilitate change in a mechanistic way. Consequently, leaders begin to think that by changing their structures, systems, strategies, styles, and skills, they will change their organizations.

"Look—management has been restructuring again."

Three Types Of Assets

In any organization there are three types of assets: physical, financial, and human. While all three are vital to the organization, they are in no way equal. Human assets are the primal source of the culture.

Because factors relating to human resources are difficult or uncomfortable to address—and often challenging to measure—most attempt to adapt through a typical accounting/mechanistic approach (bottom-line, expense-driven).

Organizations' attempts to implement change through reengineering and downsizing, even in the best of circumstances, don't recognize the value of their human resources. In most cases, these programs actually become counterproductive to the long-term gains and productivity of the reengineering effort and, ultimately, the enterprise.

Ideally, any change in the organization must be implemented simultaneously with a change in the culture (collective paradigms). In other words, individuals' paradigms must be shifted at the same time the organization begins its transformation.

Unfortunately, few organizations are equipped

to assist employees in making these paradigm shifts. As a result, both the employees and the organization lose. As individuals and organizations, we must gain an understanding of how to make these shifts if we hope to grow, prosper, and master an ever-changing world.

THREE LEVELS OF EFFECTIVENESS

To become masters of change, we must understand the three levels on which all organizations operate. If a change effort does not address all three levels, the cultural intervention will be less effective. These three levels are: personal, interpersonal, and organizational.

Personal Effectiveness

Truth: All lasting and successful change happens from the inside/out.

Wise leaders understand that people are the organization's most important asset. To create successful change, you must put a major emphasis on the people of your enterprise. While the physical, structural, and financial assets are important, they are just the *tools* people use to perform and produce.

Interpersonal Effectiveness

"Both the individual and society derive their basic meaning from the relations that exist between persons." —Revel Howe

The interpersonal level is every bit as powerful and important as the personal level. At the interpersonal level, we begin to interact and relate with others in our social environment.

One of the major challenges in today's workplace is

Levels Of Effectiveness

(Pyramid labels, bottom to top: Personal, Interpersonal, Organizational)

that we are expected to operate as cohesive teams; yet we have not been given the proper tools, techniques, and training to perform effectively.

Organizational Effectiveness

"Where there is no vision...the people perish."
—Ancient text

The organizational level is where we have typically attempted to address change. This level contains the systems, strategies, cycle times, compensation plans, etc., which are most commonly addressed. Yet more sustainable power at this level lies in providing the members of the organization with greater vision, mission, values and purpose. While organizations have often paid lip service to these concepts, most are light years away from living them.

WHERE DID IT ALL BEGIN...AND WHERE DO WE GO?

We haven't "just arrived" where we are...it has been a long-term process. Let's look at our history to gain a perspective on where we are today.

The Industrial Paradigm

The Industrial Age contributed greatly to the quality of life in America. It overtook the era of physical power, and allowed leaders like Henry Ford to forge the way into a new era. In the Industrial Age, we began to utilize tools and processes that geometrically increased our productivity. But like everything in life, the Industrial Age had a downside as well.

The downside of the industrial age was that, at some point, organizational leaders began to think of employees as part of the machinery. During this time, the ideas and philosophies of Fredrick Taylor were popular. One of these ideas was that people don't care what they

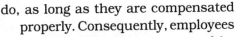

do, as long as they are compensated properly. Consequently, employees began to be treated as part of the physical assets. The thinking was that as long as employees were kept "well-oiled" with a paycheck, they would be happy and productive.

The Need For Creativity. Instead of being recognized as creative beings, employees were given repetitious, nonchallenging work that required little or no thought or creativity. Assembly-line technology made people interchangeable cogs in the line.

Truth: The human spirit will not fully invest itself in mediocrity.

Because of this truth, employees began to "check-out" mentally while in the workplace, and their creativity began to die.

People have an intrinsic need to be creative, and to create. When this need is not fulfilled in the workplace, the energy is taken elsewhere.

When our passion and energy leave the workplace, it is sad. The truth is, we spend more time earning our living than we spend with our family or for ourselves. Consequently, when not allowed to be creative in the workplace, we spend the majority of our lives disconnected from our passion.

The influence of Taylor's philosophy eventually gave way when companies began to discover that people not only wanted to be fairly compensated, but they also wanted to be fairly treated. The much-cited Hawthorn studies supported the theory that people liked to feel involved and valued, and thus, many individuals and organizations began to shift their paradigms.

"Man can bear almost any how...if he has a strong enough why."
    —Friedrich Neitzsche

The Need For Meaning. Abraham Maslow's work provided the impetus for another paradigm shift with his "Hierarchy of Needs." His theory described mankind's need for "self-transcendence"— the need to "transcend" the mundane and repetitive and take an active part in creating something meaningful.

| Self-actualization And Fulfillment |
| Esteem And Status |
| Belonging And Social Needs |
| Safety And Security |
| Basic Physical Needs (food and shelter) |

Since moving from the industrial age, organizations have improved at investing in the human asset. But many improvements must still be made in our ability to enroll people in something meaningful.

Most individuals find it very difficult to find meaning in any action or change that is *imposed* upon them. You will not succeed in your attempts to change your organization or its culture without understanding that the personal level is the most critical and vital to achieving long-term success. Reengineering is the last effort of the "command and control" mechanistic approach to change.

> *Truth: Reengineering works only to the degree that we reengineer our thinking and reengineer ourselves.*

The New Era

Many experts tell us that we are in the Information Age, but I believe that the Information Age has come and gone. For a time, we believed that "information is power," but this is untrue. Information is all around us; we are inundated with it. In fact, recent statistics state that information is doubling every three years.

> *Truth: Information is nothing more than unorganized facts and data.*

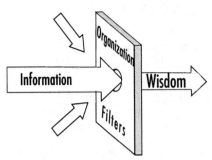

Information is not power. You can read countless management theory and organizational change books. You can jump on the World Wide Web and be overwhelmed by more information than you can ever comprehend; however, this will not make you or your organization powerful.

The truth is that *wisdom* is power. What is the difference? Wisdom is information that is organized and aligned with universal laws like cause and effect.

Truth: Wisdom is power! Wisdom is information that is organized and aligned with universal laws.

I believe that we are moving from the Information Age into the Spiritual Age. In this era, each and every one of us is beginning to understand who and what we truly are. Wisdom tells us that organizational behavior follows individual behavior—after all, organizations don't behave, people do.

Consequently, we must begin to act accordingly. People's spirits must be valued and nourished. For organizational change to produce outstanding results, organizations must invest heavily in the human spirit...the human asset.

A CHANGE EXAMPLE

When my company works with an organization in a Culture Design™ intervention, we approach all three effectiveness levels (personal, interpersonal, and organizational) simultaneously and congruently. We never lose sight that the greatest emphasis and highest leveraged portion, of any intervention is to address the human asset. While a Cultural Design intervention is too complex to cover in its entirety in this chapter, I will briefly address each of the three levels.

Personal Accountability And The Cultural Design Process

The greatest good and the highest leveraged action you, I, and our organizations can take is to accept personal accountability for our current and future results. In our diagnostic work, we find that the paradigm of "management (or my company, my boss, the union, etc.) did something wrong or unjust to me" is all too prevalent. When we as leaders, managers, and employees begin to accept personal accountability for our outcomes, our world begins to change. Again and again, I have seen the paradigm of personal accountability make major impacts for individuals, teams, and organizations.

Truth: Accountability breeds responsibility. I will be less than responsible if I am not held accountable.

Personal accountability makes us more responsible. Many people think that when I talk of accountability and responsibility, I am just playing with semantics. I can assure you I am not. Accountability is "end-results oriented" while responsibility originally meant the ability to respond.

Here is an example: Let's say that Jim and his manager, Jane, have an interaction that is less than pleasant—a disagreement regarding the last promotion that was awarded in the team. Now, both of them *responded* to each other in a certain manner, but who is *accountable* for the fact that it ended in an altercation?

Nine times out of ten, Jim will say it was Jane, and Jane will say it was Jim. Sound familiar? But the truth is that they both are truly accountable for what transpired. In other words, "it takes two to tango." Furthermore, Jim will probably tell you that he was treated unfairly and he deserved to receive the promotion. Maybe...maybe not.

This type of thinking will only result in resentment and further disempowerment of Jim's results. In all probability, Jim will not be as productive, and most likely his resentment will adversely affect the people with whom he works. The bottom line is that with this approach, Jim is hurting no one but himself...and he is helping nothing and no one.

Be Accountable

But what if Jim takes full accountability (end results) not only for the altercation but also for not getting the promotion? Will this affect the way Jim responds to the situation, to Jane, to co-workers, and the company? No question! Most likely, Jim will move forward...working more diligently on the things he needs to improve to achieve the next promotion. And this approach will have positive effects on Jane, his co-workers, and the company as well.

Unfortunately, this is not a popular mentality or approach in our world. It takes a tremendous amount of courage to take accountability for our personal and organizational results. To the degree that you assist individuals within your organization to shift their paradigms regarding accountability, your culture and your world will begin to shift.

INTERPERSONAL CONNECTION THROUGH THE CULTURAL DESIGN PROCESS

"Where two or three are gathered in agreement...nothing is impossible."
—Ancient text (paraphrased)

We live in a time where we are all expected to do more with less. On a weekly basis, I talk to individuals around our country who are faced with new demands. This presents some key challenges for the successful companies of tomorrow—and many opportunities.

Truth: Interpersonal effectiveness will never be achieved without first exploring personal effectiveness.

A major portion of our cultural work over the last two years has been directly related to "team" issues. Why? There are three reasons:

- We live in a world that is changing at lightning speed.

- We have attempted to adapt to new environments, processes, procedures, and team members while neglecting the human asset.

- Most of us have never been given the tools to communicate or form deep relationships.

Laying The Foundation

Recently my company was asked to work with a leadership team, over a six-month period, in an effort to improve the team's effectiveness and productivity. Our approach was to spend two full days with the team up-front, and then follow up and reinforce one day per month over the following six months.

After the first two days, many people didn't understand why we had spent 16 hours in a "team building event" addressing personal values, beliefs, and accountability. Even though I had explained the inside-out approach, and the team members had intellectually understood and agreed, they had not yet experienced it emotionally.

However, as I talked with the vice president over the next few weeks, she reported being totally amazed at how *differently* the team members were *interacting* with each other.

Personal Growth → Interpersonal Growth

When we regrouped after the first month, many team members expressed how they now understood that many of the differences in their team had been the result of *personal value* differences. Furthermore, they realized that because they understood themselves more clearly, they were more willing and able to understand their teammates.

Trust And Honesty

As personal agendas clarify, one of the most prevalent interpersonal issues we uncover is the lack of trust. There are obviously many factors that contribute to this phenomenon, but I believe

PERSONAL VALUES
Service
Achievement
Religion
Courage
Trust
Honesty
Responsibility
Respect
Dedication
Loyalty

the largest driver is our inability to connect and to be honest in our workplace.

Through the years, we have created environments where honesty and connection are not valued, and in many cases, not desired. We have experienced countless examples of individuals who were motivated to tell untruths about the current state of business affairs to avoid the "repercussions" of the truth. The space ship Challenger disaster of the 1980s quickly comes to mind.

You Need Honest Information Exchanged

Last year we worked with a manufacturing organization whose management was repeatedly told that a critical part they were building was "on the way to the paint shop," when in reality it was days, even weeks, from the paint bin. Why does this occur?

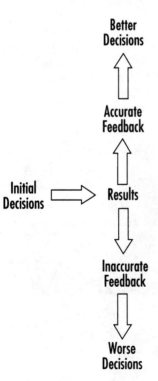

Better
Decisions

Accurate
Feedback

Initial
Decisions

Results

Inaccurate
Feedback

Worse
Decisions

In an environment that is non-connected and where relationships are poor, self-preservation and security become of major value. Consequently, my company works in many environments where the major customer is "my boss." This mentality can be observed when employees tell their up-lines what they *think they want to hear* versus the truth. This behavior is not only detrimental to long-term relationships and trust, but it makes it next to impossible to achieve high-performance results.

Because of the misinformation continuously being spread in our environments, often times we don't *really know* what processes do and do not work, or how much time certain production applications really take. Consequently, deadlines are missed across the board because true cycle times are not known.

To compound this problem, when we ask for funding or time-frames for our projects, we often falsify what is needed. Because of our lack of trust, we believe this "padding" will allow us to get what we *really need* to accomplish the job successfully.

Unfortunately, relationship disconnects are not limited to the boss/employee, boss/company relationship. I contend that a majority of the team challenges we are faced with today are the result of the lack of honest and complete information. For instance, I recently conducted a Dialogue Workshop with a client. At its conclusion, a participant told me, "I repaired a relationship that had been broken for years as the result of a misunderstanding...without question this will positively impact our results together."

Truth: If you don't talk it out...
you act it out.

Trustful Communication Needed

At the interpersonal level, we must begin to assist each individual to create deep connection, trust, and dialogue. This is not a new issue; in fact, I would guess that most of us have heard about communication for as long as we can remember. Consequently, we may trivialize its importance because we really don't know how to effectively communicate and build relationships in our business environments.

For those who may think communication is a worn-out topic or a common catch-all, I refer to the June 1996 issue of the *Harvard Business Review*.

In this issue multiple CEOs of major corporations were interviewed and asked to define the major challenge they faced moving into the future.

Almost without exception the answer was—you guessed it—communication.

Based on my experience, I suggest that the greatest team building event you can implement is one which will impart knowledge and train practical applications in the areas of effective communication and relationship building. When done effectively, the culture will begin to shift.

ORGANIZATIONAL VISION AND CULTURAL DESIGN

If lack of trust is the foremost issue found at the interpersonal level, lack of common vision and mission is pervasive at the organizational level. While organizations have typically done extensive work at this level, they have more often than not been ineffective. First, as previously stated, organizations have not mastered the personal and interpersonal levels of change. Secondly, while systems, compensation, structures, and strategies are all important and necessary, most organizations have done a poor job of clearly defining their purposes and visions.

Yes, I know that most leaders have gone through an exercise that has given time to these issues, but few have been effective at introducing these lofty ideals into their organizational cultures.

Vision tells us what we are going to become, what we are going to achieve and create...3, 5, 10 years into the future. If vision clarifies *what* we are achieving, mission tells us *why* that is important to us. Mission is the power that compels.

> *Truth: A purpose is more compelling than a goal.*

10-year Vision

1. All employees work in self-directed teams.

2. Knowledge is freely shared throughout the organization.

3. Customers provide input at all stages.

The Disney Lesson

A study was done several years ago of amusement parks in the United States. Brief results were as follows: Researchers visited Six Flags, Worlds of Fun, and Disney. Basic questions were asked of the employees. The roller-coaster operator at Six Flags was approached and asked,
"What is it that you do?" "I run the roller, what's it look like I do?" was the answer. The operator at Disney was asked the same question, "What is it that you do?" The answer was somewhat different: "I'm here to help families have a unique experience in the park."

Is there more than semantics involved here? I suggest there is. Where can you get more committed and involved—running the roller-coaster for eight hours per day or helping families? Obviously the latter.

Promote The Purpose

The greatest thing we can do as leaders is to articulate the highest and most meaningful purpose of our organization, and allow each employee to find his or her place within it. A great analogy is the countless hours we spend as parents taking our children to Little League and church activities with no monetary compensation. Why do we do this? In this rapid-paced world, where time is at a premium, we do these things willingly because of their intrinsic value, irrespective of the external reward.

To the degree that we create intrinsic value in our workplace, we will experience commitment versus compliance. Results have no choice but to follow.

CONCLUSION

Wise organizational leaders understand these timeless principles and laws, and apply them to every action they take. They realize that to master change, they must address causes rather than effects. Understanding their people and their cultures to be the cause, they no longer attempt to change with an outside/in approach. These leaders realize that to change their organizations, they must change themselves (inside/out) and their own paradigms. They study and address the laws of human interaction and human dynamics. As a result, they place great emphasis on the relationships and connections that bring synergistic results.

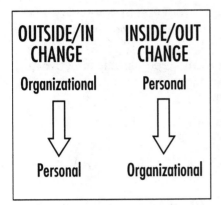

OUTSIDE/IN CHANGE

Organizational

⬇

Personal

INSIDE/OUT CHANGE

Personal

⬇

Organizational

Successful organizations address all three levels of effectiveness simultaneously and congruently (personal, interpersonal, organizational), while putting a major emphasis on the human asset.

As stated earlier, we need wisdom, not information, as we move into the new millennium. The companies that apply these principles move into an area so far beyond their competition that competition does not exist.

By enrolling each member of the enterprise into personal accountability, interpersonal connection, and a higher vision and purpose, commitment and creativity will result. Such innovative organizations will lead the field and join the ranks of the outstanding in the new millennium.

ACTION SUMMARY

► The *effects* of change may get your attention, but look for the underlying *causes*.

► Recognize that organizations are a process. Organizations don't behave, people do.

► Help people grow more personally effective and they will become more interpersonally and organizationally effective.

► Involve people's minds and spirits as well as their hands.

► Take your raw information and organize it into wisdom.

► Take responsibility for your own outcomes.

► Focus change efforts on the individual level first.

► You must provide a trustworthy environment, and a compelling vision in order for people to engage, commit, and contribute.

Part Two
ORGANIZATIONAL CHANGE

Chapter 4
RESPONDING TO MARKETPLACE CHANGE
Wayne A. Fogel & Lance H. Arrington

Chapter 5
MAKING YOUR ORGANIZATION CHANGE-ABLE™
William R. Daniels & John G. Mathers

Chapter 6
BUILDING TEAMS FOR CHANGE
William G. Stieber

Chapter 7
WEDDING TQM TO CREATIVITY
Don Rapp

Chapter 8
MANAGING CHANGE FOR ORGANIZATIONAL TRANSFORMATION
Phillip P. Andrews & Jerome A. Hahn

Chapter 4

RESPONDING TO
MARKETPLACE CHANGE

Wayne A. Fogel & Lance H. Arrington

Wayne A. Fogel (left) is a founding partner and creative director of The Arrington Group. Mr. Fogel previously served as president and chief executive officer of The Creative Factory Inc., an international education and consulting firm.

Lance H. Arrington (right) is a founding partner and chief executive of The Arrington Group (TAG), headquartered in Winter Park, Florida. Prior to founding TAG, Mr. Arrington served as president and chief operating officer of Philip Crosby Associates.

The Arrington Group is a national management education consulting firm that works with a select group of clients engaged in creating outcome-focused, process-based organizations. A significant part of TAG's work is focused on the human issues associated with helping the people of the organization transition through change.

Lance Arrington and Wayne Fogel, The Arrington Group, 1245 W. Fairbanks Ave. #200, Winter Park, FL 32789; phone (407) 647-5516; fax (407) 647-2901.

Chapter 4

RESPONDING TO MARKETPLACE CHANGE

Wayne A. Fogel & Lance H. Arrington

"If you don't know where you're going, then any road will do."

—The Cheshire Cat in *Alice in Wonderland*

Before we can plan a journey, we must know:
1. Why are we going?
2. Where are we starting from?
3. Where do we want/need to go?
4. When do we have to arrive?

Only after we know the answers to these questions can we determine who will go, how to get there, what the travel budget should be, etc.

Before you can craft an effective organizational response to marketplace change, you must answer a similar set of questions:

- Why are you trying to change?
- What is your present position in the marketplace?
- What do you need to accomplish through this change?

• By what date do you need to complete
this change?

Unfortunately, most organizations tend to
embark upon change without going through the
hard work of answering these questions. Examining why is all too uncommon. Simple cost reduction
programs, in which everyone is asked to cut costs
by X percent per year for Y years, are all too
common.

ORGANIZATIONAL ECOLOGY™

We have learned that in the natural ecology
we cannot change one thing in isolation. Every
change involves the whole. Everyone is familiar
with the consequences of clearing the rainforests,
damming rivers, etc. In each case, if the total
impact is not considered, the potential for disaster
is high.

Equally, organizations embarking upon major change need to be understood as organic
wholes. Organizations have an ecosystem as interrelated as any in nature. The Organizational
Ecology's elements include organizational structure, culture, social
systems, administrative
and core processes, its
physical environment, and
feedback and communication systems.Trying to
change just one of these
without expecting to affect all of the others is an
exercise in futility. (The
Organizational Ecology
model is portrayed in the
figure to the right.)

As in every ecosystem,
change affects primarily
the living organisms (in

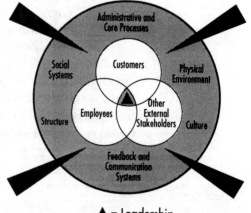

▲ = Leadership

Model Of The Organizational Ecology

this case, the people) within the organic system. The interaction of the people of an organization with each other, customers, suppliers, management, and other external stakeholders controls how an organization will function in its marketplace.

NO SILVER BULLET

In the effort to achieve competitive advantage, it's tempting to hunt for the easy solution. If we want a more competitive company, we must transform the entire organization, not simply paste on a solution. Yet, we continue to seek quick, relatively painless solutions. These solutions are "silver bullets."

> "There is always an easy solution to every human problem—neat, plausible and wrong."
> —H.L. Mencken

Management hunts for silver bullets that will solve the company's problems. After the silver bullet does its work, the company can go forward happily ever after. We won't really have to change how we do work. Our concept of our organizational structure can remain the same. Tweak, yes; but massive change, no.

The three most popular initiatives today are downsizing; total quality management/continuous process improvement; and reengineering. All of these can be part of a total solution, but none will achieve the impact needed unless they are all used as part of a total approach.

The true solution is not the silver bullets or any other piecemeal improvements. It is the transformation of your organization from one that is activity-focused to one that is outcome-focused.

An outcome-focused organization emphasizes those things that provide value to the customer, not to the hierarchy of the organization. Only a biological, holistic approach and a long-term commitment to achieve this goal can provide permanent results.

THE CYCLE OF CHANGE

We're going through a time compression now in our history, in our economy. What used to take 10 years to evolve has gone to 5, then 4, 3, 2, 1, and now six months. And so the idea of management as some sort of science, with certain principles from which you never deviate, no longer applies. The only practice that's constant now is the practice of constantly accommodating to change—and if you're not changing constantly, you're probably not going to be accommodating to the reality of your world.

—*William G. McGowan*

William G. McGowan, chairman of MCI Communications Corporation, made this observation in 1986, and the pace of change has continued to increase. Change is continuous for virtually all organizations today. Since change is inevitable, we need to learn to deal with it in a constructive manner, rather than regarding it as something to be endured or "gotten through."

Constructively implementing change requires that we understand it as a system. The Cycle of Change shows the four phases of change: marketplace success, marketplace change, organizational response, and individual response. Of these, only marketplace change is guaranteed. The marketplace will change whether or not we choose to respond. If we choose to respond, then our people must adapt to the new reality. Only when *both* the organizational response and the individual response are effective can marketplace success be achieved. Even then, it will not be a stable state.

Typical Responses To Change

Once organizations accept that change in the marketplace will occur, they must decide how to

Insanity—continuing to do the same thing while expecting different results. A. Einstein

respond. The first effort in many organizations is to redouble their efforts to do what has made them successful in the past. Eventually, all comes to naught. Working harder at the old success factors doesn't create success.

Then they pursue silver bullets. Again, despite the best efforts of everyone involved, most of these efforts achieve very little.

While there are obvious exceptions, the simple truth is that the degree of difficulty organizations have making real change is directly proportional to the degree of success they have experienced in the marketplace over time. Charles Handy provided an elegant presentation of this in his book *The Age of Paradox*. He provided us with the sigmoid curve.

NOTHING GOES UP FOREVER

Point A to point B marks the period of marketplace success. The longer the time of continuing success, the more the curve looks like a straight line. When the curve begins to top, it is tempting to believe that with a little more effort we can straighten it out again and go back to our 'natural' growth rate. Financial analysts are continuously guilty of projecting growth for an industry into the future based upon past performance. Unfortunately, the curve does bend.

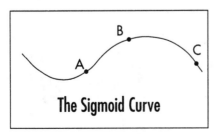

The Sigmoid Curve

The choice for any organization is to either go down the far side of the curve or embark upon a *new* curve. Most companies choose to stay on the same curve and somehow make the old solutions work in the new reality. This is why 11 of the 12 largest companies in the United States in the year 1900 are now gone—out of business or acquired by their newer, stronger and more aggressive competitors. These were steamship companies that did not understand that they were in the transportation business; steel companies that did not understand that they were in the materials business; and so on.

The individual companies that survive the present turmoil in the marketplace will be those who create basic changes rather than react to them. These companies will not fall into the trap of continuing the old patterns with greater effort. Rather, they will recognize the implications of the Cycle of Change and focus their energies on their own responses and those of their employees.

PHASES OF EFFECTIVE CHANGE

The process of crafting and implementing an organizational response to marketplace change includes three distinct phases:

- **Refocus** on the needs of the customers and other stakeholders.
- **Realign** the Organizational Ecology to provide value to the customers.
- **Reengineer** the new core processes for maximum efficiency, flexibility, quality, and responsiveness. (Only preparing for *this* phase will be covered here.)

These three phases form the basis of organizational transformation. The first two phases provide the foundation and grounding that are necessary to make the third phase succeed. Reengineering and other initiatives are then required to optimize the performance of the newly transformed organization.

REFOCUSING ON THE NEEDED CHANGES

Refocusing creates the plan for, and defines the expected outcomes of, the transformation process. In doing this, it prepares the organization for success by providing:

> "The will to win is important, but the will to prepare is vital."
>
> —Joe Paterno,
> Head Football Coach,
> Pennsylvania State University

- an analysis of the marketplace environment
- an assessment of the organization's character and readiness for change
- an analysis of the stakeholders' present and future needs
- a model of an organization that can meet these needs
- an analysis of ongoing improvement initiatives and their costs

The Refocus step is much like developing an architectural rendering and model of a new facility. You can accurately determine the costs and benefits without even breaking ground! Embarking on a major improvement initiative without doing the analysis in advance is the equivalent of starting the foundation of a new building without a set of plans. "Just doing it" doesn't get it done.

Determining The Direction Of Change

"My interest is in the future because I am going to spend the rest of my life there."

—Charles F. Kettering

Being interested in the future is the easy part. Determining what it will look like and how our organization will fit in is where the rubber meets the road. This is what leaders of organizations should spend a great deal of their time doing.

Historically, most executives have tried to blaze new trails by following clearly laid out roads–asking for demonstrations of success by a dozen other organizations before committing to a path of action. While this can lead to short-term security, it does not lend itself to long-term organizational success.

Fortunately, there are ways to determine direction without following the path of the herd. One such method is to develop a strategy for change. The self-evaluating techniques of the methodology ensure an informed decision to proceed at the end of the refocus phase. This is extremely important to prevent committing massive resources to what will become a failed effort. None of us need to be the creator of the next Edsel.

When management understands their role in change, developing the direction of change involves three distinct steps:

1 **Develop/refine the organization's mission, values, and vision.** While this may seem esoteric, it is critical to visit not only the formal, stated versions of these, but also the understood ("real") values and mission of the organization.

The real mission of an organization is not what is posted up on the wall, but what would drive the organization to drop

The Old Vs. New Organization	
Old Rules	**New Rules**
Individual emphasis	Team-emphasis
Information-hoarding	Information-sharing
Internal focus	Customer focus
Hierarchical	Lateral

everything else and focus all of its efforts on the task at hand. Understanding the difference between the "real" and the stated is critical to the future. If you are trying to create an entrepreneurial spin-off of a bureaucratic parent organization whose values are "don't rock the boat," "follow the book," "dress correctly," and "get your reports in on time," you face a nearly impossible task unless the conflict is dealt with in unequivocal terms. Not addressing these issues will assure failure.

2 **Identify core business areas (CBAs).** These are the business areas within which the organization does or will operate. To a large degree, these are business areas in which the existing and potential customer base perceives that the organization has (or should have) expertise. This perception on the part of the customer gives the organization distinct advantages in achieving market entry. If the customer does not perceive expertise, market entry will be very difficult. If the customer does perceive expertise, even if it is not present, market entry will be relatively easy.

3 Develop a business model. This answers the question, "What do we want to be at the next stage of our growth?" By developing a business model, we can determine how to serve our core business areas. Do we want to maintain a functional organization or go to a process-based one? Should we take advantage of new opportunities through the existing organization, or are they best exploited through a new, entrepreneurial subsidiary?

REALIGNMENT: DESIGNING THE NEW ORGANIZATION

At this point, it is time to get on with the work of transformation by realigning the organization to serve its core business areas effectively. Realignment is intended to move an organization from a functional structure to a process-based structure that is oriented around start-to-finish, customer-to-customer processes.

A diagram of a process-based organization is shown at the left. The organization is built around the processes that the customers see adding value to *them*. It is not built around the traditional line and staff functions.

Developing the design for this type of organization is a task best undertaken by the people who will lead the new organization. For this reason, we recommend that top management identify the high-level process owners of each of the Core Business Areas identified during strategy develop-

Process-based Organization

ment. These "owners" can then be put on a task team to design the new process-based organization and develop a comprehensive plan for getting there.

With few exceptions, this will be a full-time assignment that may last for several months. The people selected will be the hardest to spare, but their involvement in designing what they will run is critical. Without their participation, the needed buy-in by these people may not be achieved.

Documenting Key Processes

The first job of the high-level design team is to finalize the identification of the core processes within each Core Business Area that add value in the eyes of the customers, and then analyze each of these processes. Process analysis should include:

- Developing a process flow chart that shows each step of the process.
- Developing a process map that details each step showing movement, departmental involvement, skills and knowledge required for each step, special requirements, etc.
- Collecting process performance data.

- Develop flow chart
- Develop process map
- Collect data

Once the core processes have been identified and analyzed, it is time to analyze the work now being done. Look at each job classification involved with the processes and determine how much of a typical workday is devoted to work that adds value from the customer's point of view, how much time is devoted to other work that does not add value

(NoVA™), and how much structured idle time (SIT™) is included in the job. Honest analysis shows that as little of 10% of the workday is devoted to value-adding work in most companies.

You cannot simply eliminate all NoVA work. Essential reports must still be prepared, new systems must be developed, paychecks must be issued, and so on. However, it is realistic for most companies to double the proportion of time devoted to value-adding work *if* they are willing to roll up their sleeves and make it happen.

Designing New Customer-oriented Processes

Having completed this stage, the design team can lay out new customer-oriented processes, design the performance measurements for each process, determine the knowledge and skills required to operate the process, and develop a team

that has the necessary abilities to operate either the entire process or a significant portion of it (e.g., the entire line extension process for an electric utility). The team can then be replicated as many times as is necessary to perform the work of the organization.

It is important that each team be a single unit. Everyone on the team should report to a single leader and be tasked with doing the work of the team, not performing a job. This requires eliminating functional tasks and organization and replacing them with teams that fulfill customer needs.

Having determined what the new organization will look like, the team should develop the information and staffing systems that will support the new processes and way of working. Systems that were designed to support a functional hierarchy with an emphasis on individual performance may be counterproductive in a process-based, team-centered organization.

IMPLEMENTING THE NEW ORGANIZATION

Concurrently, the transition management plan developed as a part of the organizational strategy for change should be implemented. It is important to do this as soon as possible after assigning the high-level design team. More change efforts fail because people do not fully accept them than for any other reason. Individual transition training should immediately follow the development of the new organizational structure. While everyone will want more detail than is available, providing people with knowledge of the transition and the tools to deal with their own transitions is critical as soon as the people of the organization perceive that change is coming.

Finally, the high-level design team must complete the implementation plan and schedule. Once these are evaluated and accepted by the organization's leadership, they should be shared

> "Even if you're on the right track, you'll get run over if you just sit there."
> —Will Rogers

with all the people of the organization. Continuous communication is essential to (1) help provide the information individuals need to manage their own transitions, and (2) counter the rumor mill that can wreak havoc within the organization.

Organizations should heed Will Rogers' advice (see box) as they go about the business of implementing their new designs. At each step, during each day, and often several times a day, people will come up with reasons to study rather than act. It is important that leadership accept the fact that not everything will work out as expected, but continue to push forward, find the weak points, correct them, and move on. Sitting and studying guarantees failure–continuing hard work and forward motion are virtual guarantees of success.

Implementation consists of three phases:

- piloting
- full-scale implementation
- evaluation and preparation for reengineering

Some overlap may occur within each phase and from phase to phase. For example, high-performance work teams may be introduced in the pilot phase and then extended during the full-scale implementation phase.

1 Pilot Testing New Processes. During the piloting phase of implementation, two major activities are undertaken. The first of these is to implement any short-term improvements that have not already been implemented. Quite often, this will have been done earlier to help free up the money and people to do the work necessary for organizational transformation.

The second major activity is to pilot and debug the new core processes that will be central to the new process-based organization. This is important for two reasons—first, it provides an opportunity to test the new organizational design against reality. Unless a miracle has occurred, there will be problems. You can fix those as you go along. With persistence, you can resolve the problems and have the pilots up and running effectively. At this point, the second reason for piloting becomes apparent. As the people in the pilot see the new way of working as both more productive and more fulfilling, they become internal salespeople for the redesigned organization.

High-performance work teams should be introduced concurrently with the piloting work on the new processes in order to carry them out. Going to high-performance work teams is an activity that requires a great deal of time, effort, and education. Simply announcing them accomplishes nothing except creating a feeling of frustration among all the people involved, both managers and employees. (Also see Chapter 6 on teams.)

2 Full-scale Implementation. When to do this is a matter of judgment. An organization should feel reasonably comfortable with the new processes. However, the tendency for perfectionism must be resisted. All potential problems will never be fully addressed to everyone's satisfaction. This is the time when the greatest

---

Full-scale Implementation Plan

- Introduce the new process-based organizational structure.

- Implement the new core processes across the organization.

- Implement the new information systems that support the new way of working.

- Implement the new process measurements to quantify performance and identify problem and high-performance areas. Both must be analyzed: problem areas so that the problems can be eliminated and performance restored, and high-performance areas so that the benefits can be spread across the entire organization. Exploiting unexpected high performance normally provides many times the benefit of normal problem solving.

- Implement the support and administrative processes that work with and assist the carrying out of the new core processes.

- Implement the new people systems that reward team rather than individual behaviors to support the new way of working. In most organizations, the new people systems follow rather than lead the implementation. This allows a higher degree of certainty of structure before you alter what many people consider to be entitlements.

- Provide training to support all of this. Training should be provided on a 'just-in-time' basis. In other words, it should coincide with and overlap the introduction of doing work in the new way. Trying to do the training in advance will prove futile because adults learn only what they can apply. (Months of theory do little to help musical ability, unless the individual sits down and plays.)

---

resistance to change will occur, and it is critical that forward movement not be stopped.

Full-scale implementation is putting in place what was previously designed and debugged. Normally, it cannot be done in one fell swoop, but must be phased in over a period of time. (See box above for what this work involves.)

3 **Preparation for Reengineering.** The last phase of implementation is the evaluation and preparation for reengineering. Note that some aspects of reengineering are discussed in detail in other chapters of this book. This section addresses only those activities involved in preparing for the reengineering process.

Benchmarking

The first action in preparing for reengineering is to establish baselines for each core process. This is done using both internal and external standards of performance.

- Establish the internal standard of performance for each core process by identifying the best-performing process (and/or subprocess) team across the organization. Determine the team's performance and the methods of achieving it, and then compare it to the performance and methods of the rest of the organization.

Measure performance, and compare it to best-performing team.

- Establish the external standard of performance for each core process through benchmarking. Many organizations and industries share the infamous "not invented here" syndrome. While the organization and specific technologies may be different, the methods of carrying out a process are not. For this reason, it is essential that information from outside the industry be considered. The knowledge needed for a breakthrough in core process performance is almost always found in areas outside the existing industry.

Once the standards have been established, it is time to quantify the performances of the existing core processes (and subprocesses as appropriate) and compare them against these standards. Those areas that fall short should be brought up to the internal standards as quickly as possible. Where the internal standards fall significantly short of the external standards, reengineering of the internal processes is indicated.

CONCLUSION

Real organizational change is hard, ongoing work. It must involve all parts of the organization and its entire system/ecology to be effective. Otherwise, it will be just one more 'silver bullet.' And most of us have had enough of those in our lives.

However, just as the work is hard and real, the payoffs are hard and real. Typically, organizations that carry out what we have outlined in this chapter see the following:

- A 20 to 40 percent reduction in operating costs
- Radically improved customer satisfaction
- Shorter turnaround times
- Greater employee involvement and satisfaction

Once you have "accomplished" your organizational transformation, it will be time to start again, for the marketplace will continue to change. If, however, you have done it right this time, you will have an organization that is proactive about change. In fact, change never stops in an organic organization that is in a fluid environment. This will provide a long-term competitive advantage— and isn't that what we are all seeking?

ACTION SUMMARY

▶ Assess your position in the market-place and where you want to be.

▶ Determine positive reasons why you want change.

▶ To create change, start by refocusing on your customers. All changes should provide extra value for them, on their terms.

▶ Involve other stakeholders like employees.

▶ Develop or refine your mission and values statements.

▶ Develop flow charts of your processes and planned processes.

▶ Set up pilot programs to test new process-oriented teams.

▶ Benchmark yourself internally and externally.

▶ Develop a full-scale implementation plan.

Chapter 5

MAKING YOUR ORGANIZATION CHANGE-ABLE™

William R. Daniels & John G. Mathers

William R. Daniels (left) is a senior partner of American Consulting & Training, Inc. (ACT), which he co-founded in 1979. For more than 25 years, he has helped managers, teams, and organizations develop the skills necessary to manage continuous change. Mr. Daniels helps his clients cope with change by addressing their most immediate and critical business needs, and in the process teaches them management skills needed for long-term success. He is the author of several books, including: *Breakthrough Performance: Managing for Speed and Flexibility*, and *Group Power I: A Manager's Guide to Using Task Force Meetings*.

John G. Mathers (right) is a senior consultant of ACT. He has worked with top executives for more than 25 years to facilitate their decision making on issues of strategy, organization, and diversification. Mr. Mathers' work focuses on decision-making processes based on teamwork and technology. To support speed and quality, he employs electronic meeting technologies to capture and process management discussion, organization design, and decision making as it occurs. He has been instrumental in the design of ACT's proprietary software product that assists teams in streamlining their work for improved productivity.

Recent ACT clients include: Intel, Motorola, Genesco, Space Systems/ Loral, Philips Semiconductor, Levi Strauss & Co., Pepsi-Cola International, University of California, Bank of America, and Bristol-Myers Squibb.

William R. Daniels and John G. Mathers, American Consulting & Training, 655 Redwood Hwy., Suite 395, Mill Valley, CA 94941; phone (415) 388-6651, (800) 995-6651; fax (415) 388-6672.

Chapter 5

MAKING YOUR ORGANIZATION CHANGE-ABLE™

William R. Daniels & John G. Mathers

"We have got to address the issue of making the work force sufficiently skilled to deal with [advancing technology]."

—Alan Greenspan, the Federal Reserve

The human factor is the balance point by which private enterprise in the United States will define itself well into the next century.

Our twenty plus years of consulting work with thousands of managers and individual contributors, in every segment of private and public enterprise, has convinced us that new methods of on-the-job training must be employed for the human factor in organizations to keep up with technological changes.

THE FIVE PRACTICES OF THE CHANGE-ABLE ORGANIZATION

Through observing corporations that have grown 20% or more in revenues, profits, and infrastructure for more than three years, we have identified the core practices of high performance. We have come to believe in the power and resilience of the type of management structure that underlies these high-performing corporations—what we call *Change-ABLE* organizations.

There are five key management practices which, when undertaken in concert, support continued growth and increasing productivity. These five practices are:

1 **Linked Teams**. The management hierarchy operates as a system of linked teams. Groups of overlapping managers form the channels of communication by which the organization governs itself.

2 **Performance Plans**. The planning system requires every team of managers, every individual manager, and every individual contributor to have a performance plan. Performance plans coordinate every individual's performance throughout the organization.

3 **Work Reviews**. Management teams systematically and frequently focus on work review. Managers work together to evaluate and control each other's organizational sections.

4 **Group Decision-Making**. Management teams use rational group decision-making processes. Group intelligence allocates and controls the use of organizational resources.

5 **Breakthrough Systems**. Individual contributors are in breakthrough systems at the base of the hierarchy. They manage their own behavior with reliable feedback systems, and immediately and accurately report what has been accomplished.

Each of these five practices can be found—to varying degrees— in every organization. However, the application of each practice may not be stable enough to produce consistent results. Also, the fact that many organizations apply some, but not all, of the practices, guarantees inconsistent or poor results.

Here is a brief overview of each of the practices as installed in high-performance organizations:

Linked Teams

Linked Teams have four key attributes. First, the focus of performance objectives is on team results rather than handling actions on a one-on-one basis (i.e., there is an admitted dependence). Second, there are regular one-on-one and team meetings. Third, the team recognizes and understands its links into the organization's formal authority. Fourth, the team recognizes its links across the organization to other task force and cross-functional teams.

Performance Plans

Performance Plans have five attributes. First, there are seven or fewer objectives. This makes the plan memorable and memorizable (i.e., it can be communicated in three minutes or less). Second, the total Performance Plan represents 80% or more of the individual manager's job responsibilities (i.e., the plan is comprehensive). Third, the objectives are outcome-oriented and metrics-based. Fourth, key partners (i.e., those individuals across and outside the organization who are crucial to accomplishing the objective) are aligned with the identified outcome. Fifth, the objectives are prioritized. A hundred percentage points are distributed among the outputs in the plan to show their relative importance.

- Focus on team rather than on individual relationships
- Regular one-on-one and team meetings
- Recognized team links to organization's formal authority
- Linkage across the organization to other teams

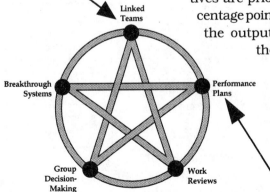

- Seven or fewer memorable objectives
- Comprehensive (80% or more) of Job
- Outcome-oriented & metrics-based
- Aligned key partners
- Objectives prioritized

Work Reviews

Work Reviews have four key attributes. First, the review compares results against the Performance Plan. Second, the review of each objective and its results is represented graphically in an easy-to-understand format. Third, the focus of the review is exception-based (i.e., issues—rather than status-oriented). Fourth, the review is action-oriented (i.e., each issue is followed by a recommendation for team action).

Group Decision-Making

Group Decision-Making has four key attributes. First, the team selects and utilizes a rational decision-making process (i.e., consensus or consultative decision-making). Second, regular meetings have a decisive, predefined agenda (i.e., "pass-downs," Work Reviews, recommendation reviews, and news). Third, all members of the team "advocate and inquire" in all peer inter-actions. Fourth, team members may "agree/disagree and commit" to actions stemming from rational decision-making.

Breakthrough Systems

Breakthrough Systems, at the Individual Contributor level, has three key attributes. First, each individual contributor has a clear expectation, aligned with the team leader. Second, each individual contributor has

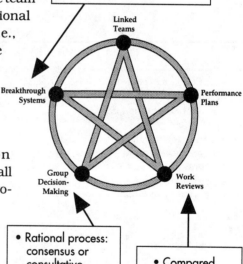

For individual contributors:
- Clear expectations
- Self-monitored feedback
- Control of resources

Linked Teams

Breakthrough Systems

Performance Plans

Group Decision-Making

Work Reviews

- Rational process: consensus or consultative
- Decisive pre-defined agenda
- Advocacy *and* inquiry
- Agree/disagree *and* commit

- Compared against plan
- Graphically presented
- Exception/ issues focused
- Action-oriented

his or her own feedback system for regularly checking progress toward their objectives (i.e., every few hours). Third, all individual contributors have the resources needed to accomplish their expected results.

INCREASING ORGANIZATIONAL PERFORMANCE

The organizations that were Change-ABLE before we met them had varied histories. Some came to the key practices through trial and error. Others started out with the whole system in place as a requirement of their early leaders.

In our consulting practice, we have had the privilege of working with companies desiring to move from their current slow or low performance levels—what we refer to as "stuck"—to a higher performance level. No management book can guide such a shift in culture, and we have not attempted to prescribe what we believe are oversimplified solutions.

We have had some success changing stuck organizations to Change-ABLE ones, and we have used a variety of approaches—depending upon the organization's understanding of its immediate needs. Our experience has taught us that there is no one way to move an organization from a stuck culture to a Change-ABLE one. There are, in fact, many ways. Sometimes we've started working on strategy with the executive team. At other times, we've started at the bottom of the organization, working with first-line managers and individual contributors to implement Breakthrough Systems.

Unprofitable Approaches To Becoming Change-ABLE

We've also been part of unsuccessful efforts, which resulted in no appreciable organizational change. As a result, we have learned there are at least three methods that don't work very well.

> "As the problems are new, we must disenthrall ourselves from the past."
> —Abraham Lincoln

The turnaround artist is one unsuccessful approach. Though almost everybody says they know better, most of us still hope to find a "quick fix." We want some obvious method we can quickly learn that will yield immediate results—so we go for the dramatic turnaround.

Such leader-dependent efforts at organizational change almost never have a long-term beneficial effect on organizations. The quick results are usually gained at the expense of employees and customers. It often seems as if the turnaround leader came into the organization, removed half of the resources (i.e., people, capital, or budget) and told those remaining to now produce twice the results. Costs are temporarily reduced, but the long-term result is a crippled organization. After a couple of years, the organization is in worse condition than it was before the turnaround began.

Approaches that take people off-line a long time don't work either. Today's organizations just don't have the time to sit around thinking about their processes.

When being stuck has resulted in organizational crisis, the idea of stopping to think about it is unacceptable. It's difficult to find the time for goal-setting, team-building, or organizational-culture training programs when you feel the organization is about to lose some of its biggest customers or fall into Chapter 11. It is also unlikely that the organization will tolerate massive programs operating as separate, parallel organizations. This is often the way implementation of total quality or reengineering is attempted—which might explain Michael Hammer's statement that 70% of reengineering efforts fail. Typically, these programs run into a wall in about three years. They are not seen as essential, but rather as competitors for the organization's vital resources and a distraction from the organization's real work. These efforts at change seem like diversions—employees are working hard, but not on work directly linked to the organization's goals.

A third ineffective approach to organizational change is to give attention to only part of the key practices. Many organizations do one or two of the five practices quite well. But that isn't enough to get the necessary swift and flexible performance. Just getting everyone to write a performance plan won't cause an organization to become Change-ABLE. All by themselves, Breakthrough Systems for individual contributors will not make a stuck organization govern itself intelligently. Any one of the practices by itself is not effective. Only when all five of the key management practices are adopted does a stuck organization become something altogether new.

A PROFITABLE 4-STEP APPROACH TO BECOMING CHANGE-ABLE

In our experience, an effective effort at becoming Change-ABLE has to have four key characteristics: (1) widespread participation; (2) immediate "online" applicability; (3) using existing meetings to implement numbers 1 and 2; and (4) all five key management practices.

> "A good employee is a valuable resource who can easily be lost forever if placed in a job that is not personally fulfilling and challenging and that does not offer a genuine opportunity for contribution."
> —Tom Potts & Arnold Sykes, *Executive Talent: How to Identify & Develop the Best*

1 **Widespread Participation.** Management can not "do change" to the organization. People control their own behavior. They may *allow* themselves to be coerced into changing their behavior. Coerced behavior, however, is usually slow and awkward, as it is based on latent resentment and fear. Involuntary behavior doesn't have the flexibility and precision representing the practices of the Change-ABLE organization.

The motivation to take prompt action comes from people who understand and are committed to the organization's purpose—people who know what the organization expects. The Change-ABLE organization appreciates anything employees do toward accomplishment of that purpose. The Change-ABLE organization is made up of participants, not rule-makers and rule-followers.

2 **Immediate "Online" Applicability.** An effective change effort ought not to start with too much time-out for talking. Since the change

ultimately has to happen "online" (i.e., in the midst of people doing what it takes to make the organization effective), it is a good idea to start the change effort online. If the effort must begin with talking, start talking about solving the real problems. Since change requires people to alter their own behavior, request behaviors relevant to solving the problems their current behavior causes. It's important to get into the organization's politics and power plays right at the start because successful change requires the use of all the organization's political and social power.

"We can sit here all day until the person who has the hidden agenda speaks up."

3 Meetings Reinforce Culture, And Points 1 & 2. Getting online to change the organization is not difficult: Join its regular meetings. Weekly staff meetings are an effective place to start. Because of the wasted time in most meetings, there's plenty of time available for doing something more useful! Other regular meetings may be important as well: the quarterly work reviews (even if they are ineffective), or the annual planning sessions (even when they seem empty of meaning).

Also look for any regularly held "informal" meetings, because it's at these meetings that the work actually gets done. These informal meetings are often cross-functional meetings and are held at lower management levels. They usually include a mix of managers and individual contributors.

After extensive observation of regular meetings, it has become clear to us that this is the way an organization reinforces its current culture. If these meetings are changed, change can be leveraged all over the organization. They are the windows to the organization's culture, and the classrooms in which that culture is taught—over and over every week. No training seminar can ever override what is being taught in these real classrooms. Change the organization by changing what its regular meetings display and teach!

4 **Use All Five Key Management Practices.** Finally, commit from the beginning to all five of the key management practices. In isolation, none are new or unique. Most organizations do at least one or two of them. But the results are very different when only one or two of the practices are in place. The swift and intelligent performance of the Change-ABLE organization requires all the practices to be done in unison. Doing them simultaneously creates an organization that is altogether new.

CREATING CHANGE: AN EXAMPLE OF SEQUENCED ACTION

As we noted earlier, there are as many ways of moving an organization as there are organizations. However, one scenario that we have employed successfully over the years has this series of five steps implementing the five key managaement practices of a Change-ABLE organization.

1 **Linked Teams.** Start by "rostering" the organization reporting to the manager who wants to champion the transformation. Rostering is simply getting out the organization charts and finding out who is supposedly reporting to whom.

Usually, the charts don't tell the true story of how the organization is operating. In reality, lots of people have been more or less consciously promoted, demoted, and even terminated-in-place. Look at what regular meetings are being held and who is attending them. The structure will reveal itself as an operational reality through the leadership and attendance of the regular meetings. Pay attention to how the meetings link to each other through their leaders and members. Where they are linked in this way, you have the beginnings of an effective hierarchy. Where the linkage breaks down (usually because meetings are not actually being held) there is a need for structural repair (i.e., convening the missing meetings).

Don't even consider restructuring the organization! Any action will be a source of confusion and create the potential for a covert power play. Let the real operational reality come into view as the bright lights of decisive regular meetings focus on structural inefficiencies. If no regular meetings are being held—a rare case— then convene them as defined by the current organization chart. State the purpose of the meeting as a chance to talk about how the work is getting done.

2 **Performance Plans.** In each of these meetings, initiate the process of forming a management team. Draft the leader's Performance Plan. Make sure the draft contains all of the essential characteristics of a good Performance Plan. Then make it the main agenda for one of these regular meetings. Ask the team members to consult with the leader until the plan states the results they want to accomplish as a group.

Next, the leader should request that each team member create an individual Performance Plan, using the same format. Mention that these plans should be specific enough to use in work reviews. Team members should be encouraged to test their plans, with both the leader and their teammates.

With this accomplished, the management team should meet to align their plans with the leader and with all the group members. At this alignment meeting, the management team will look for overlaps and disconnects between the plans. Revise plans until the roles each member is supposed to fulfill to ensure achieving the results stated in the team's plan (i.e., leader's plan) are clearly identified.

Start this Performance Plan alignment process with the positive attitude that it can be done in a couple of weeks. Sometimes it can! And don't be discouraged when it takes two months. Big attitudinal and behavioral changes take place in this process when working in a stuck culture. This is the right focus of attention—the right set of issues to be talking about. Be prepared to see the group quickly identify and solve some problems long overdue for attention. These real-world solutions are the early successes that build confidence in the new practices.

3 Work Reviews. As alignment of performance plans nears conclusion, begin doing Work Reviews. Don't wait for perfect plan alignment before starting the Work Reviews. The effort to keep plans aligned is never going to cease—it will always be an underlying purpose of every regular meeting. As soon as the group accepts one of its members' Performance Plans, schedule that member for a Work Review.

Work Reviews should begin as an agenda item in the regular meeting. Set some meeting time aside to review the work of one or two members. These first reviews will often take up to an hour each. The group will discover problems. The metrics for measuring progress may be inappropriate, or the data being displayed may be inaccurate.

Over a period of a few months, each member's Performance Plan and Work Review will come into focus. Eventually, team members will be able to meet the criteria of displaying their status in four minutes or less, and getting their critical issues addressed in about fifteen minutes. The team will then be able to make a complete round of all its members' Work Reviews within a couple of weeks—as part of two regular weekly meetings. This is the mark of mature teams.

It may take quite awhile to reach this point—maybe even a year. Don't be impatient. Not a minute of this time is wasted. Every word, every correction, every small step in the direction of a more current and valid presentation of the issues affecting the organization's performance is signifi-

"Obstacles are those frightful things you see when you take your eyes off the goal."
—Hannah More, English social reformer, 1775

cant progress toward becoming Change-ABLE. Getting regular meetings to focus on Work Reviews and the associated decision making is the most difficult of the practices to get in place. It is, however, the core requirement for management as we proceed into the 21st century. Are we going to share purpose, goals, resources and accountability—or not?

4 Group Decision-Making. At every step of the way, apply rational Group Decision-Making. The leader of each group must insist on consultation from the team members regarding every decision, starting with the five practices:

- Should we adopt these five practices?
- Is the leader's plan right?
- Are the members' plans right?
- Are the metrics correct?
- Are the graphics helpful?
- Are the data valid?
- Do we think the performance being reported should be approved, corrected, or supported in some other way?

While these decisions are being made, the leader teaches the group to check for understanding—not agreement. By model and explanation, the leader teaches the members the importance of inquiry—asking questions to make sure you understand and are understood by others. The leader then models and teaches team members not to argue until there's mutual understanding—understanding of how much disagreement actually exists. Only then can we intelligently explore these disagreements. Disagreement must be made not only acceptable but desirable.

Finally, the leader needs to follow up in these meetings to make sure the members are exhibiting the behaviors of commitment. Check to see that decisions are correctly explained to the rest of the organization, and that compliance is defined

"To be able to ask a question clearly is two-thirds of the way to getting it answered."

—John Ruskin

through the focus and allocation of the organization's resources.

By the time these practices are in place, the organization will already have felt one or more jolts putting it into a more rapid and intelligent level of performance. Don't be fooled. Moving into high gear has not yet taken place—not until the fifth practice is in place.

5 **Breakthrough Systems.** Once a "critical mass" of managers— about half of the management meetings—are doing Work Reviews, implement Breakthrough Systems. Begin by putting the idea on the agenda in meetings of first-line managers (i.e., people who manage individual contributors). Place it on the agenda as a recommendation for review. Get the first-line managers to consult with their leaders about whether or not, or how, the implementation should take place.

Several different ways of introducing Breakthrough Systems have proven effective. Workshops for teams of first-line managers and their direct reports (individual contributors) provide a quick start. In the manufacturing setting, such workshops usually introduce the idea through simulations—exercises allowing the teams to experience working in Breakthrough Systems. The teams can then spend time deciding how to put Breakthrough Systems in place for their own work...usually by the next day.

The simulation may be different when working with project teams (who are often more directly focused on charting project tasks and critical path). But the outcome of commitment to breakthrough systems is the same.

Everybody involved with the project—marketing, product design, engineering, suppliers, customers, sales and service, etc.—is

invited into one big war room for a day to review, revise, and authorize the plan. Deliverables, schedule, management structure, and the change approval process are discussed in as much detail as possible. The final result is a plan with a short cycle of deliverables establishing expectations individual contributors can use for their self-management in Breakthrough Systems. At the end of the next week, individual contributors attend their first weekly "Done/Not Done" meeting, a form of work review that is appropriate for their kind of work.

No organization we have worked with has ever failed to shock itself by the results of getting Breakthrough Systems linked up with the other four practices. The difference this linkage makes is extraordinary. Things will begin to change quickly (see at right).

SUMMARY

This is only a high-level overview of one way to move an organization toward becoming Change-ABLE. The details of all forms of resistance that emerge and all the possible ways of dealing with that resistance are not addressed in this article. But it would be untruthful to represent any process we know of as easy, quick, or certain.

The complexity of organizational change is staggering—all individuals go through the process of significant role change in their own unique way. And not everyone makes the change. There is nothing sneaky about this process, however. Everyone is asked to reconsider the purpose of the organization, to decide whether or not to contribute to that purpose, and to continuously participate in deciding how to make their contributions. Some choose not to be a part of the new organization. Others find the change demanding, enlivening, and uplifting.

You'll Know Change Is Happening When...

- The organization spontaneously begins redesigning itself for streamlined performance.
- Customer suspicions and doubts start dissolving and partnerships emerge.
- Suppliers temporarily go a little crazy as you become a more significant and demanding customer.
- Competitors get scared and start using larger caliber ammunition.
- A new set of problems quickly comes into focus. They are real problems, but they are the kind of problems you want: the problems of success.

Taking Your Step Toward A Change-ABLE Organization

The process we have described has all four of the characteristics we believe are required for any successful effort. It involves everyone. It has immediate online application. It uses existing meetings to implement the first two steps. And it ties all the key management practices together.

The sequence we described has an internal logic. It pulls the organization's hierarchy together as a system of meetings. It aligns Performance Plans; starts using the plans for Work Reviews; takes each step using rational Group Decision-Making; and implements Breakthrough Systems. This logic can help you choose to begin.

Other sequences will also work, because the practices make up an interdependent system. You can start with any one of them and work your way to the others in a variety of ways. As long as all the practices are adopted as soon as possible, the change effort will maintain its relevance and acquire more and more of the organization's support.

You can start at any level in the hierarchy. Of course, the ideal place to start is with the highest level executive team. Starting at the top produces the biggest changes in the least amount of time. But we have been part of successful change efforts that have begun at the middle—and even the lowest—levels of the hierarchy.

We have seen several large projects transform themselves into Change-ABLE organizations, while nested within organizations that were bureaucratic, entrepreneurial, or autocratic. In such cases, after two or three years, the Change-ABLE organizations are usually cast off by the parent organization—sold or in other formal ways separated from the parent. We consider this result only a partial success.

Finally, we want to make it clear that we do not think organizations must evolve through certain "stages" to become Change-ABLE. It can be argued that there is a historical progression from the association, to bureaucracy, to autocracy. But this does not imply a natural course of development requiring replication in each organization. We believe everyone should progress directly to the health and effectiveness of the Change-ABLE organization.

CONCLUSION

As Alan Greenspan, chairman of the United States Federal Reserve, pointed out in testimony before the House Committee on Banking and Financial Services, we are in the "midst of a quickening of the process" of change brought about by technological advances. How we respond to the change—and how we manage it in the next *short* decade—will define our future...and maybe the future of economic democracy worldwide. As Chairman Greenspan noted:

> I think it is essential that we focus on this in a manner which addresses the fundamental causes of the problem—getting human capital, as economists like to call it, up to levels which enable the physical capital to function—but recognizes that, as difficult as technology is in many respects as we change the structure of our economy, it has propelled the United States to the highest standard of living the world has ever known. If we proceed in that regard, I suspect we are going to find that we will maintain that position well into the 21st century.

Getting human capital up to levels which enable physical capital to function is the task of leadership for the next decade. The method for achieving this is implementation of the integrated system of Linked Teams, Performance Plans, Work Reviews, Group Decision Making, and Breakthrough Systems.

Wherever organizational change has been participative, online, and aimed at adoption of all five practices, there has been a significant improvement in the organization's performance and an acceleration in its growth. The organizations we have worked with have become noticeably more successful. So, we grow in our confidence as we recommend to all managers and individual contributors, go for it! Get Change-ABLE!

ACTION SUMMARY

▶ Create an accurate organizational chart showing real reporting relationships. Fill in existing lines of communication that have not been acknowledged.

▶ Don't restructure the organization, just bring what really works to the forefront.

▶ Use existing meetings to draft Performance Plans, individually and as groups.

▶ Use regular Work Reviews to align Performance Plans with performance.

▶ Use Group Decision-Making to involve all team members.

▶ Implement the Breakthrough System of clear expectations, alignment of individual and team goals, self-monitored feedback, and control of resources needed to do the job.

Chapter 6

BUILDING TEAMS FOR CHANGE

William G. Stieber

William G. Stieber, PhD, is the owner of InterPro Development, Inc., a consulting firm that assists corporations in their quests for improvement and change implementation. He has been recognized for his leadership in quality improvement and other large-scale improvement initiatives in numerous organizational settings, and in 1994, served as a Senior Lead Examiner for the Pennsylvania Quality Award. He is also a certified Deming Method consultant.

Dr. Stieber has extensive experience in training and development, organizational design, and in developing team skills—from group dynamics to meeting management. Many of his assignments have included implementation of total quality and organizational redesign processes involving design, and self-directed and process improvement teams. InterPro's clients include Blue Cross and Blue Shield, ICI Americas, Merck and Co., the Federal Reserve Bank, Peabody Western, Kiwi Brands, SmithKline Beecham, and Zeneca.

Dr. Stieber received his PhD in Psychoeducational Processes from Temple University. He is a member of the American Society of Quality and Participation, American Society of Quality Control, American Society of Training and Development, and the National Speakers Association.

William G. Stieber, PhD, InterPro Development, Inc., 2865 S. Eagle Road #388, Newtown, PA 18940; phone (215) 860-6098; fax (215) 860-4398; e-mail Stieberpro@aolcom.

Chapter 6

BUILDING TEAMS FOR CHANGE
William G. Stieber

"We must all hang together, or assuredly we shall all hang separately."

> —Benjamin Franklin, speaking as a member of the first American change team (about the Revolution)

A TALE OF TWO COMPANIES

Two organizations, Company X and Company Y, are revamping their management and supervisory structures, their data processing centers, and their customer service departments, as part of reengineering efforts.

Both businesses have about 1500 employees and experienced a period of rapid growth in the early 1990s. However, the companies are struggling to maintain profit margins and retain good employees, especially since a major corporation has opened a new plant in the area.

COMPANY X: TOP DOWN CHANGE

Knowing that change was imperative, The CEO at Company X directed his three top managers to work with him to come up with a plan that could be quickly and easily implemented. He referred to this group of four individuals as the reengineering team.

One month later, a memo was distributed to midlevel managers and supervisors. The document outlined the company's new goals and assigned a date by which each new plan would be implemented. The next day, department supervisors assembled for a staff meeting and were handed instructions about the alterations in production and customer service procedures. The new supervisory and reporting pyramid was revealed and the meeting ended with a pep talk by the CEO.

Explanations Needed

The next day, many supervisors approached their managers with questions: Why was their reporting structure changed? Why were production goals altered, and were more people going to be hired to meet the goals? The data processing department supervisor was alarmed about the increased number of written reports she was expected to produce. The customer service supervisor didn't understand why their telephone procedures were being revamped. No one had complained about them, so why the change?

One by one, the managers went back to the restructuring team to ask for clarification. Piece by piece, the plan was reexplained

---

Poor Grades On Communication And Planning

- Only 37% rate their companies positively on their communication efforts regarding the change process; 20% said "poor" or "very poor."
- Only 42% did a "good" to "very good" job of planning and organizing the change effort; 18% indicated either "poor" or "very poor."

From a Hay Group survey of 927 human resources professionals whose companies had undergone a significant strategic or organizational change in the past two years.

"Please, no more changes!"

and the supervisors attempted to pass the information on to their direct reports.

The managers responsible for training the supervisors scheduled after-hours sessions, which created difficulties in many departments. Since when, the supervisors wanted to know, do we hold training workshops on Saturday? And why are we doing this anyway?

Morale Shot

Within weeks, several managers and supervisors were updating their résumés and approaching recruiters. With the new plant coming into the area, perhaps some new job opportunities would appear on the horizon. Meanwhile, the CEO and his "team" couldn't understand what the fuss was all about. Nevertheless, within a year, employee morale was at an all-time low. The CEO fired two top managers, claiming that their inability to work as a team hampered the implementation of much needed changes.

COMPANY Y: INVOLVING WORKERS

Meanwhile, on the other side of town, top management at Company Y was facing the need to overhaul their product delivery system. Plus, their computer support software in customer service was rapidly becoming out-of-date. The CEO, who had attended a seminar on using teams to facilitate change, called in a consultant to help upper-level management reach consensus about their mission, strategy, and goals.

Values And Goals

Before management changed their current organizational structure and systems, they asked themselves what they were trying to accomplish. If they decided to redesign the organization to emphasize teams, what would the teams do? What improvements could the company expect? The consultant helped managers determine what worked well within the company's departments, systems, and strategic direction, along with determining what long-standing problems needed attention.

The CEO brought in an outside consultant because he wanted objective opinions and impressions. The consultant also provided educational and facilitation support to a team of company employees assembled to help redesign the organization.

The CEO of Company Y also formed an ad hoc team to explore the company's vision for the future. While everyone knew that change was needed, he believed the company needed a new vision, one that would guide the hard task ahead of them.

Time To Team

Within two months, Company Y had a redesign team in place. While it took an additional six months to come up with a final plan to redesign the company, two self-directed teams were initiated immediately. One team was directed to handle payroll; the other was in charge of purchasing procedures.

The consultant recommended a team-process trainer who could work with participants and help them make the transition from individuals with a supervisor to a self-directed team. Both teams were asked for ideas for permanently streamlining their procedures to increase efficiency.

In essence, these teams became the pilot project for Company Y, with an implementation team closely following their progress and watching for obstacles in their path. No doubt about it—change was in the air at Company Y. The *process* of change was communicated to employees at all levels through the company newsletter. Members of the newly formed self-directed teams were asked to write articles about their experiences. Employees in other departments were informed that these were pilot projects expected to benefit the company in the long run. In other words, top management at Company Y began involving all employees in implementing the changes.

As the months passed, additional teams were formed to explore the status of other departments. Within two years, Company Y had restructured, streamlined many procedures, and improved customer service and product delivery. All these improvements were accomplished by using teams, while morale stayed high.

PRINCIPLES OF SUCCESS

Company X and Company Y both dealt with necessary changes. Yet their experiences were very different because they approached the challenges using different change models. The box at the bottom of the page shows the principles their experiences illustrate.

Company X, Theory X

The CEO of Company X attempted to institute change quickly, which can appear advantageous in some circumstances. The weakness in his plan, however, was that change was directed from the top and lacked clear focus.

When employees asked why a particular system or procedure needed to be changed, they posed a logical question. They were neither convinced that change was needed nor impressed by directives imposed from "on high." Changes were implemented without adequate preparation and a sense of experimentation was sorely lacking. When two managers were fired at the end of the first year, the middle managers wondered if they'd be next.

6 Principles For Successful Change

1. Change for its own sake is not necessarily positive.
2. Diagnose problems before you treat them.
3. Involve people at all levels of the organization.
4. Train team-building techniques as you institute teams.
5. Try pilot team projects and assess how well they work.
6. Communicate, communicate, communicate.

Company Y, Theory Y

The CEO and top management at Company Y also recognized the need for broad changes in procedures and productivity. However, they wanted to identify their strategic direction before they proceeded.

In addition, they wisely believed that participation should be wide, rather than narrow. Their outside consultant guided them and ultimately helped save money as they redesigned the organization. They used their pilot projects to assess the way teams could be brought into the organization. In this company, the "surprise factor" was minimized. Employees were involved in all aspects of the change effort. Each step of the change proceeded with a team in place.

> "All changes even the most longed for, have their melancholy; for what we leave behind is part of ourselves; we must die to one life before we can enter into another."
> —Anatole France, French writer

INDIVIDUALS VS. TEAMS

Company X's CEO was a proponent of rugged individualism. Though well-educated and highly successful, he remained ignorant about the true function of teams. To him, teamwork meant that each individual carried out tasks that were assigned by someone else, no questions asked. If these individuals performed well, they were good team members. Ultimately, he was the leader of the team, which to him, included the whole company.

The top managers, whom he believed were unable to work within a team structure, were understandably confused about their functions. As happens in many companies, upper-level management attempted to carry out policies they weren't clear about in the first place. Company X had set itself up to fail.

The CEO at Company Y and many of his managers had a better grasp of the change process. In addition, they had kept up with trends in organizational design and development. This CEO, together with the managers he hired, looked at the challenges facing them down the road and were willing to leave the past behind. They also understood that teams can help bring out the best in individuals and companies.

Teams Are The Future

In the current business climate, almost all business owners, managers, and supervisors acknowledge the need for teams. Teams also have advantages in implementing change during critical periods.

Today, "teaming," "team-building," "team leader," and even "virtual team" are common terms in organizations of every description. But it was not always so. It's no exaggeration to say that the concept of team building in U.S. industry was born as a result of a desperate need for rapid improvement. Economic and social pressures combined to change the nature of the workplace. Now millions of men and women have participated in this ongoing evolution of the nature of work itself.

"When they said joining the team meant we'd be riding the constant whitewater of change, I didn't think they meant it literally."

Evolving Teams

Where once the term "teamwork" was borrowed from the athletic world, today it is firmly established in the lexicon of business culture. The concept of teamwork wasn't absorbed into corporate thinking overnight, but it appeared at a critical point in our history.

For the last 300 years or so, we've evolved from the pre-Industrial Revolution era, where individual artisans designed and produced a product from start to finish. Apprenticeship fit that structure, but teams were not part of the profile. The assembly-line system, which assigned small pieces of the production process to individual workers, was nothing short of revolutionary. That production process changed the nature of work forever. However, like many developments that lead to greater efficiency, the rapid growth of assembly line production came with a price.

WORKER ALIENATION

During the 1960s and 1970s, social scientists warned us about a new concept—alienation from work. They told us that factory workers who spent eight hours a day assembling one piece of a car, television set, kitchen cabinet, and so forth, easily became detached—alienated from—not only the end product, but from the company as well.

Corporations had no powerful motivation to change the entrenched assembly line methodology, because it had succeeded *in the past*. Thus, companies failed to address fundamental weaknesses that ultimately threatened their continuing ability to compete.

FOREIGN COMPETITION

During the 1980s, the United States was rudely awakened from complacency and was faced with the need to change its production methods in order to improve quality and service. Only as we found ourselves losing our long-held competitive edge to the Japanese and others, did our large corporations began to emphasize innovation and explore a variety of "new" management techniques.

From the early 1980s to the present, we've lived in a time of trial and error as we accepted the need to change. The resulting philosophies and techniques are compatible with our changing cul-

> "The idea whose time has come is the team-based workplace, where work is designed for maximum productivity and maximum human involvement. What is needed now is a new generation of managers with true vision and a belief in people that expands the pace and scope of this change."
> —John Schuster, *Hum-Drum to Hot-Diggity*

"We know where most of the creativity, the innovation, the stuff that drives productivity lies—in the minds of those closest to the work. It's been there in front of our noses all along while we've been running around chasing rabbits and reading books on how to become Japanese—or at least manage like them."

—Jack Welch

ture, one that now emphasizes diversity, interdependency, and personal empowerment.

In the last decade, prominent companies from Motorola to Xerox have realized that improving quality and service required changes in the processes of production. The growth of team-based production entered the workplace. So far, it shows no sign of abating. In fact, research confirms that teams may be the optimal way to guide organizations through a pressure-filled atmosphere where change is demanded.

THE VERSATILITY OF TEAMS

Many organizations now realize that change is more quickly and smoothly implemented if many people are involved. Teams can help in key areas like process improvement, problem solving, generating ideas, improving performance, and so forth.

Nowadays, teams identify areas where change is needed, suggest and plan for change, implement change, and measure progress and success. In other words, teams are formed at every level of an organization for almost every purpose. Some teams are temporary, formed to initiate and complete one task. Others become a permanent part of an organization's structure.

WHY TEAMS SUCCEED

Why various kinds of teams work as efficient tools to promote change remains a key question.

Part of the answer goes back to the vertical,

top-down structure that once dominated many corporations, businesses of all sizes, and not-for-profit associations. In the vertical organization, the ability to respond rapidly to customer needs—whether the customer is an individual consumer or another company—is impaired by the structure itself. The rapid response and fast course changes demanded by global competition are nearly impossible when lines of authority are removed from the processes of production and delivery. It's become increasingly

> ## Team Facts
> - The average North American team consists of 10 individuals, with eight members being the most common size.
> - The average team member reports being on a team for 25 months, with overall length of service ranging from one month to nine years.
> - 57% of team members are required to participate on teams; 41% participate voluntarily (2% didn't know).
>
> Zenger Miller, San Jose, CA.

clear that change carried out through a vertical structure often is inefficient and, even worse, slow.

From past experience—sometimes painful—we know that in a vertical organization change can lead to a dependence culture. Each person waits for new "marching orders" before taking action. Employees can become especially confused and frustrated as they wait for direction and guidance. Teams are a natural and logical antidote to the chaos that develops when the winds of change are blowing.

TYPES OF TEAMS

The word "team" is used so frequently nowadays, that many people are unaware of the variety of team structures and purposes. Just as there are many different kinds of athletic teams, there are numerous types of organizational teams. Whether permanent or temporary, each kind of team has its own structure and lines of authority.

Following are a few examples of the kinds of team approaches that have proven effective in responding to rapid changes in our culture and the global marketplace.

Process-improvement Teams

Also called *quality improvement teams*, these teams are usually

Teams Necessary For TQM To Work

Total quality efforts often focus on statistical process control and other engineering aspects. Recent findings suggest that the benefits of TQM all come from the same basic sources. When employees' participation is sincerely solicited, with a focus on customer satisfaction, things start to work. For instance, a recent study found that 64% of companies that integrate total quality *and* teams reported success. But only 30% of firms that didn't integrate teams in TQM achieved success.

Incentive magazine.

temporary. They developed from an increased emphasis on continuous improvement. This, in turn, was a response to a perceived need to measure and improve current levels of quality and service.

Process-improvement teams often are independent of the organizational structure, although management has a sponsorship role. Based on a philosophy of trust and respect, employees define the system used to improve performance and measure results. Members of the team may come from one or more areas within the company. These teams usually focus on a single problem or process.

Because of its temporary nature, members of a process-improvement team may spend a relatively small amount of their workweek on the team's project. On the other hand, members may devote significant time over a concentrated period until the process improvements are designed and implemented.

Cross-functional Teams

These teams are created to manage a process across various functions. A typical cross-functional team may be created to manage a product line in a way that guarantees that the customers' needs remain in clear view at all times. Members of this team generally retain other functional reporting relationships and they balance these responsibilities with their work on the team.

It's not uncommon for people just learning this approach to experience conflicts and confusion. However, these are usually wrinkles that can be ironed out when the team's purpose becomes clear. In some organizations, cross-functional teams work on process-improvement efforts, although they generally don't manage the entire process.

Reengineering Or Design Teams

This type of team is created when large-scale change is contemplated or mandated. In recent years, reengineering often has brought about radical or dramatic change, usually in core processes and even in mission and philosophy.

Reengineering or design teams are put in place over the long term to gather data from customers and employees, as well as data about work flow. Using this information, members then design changes in the total system in order to meet future needs. Reengineering or design teams are responsible for changes in basic functions, including the ways in which jobs are performed; information is gathered and stored; decisions are made; employees are recruited, trained, and compensated; and how the organization evaluates and improves itself.

Unlike many other teams, reengineering groups often meet over a period of many months. They may even work full time on the project until the final organizational design is proposed. In some cases, team members are involved in the implementation phase of the reengineering project.

Self-directed Teams

We live in the age of empowerment, both personal and corporate. Within many organizations, teams are their own leaders. They manage their work activities, from planning and scheduling to budgeting, quality, and safety. Many organizations have moved toward empowerment-oriented structures, which can identify the need for change and respond quickly.

Self-directed Teams Work

In a study of over 1000 employees, self-managing teams were more effective than comparable traditionally managed groups that performed the same customer service, technical support, and administrative functions.

Human Relations, 1994, Vol. 47, pp. 13–43.

A first-level, self-directed work team is supervised by a person who takes on the role of coach. He or she helps team members take on tasks traditionally associated with supervision. Over time, team members make their own job assignments, select new team members, and take on administrative duties.

Advanced self-directed work teams take on additional responsibilities, including peer review, preparing budgets, and handling hiring and firing for their own departments. In essence, they operate much like a small business unit.

The Virtual Team

A relatively new term, this type of team is comprised of individuals who may work on opposite sides of the country. Team members make use of the latest communication technology to keep in touch and coordinate work. By eliminating the need for proximity, the most willing and talented people in an organization can be asked to serve on a team that's implementing change. We'll no doubt hear more about virtual teams in the future, as organizations seek more innovative ways to use new technologies.

A Virtual Example

When engineering giant Bechtel wanted to assemble a team for a special project in Quebec, the experts they wanted were not easily available. The experts had other responsibilities and were spread throughout offices around the country.

So, Bechtel created a "virtual team" of experts linked by computers, fax, and phone. Engineers were able to see the same plans and discuss modifications at the same time. One practice that Bechtel believes helped the team succeed was that a preliminary face-to-face meeting was held. This allowed the team members to align their approaches.

THE WHOLE IS GREATER THAN THE SUM OF ITS PARTS

Whether teams are put into place on a temporary basis or become a permanent part of an organization's structure, they tend to empower individuals and unleash new energy. Research has shown that working in teams leads to greater willingness to take on increased individual

responsibility. Teams also foster
creativity and flexibility. Better
decisions are usually the by-product of a team approach to problem
solving and management.

Frontline Involvement

Most companies learn that
people whose jobs put them in
contact with a company's customers (internal or external) are
in the best position to meet users' needs. If we ask these
employees to take responsibility
for procedures that meet internal or external needs, we usually
see positive results.

In our "tales" discussed earlier, Company X was directing
employees to use systems that
may not have worked well in individual applications.

Company Y, on the other
hand, recognized that this was
an outdated way to increase productivity. Before implementing
changes, they formed teams
within departments and gave
them a mission. Tell us, they
said, how you can take responsibility to better serve our
customers.

Company X had many confused employees. Disgruntled,
employees had little choice other
than to wait to be told what to do
next. As changes were instituted,
these employees felt like experimental pawns, never sure that
they could perform at expected

Change Takes Time And Training

The mistake many companies
make is thrusting too much authority and responsibility on employees without giving them reasons to cooperate and first training them in the needed skills.
That can be damaging to a
program's success as well as create high stress levels and low
morale on the front line.

To be realistic, cultural change
must evolve over three to five
years, according to one manager. The key is cultivating a
management mindset for change.
Rather than starting with employees, managers have to train their
workers to acquire basic administrative skills—and then the hardest part, learn to let go.

Train frontline employees in
areas like facilitator skills, conflict resolution, and how to give
and receive feedback. It's also
important to train staff in new
areas—for instance, how to
coach rather than manage, group
processes, conflict mediation,
problem solving, data analysis,
and facilitation.

When teams complete basic
training and have reached an
empowered level, they should be
capable of making the decisions
that impact their work.

—The Customer Service Group

levels. This triggered even greater resistance to change efforts.

The way Company Y put teams in place helped its employees shift from a dependency attitude to an initiative-based and action-oriented mind-set. It sounds paradoxical, but a team culture actually fosters independent thinking, initiative, and commitment among employees far better than the top-down, lone-wolf approach.

GETTING STARTED WITH TEAMS

Every team needs a sense of purpose and direction. Each member must be clear about the mission—why they came together in the first place. Most of us work more effectively if we can define our mission, goals, and guiding principles. An employee might say, "What's the point? Why are we here?"

Change And Trust

Traditionally, trust levels fall during times of change. Lack of trust is a significant issue. As many organizations downsize, employees feel less secure in their jobs. However, this negativity is minimized when people within the organization work in teams.

During the start-up phase, the team should create its own mission and guiding principles that direct them in their work. This step is as needed for a short-term, temporary team as it is for a long-term or permanent team. The start-up phase of any team is similar to establishing a charter. Sometimes we call this phase the "chartering process."

All team members must understand why they have come together and then proceed to establish a set of ground rules by which to operate. What is expected of each member? How will they communicate with each other? How often will they meet?

> "Teamwork is neither 'good' nor 'desirable.' It is a fact. Wherever people work together or play together they do so as a team. Which team to use for what purpose is a crucial, difficult and risky decision that is even harder to unmake. Managements have yet to learn how to make it."
> —Peter Drucker

Skills And Strategies

Part of what is expected of a team is, of course, to accomplish the task at hand. The mission defines the task. It's usually up to the team to determine the strategies and methods they will employ to reach their goal.

Individual roles are defined as well. For example, process improvement teams can include members from a range of departments and disciplines as well as members from the same work unit. Team members may each possess different skills, but they are brought together to improve a specific process.

Design and reengineering teams are always comprised of people from various departments and functions. Members of these teams investigate both internal and external forces that influence the organization. Their task is to challenge outdated ways of accomplishing the organization's goals. This often means changing the way work is performed. Therefore, bringing individuals together with different but complementary functions insures a better mix of information and ideas.

Team Successes

• In a steel manufacturing operation, small design teams redesigned work flow processes leading to substantial increases in productivity in existing plants and smooth transitions in two new plant locations.

• One team standardized processes to reduce paperwork 66% and product development time from 28 weeks to 9 weeks.

The Right Attitude

In addition to bringing individual abilities to the table, team members must also bring a willingness to work with people they may not know well. Members of self-directed work teams may interact regularly and be accustomed to working together. Other teams are comprised of relative strangers.

It's important that interaction is effective. This should include an agreed-upon strategy to resolve conflicts as they arise. This is part of team

Conflict Is Expected

As teams evolve, they generally go through stages. These can include:

- Forming,
- Storming,
- Norming, and
- Performing.

The conflict of "Storming," helps create the effective norms which help the team perform.

bonding, a necessary step for moving forward with the team's mission. Commitment to the mission and the team tends to run high when employees know and care about each other.

MEETINGS, BLOODY MEETINGS

One way team members form a bond is by regularly meeting together. Meetings are a necessity of today's organizational life. Most of the time, no one individual has all the information and knowledge needed to make decisions about complex issues facing organizations today.

Striving For Consensus

Meetings also facilitate a consensus style decision-making process for teams. This can become a key component in managing the change process successfully in organizations.

On the one hand, reaching consensus may be a slow process. It requires more time than decisions reached by one person who listens to others but makes the final decision alone.

On the other hand, implementation of decisions made through a consensus process is often smoother. This happens because sufficient time has been allocated to allow each team member to become invested in the decision. Commitment to decisions is more easily obtained through healthy and open discussion. Over time, agreement usually develops within the group. You also have more people to promote the decision. While 100 percent agreement isn't necessary, consensus leads participants to support decisions, rather than just tolerate them.

Managing Meetings

Since meetings are critical to a team's success, it is especially important that they be managed effectively and productively. Meetings with nebulous goals, or held just because the time seems right, are usually viewed with a jaundiced eye. And for good reason.

Most people who have spent time in organizations are familiar with meetings that seem little more than formalities. While they may be required to attend, many employees do not see their presence as needed.

Some people believe their contributions aren't welcome and meetings serve the needs of management rather than serving the entire organization. Company X's employees dreaded meetings, which were usually held for the purpose of informing workers about policies and changes. Discussion was limited to questions about implementation.

When teams are used to implement change, the nature of organizational meetings is changed, too. However, effective meeting management doesn't happen by itself. I've seen organizations waste resources when they create teams without guidelines for team meetings. I believe using an internal or external facilitator is often valuable for helping teams accomplish task and process goals. As a consultant working with teams, I often serve as facilitator. In that role I guide participants to understand clearly why they're attending and what the goal of the meeting is.

> ### Better Team Meetings
>
>
>
> Hang up a clipboard with a blank agenda sheet. During the week, as team members identify agenda items, they can list them on the clipboard (where they also indicate the time requirement, the priority of the item, and who will present the item to the team). If items on the list are informational only, the facilitator should ask the person if the information can be shared in another way (e-mail, memo, handout at the meeting, etc.).
>
> —Deborah Harrington-Mackin, *Keeping the Team Going: A Tool Kit to Renew & Refuel Your Workplace Teams*

Clarifying Roles

Some meeting expectations are general and apply to everyone. For example, all team members are expected to listen carefully, ask questions, solicit ideas and opinions from others, and acknowledge and praise others' contributions. Most teams choose a timekeeper, whose job it is to keep meetings moving through its agenda, and a scribe, who documents discussion points and decisions. Both jobs are often rotated among team members.

Individuals use meetings to report in and get assignments. Tasks are assigned based on areas of expertise and the team's goals. All tasks should have a time-frame for completion, with each member taking responsibility for the work he or she has agreed to accomplish before the next team meeting. Most teams also design a mechanism to communicate with each other between meetings.

Within effective meetings—and teams—the atmosphere is characterized by a willingness to encourage diversity and differences among its members. In addition to assessing areas of agreement, conflicts are resolved by bringing out all relevant information and checking for partial agreement.

Evaluation And Follow-Up

Effective teams evaluate each meeting and seek suggestions for improvement. Evaluation can be handled through structured discussions or by using written forms. In either case, members should be asked a variety of questions, such as:

- How effectively did the team stay on point?
- Were problem-solving techniques appropriate for the situation?
- Was the agenda followed and were time allocations for each agenda item adhered to?
- Was group interaction effective?

The meeting evaluations should be summarized and distributed to team members, to other participants, and to those interested in or affected by the outcome of the meeting. It's important that teams have clear lines of communication with individuals or groups within the organization whose missions or tasks will be altered or otherwise influenced by the team's decisions.

When teams first begin working together, there is a natural tendency to speak only in positive terms about team meetings. However, it's important that team members be honest and open in evaluating the meeting time they spend together.

If honesty is lacking, the group risks falling short of reaching its objectives. In addition, problems identified early can be solved before the team begins the heart of its work. Periodic evaluations help teams improve their tasks and processes, which ultimately leads to higher performance.

BETTER COMMUNICATION

Company Y of our earlier example implemented a communication process that involved every employee in the company, even if they were not currently participating in teams. Just as important, however, is the need for teams to communicate with those in senior leadership positions in the company.

I've been involved in situations in which the CEO participated in communicating the implementation of design teams and self-directed work teams. He presented information about the teams to others in senior leadership positions throughout the company. Some of his talks were videotaped, enabling employees at sites across

Problem Solving And Process Improvement Tools

When teams are designing or implementing change, there may be a tendency to *talk* about issues and challenges rather than *visually describing* them.

One organization created a diagram of its process problems. This provided a level of detail so precise that to display it required the use of all four walls. The diagram was the result of brainstorming and clarification, which then led to accurate descriptions of root causes of problems.

A visual description of this type triggers ideas. It also helps teams reach specific solutions, recommendations, and objectives, which are then expressed in concrete language. By both listening to and looking at data and concepts, you reduce the level of abstraction. This enables most people to form a "holistic" picture of not only the problem, but the solution as well.

the country and overseas to learn—from the most senior person in the company—about the mission of the teams and the progress they were making in reaching their goals.

This company, like Company Y, was able to implement significant changes in its organizational structure and its work processes with relative ease, precisely because the top leadership had communicated with employees at all levels. In other words, employees could see the rationale for every implemented change. Rather than having confused, passive employees, this company had empowered its employees to become involved in changes affecting their lives.

DEVELOPING LEADERSHIP AND EMPOWERING PEOPLE

The open and productive communication that occurs in team building naturally leads to greater employee empowerment.

As new responsibilities and roles are adopted by a greater number of people in an organization, you see a gradual shift from merely carrying out directives from others to employees directing their own work and measuring the results. If results aren't adequate and don't meet the goals, then team members, who are close to the process, will explore the difficulties and design and implement changes.

As teams take over responsibilities for daily activities and decisions, the team leader's role changes too. He or she becomes a facilitator, and the person who works with the team as an as-needed advisor. Other descriptions include: mentor, information resource person, team liaison, process consultant, advisor, and even role model for others who are developing leadership qualities.

> "Never tell people how to do things. Tell them what to do, and they will surprise you with their ingenuity."
> —General George S. Patton

SUMMING UP

There is no doubt that teams can be an important and powerful tool for change. In many cases, teams have replaced outdated organizational structures and changed the way in which a company's mission is accomplished.

With their eyes always directed at better ways to serve the customer, teams can empower employees to take risks and to offer creative ideas and suggestions for improvement. Today, teams reflect a cultural shift. Teams bring greater individual responsibility, along with the ability to respond quickly and with a minimum of confusion and disruption.

Teams may not be for everyone. But organizations that want to maintain, or regain, their competitive edge, realize that involving more people in designing and implementing change achieves better and faster results.

ACTION SUMMARY

▶ Clarify your mission and goals before implementing changes.

▶ If you have existing teams, involve them in any change efforts.

▶ Make up teams of the people who will be effected by a change to deal with each aspect of it.

▶ Input from the frontline employees who deal with customers is particularly valuable to drive change.

▶ Follow the Doctors' rule: Diagnose before you prescribe change.

▶ To help teams succeed, train members in team-building techniques.

▶ Train teams to run efficient meetings with clear evaluations and follow-throughs.

▶ Develop your organization's team abilities by using pilot team projects and careful assessments.

▶ Communicate to everyone about changes. Communicate more than you think is necessary.

▶ Use visual tools like charts to communicate about process changes.

▶ Teams lead to empowerment. Be prepared to give up arbitrary control of processes.

▶ Consider using outside consultants to lend perspective and team expertise.

Chapter 7

WEDDING TQM TO CREATIVITY

Don Rapp

Don Rapp, PhD, is a consultant who focuses on opening the mind for creative thought. "There is no doubt," he says, "that creativity can be learned." Dr. Rapp's unique background helps him show organizations and individuals how to be playfully creative.

During his 34-year university career, he taught at the University of Illinois, University of Georgia, and Florida State University. A year-long psychiatric fellowship at Shands Medical Center in Gainesville, Florida, helped him better understand the human condition. Later, a visiting professorship was spent studying management and the quality effort at Yale New Haven Hospital.

His consulting has helped Caterpillar, The Center for Public Management, the Tallahassee Regional Medical Center, and many other organizations discover those creative leaps needed to fully succeed.

Dr. Rapp has been a classic juggler for 56 years, using his entertaining skills as metaphors to render speech and workshop content immediately usable and vividly memorable.

Don Rapp, PhD, Rapport Unlimited, 1806 Skyland Drive, Tallahassee, FL 32303; phone (904) 385-5627; e-mail: RappDP@aol.com.

Chapter 7

WEDDING TQM TO CREATIVITY

Don Rapp

> *Total Quality Management*
> *and*
> *Creative Problem Solving*
> *request the honour of your presence*
> *at the marriage of their children*
> *Inch Worm*
> *and*
> *Kangaroo*
> *on the soonest possible date.*

A classic story connecting the past to the future: A 58-year-old man worked for the same company for 40 years. At his retirement party, the boss presented the customary gold watch and the retiree said a few words. After the reminiscences and thanks, he gently released his frustrations, "For forty years, I have given this company my hands, my back, and my sweat. If you had only asked, I would have gladly given you my mind!"

That scene is typical of many that took place in the 1930s. Between 1950 and 1979, America's W. Edwards Deming and Toyota's Taiichi Ohno and others ushered in the quality movement. The quality movement now pervades the business world. Total quality has become the goal, and it works.

In the 1930s, an employee's mind was irrelevant to management. Today, continuous improvement requires that every worker's intelligence be focused on innovation. Today's employees are not merely hands. Now they are also minds which must be stimulated and utilized for the benefit of the company, the world, and themselves. The new world of lean production is here. (I categorize TQM, reengineering, and similar terms as "lean production.")

A MAJOR PARADIGM SHIFT

Rosabeth Moss Kanter, in a *Harvard Business Review* editorial, suggested that we are at a crossroads. She used the term *crossroads* to indicate we are in the midst of a paradigm shift, the likes of which have occurred only a few times in the history of world civilization. The first was from the transition from nomad to agricultural life. Then came the shift to industrialization, and presently the change to the information society.

A large part of today's shift is from making *some* goods of quality to all services and goods of highest quality. We have also shifted from a model in which employees are told what they are to do, to a situation where employees take responsibility for the quality of their own production. In this new situation, responsibility and thought are premium commodities.

Even though change is normal, the speed of change today is disconcerting to all and dangerous for many. Most people see today's world as chaotic. It is, at the least, upsetting and unsettling.

The retiree of the 1930s was right—his boss should have asked him to use his mind; it takes a brain to solve a problem. Many in business today, however, are still resisting, refusing to take up the challenge of the mind. Only by using ALL of our minds can we solve the problems presented by the fast-moving changes in our world today.

This brings us to the image we started with, the marriage of the Inch Worm and the Kangaroo. This marriage is a metaphor for a new synergy, a union which represents the combination of two very different problem-solving approaches. The Inch Worm stands for the slow, unrelenting forward motion of the TQM juggernaut. The Kangaroo represents the fast, leaping, gazelle-like action of creative problem solving. As with any marriage, this one involves a paradigm shift; in this case, a change from a unidirectional (top down) approach to one of synergistic teamwork.

The Value Of Speed

In one of his columns, management guru Tom Peters discussed a study on accelerated decision making by Kathleen Eisenhardt and Jay Bourgeois. The study compared decision makers at 12 microcomputer firms. Quick decision makers accomplished in 2–4 months what took the slow decision makers 18 months.

Quick decision makers tended to consider multiple options at once, while slow decision makers reviewed one option at a time.

Peters' diagnosis: "The one-at-a-timers mull and mull—often until opportunity passes them by. When the much belabored option dies, they're left with nothing, and must fire up the cumbersome process once again."

A QUAKE, NOT A SHIFT

Some observers suggest that the word *shift* is too tame. *Quake* might more accurately describe our topsy-turvy condition.

Every aspect of our lives is shifting in ways we can't predict, toward a future we can't imagine. It takes a lot of mental and organizational agility to respond to these shifts. However—and this is the point—it takes creative ability and organizational agility to prepare for and make full use of these changes as they come upon us. Beyond that, the truly creative people and organizations are ahead of the quake-curve. They are creating the next new process, product, or service that will continue the changes.

Today, as never before, there is a worldwide need for businesses and individuals to push their thoughts toward innovation. Our global economy demands that we have available as many methods of thought and problem-solving strategies as possible.

The image of a marriage between the Inch Worm and the Kangaroo suggests that magnificent new possibilities can come from this combination of slow, incremental change joined with a leaping imagination. This is a marriage of both convenience and necessity. Like most, it begins with passionate engagement and hopeful enthusiasm for the future. This essay speaks to the concept of continuous improvement in all tasks, from those of labor or management, office or factory, planning or production, technical or human issues, to matters of money and morals.

SUPER COMPETITION

We used to compete with our neighbors. Now we live in Marshall McLuhan's "Global Village" and we compete with the whole world. We Americans, who were once the world's top producers, now compete with people from places we hadn't heard of 30 years ago. We face an increasingly sophisticated industrial world. This new competition is inconvenient at best; at worst, we lose our shirts. Working against us is our status as the world's largest debtor nation.

We Have A Choice

Cut-throat competition on a worldwide scale can lead in two directions. First is survival of the fittest—a horrible death for some companies, and a fabulous success for others. The second path, the only one worth considering, leads to ideas and acts of unparalleled efficiency and creativity. American business and industry is, at last, now serious about being in a world of free trade, super competition, and the relentless pursuit of quality on every dimension.

SOME HISTORICAL PERSPECTIVES ON TQM

The quality movement, born out of desperate conditions in post-WW II Japan, fostered by the the savvy and forethought of the Japanese, almost did us in. WW II was our victory, but the Japanese soon conquered us economically with the precision-made weapon of quality (lean) production.

"Get the confidence of the public and you will have no difficulty getting their patronage. Remember always that the recollection of quality remains long after the price is forgotten."
—H. George Selfridge

Led by Taiichi Ohno at Toyota, the Japanese perfected the ways of quality for thirty years. From 1950 to 1979, W.E. Deming worked with Japanese industry while U.S. industry stubbornly ignored his ideas about quality.

In 1979, Deming's ideas were belatedly recognized in the United States. In 1981, the Ford Motor Company was amazed to learn from their Mazda connection just how much more efficient Mazda was than Ford.

Futurist Joel Barker says that quality is a disease you must catch or you may not survive. By the 1990s, we had finally caught the quality bug and are now coming back strong into world markets.

There is no doubt that the quality approach is good for business. It helps all of us work smarter, not harder. The emphasis of lean production is single-minded attention to process. Even the most lowly employee learns how to use process principles to improve job performance. Savings are in the billions, and customer satisfaction is significantly improved.

The disadvantage of lean production is that jobs are often lost to more efficient organizations; downsizing has hurt many individual Americans. Is there a way we can continue to improve quality *and* make more jobs for people all over the world? J. Womack's research on worldwide lean production suggests a positive answer to this question. But it takes a creative mind to invent a truly win-win outcome.

RELATIVE ADVANTAGE

Consider this: Customized, handmade automobiles were the norm until Henry Ford's mass production proved significantly more efficient. Now lean production has won out over mass production technology.

The next revolution will create a new and even leaner, more creative manufacturing-marketing-service mode. This will be achieved by marrying lean production strategies to the tools of creative thought.

What will this new organization look like? Such a company will be like an athlete: agile, graceful, limber, lissom, supple, willowy, determined, strong, steady, dogged, and disciplined. It can be described poetically as a company as swift and lithe as Gail Devers running the hurdles, and as doggedly goal-oriented as Dan O'Brien training for the decathlon.

The Inch Worm and Kangaroo are two distinct thought processes coming together to reshape work and life on this planet.

Plan From The Outside In

"Since the customer is constantly changing, you don't even want to talk about your organization until you figure out what's going on outside. The idea is to monitor what's outside, focusing externally on new developments and technology, new competitors, new opportunities, etc. Then build your organization around that."

—Orin Harrari and Nicholas Imparato, authors of *Jumping the Curve*, in an *Executive Edge* interview

Carrying the metaphor one generation further, what will the children look like? One possibility, a two-inch leaping worm?

Extracting the serious part of this image, I envision a system that can progress two inches at a time instead of just one inch, and that simultaneously has the ability to leap when leaping is needed.

Already this combination is seen in successful organizations. The ability to be doggedly quality driven, while having the flexibility to leap is as big a step as was taken from mass production to lean production. Metaphors are a way to "see" the best of the present and distribute it widely. There is always a next step, or *leap*, as the case may be.

Now let's take a separate look at each partner in this odd couple.

TOTAL QUALITY MANAGEMENT TODAY

Japan's rise was triumphant. From 1950 to 1980, a forgiving U.S., the Japanese work ethic, and Deming and Ohno's relentless push for quality were responsible for Japan's phoenix-like resurrection.

Forget The Statistics

One misconception about TQM continues to linger in the American mind. TQM is not mainly about statistical analysis of variations, etc. It is mainly about worker and team involvement—utilizing the minds of workers in addition to their hands. Perhaps because of American stereotypes of Japan as a "hive" culture, better at production than creativity, TQM continues to be thought of, *by those who haven't studied it*, as the uncreative application of discipline and careful management.

Lean production was the force that created the funnel for money that still pours into Japan. During those years, I often asked myself why it was taking us so long to catch the Japanese. My explanation now is this: TQM is an Inch Worm. It slowly nudges hearts and minds to think quality as the process is continually improved. BUT, if we are starting in second place, and run at the same speed as the leader, we will always be second or perhaps even further back in the pack. We must find a way to leap ahead. Leaps also fit the American stereotype personality of honoring big results, not incremental improvements!

A paradigm shift may arrive slowly or rapidly. Lean production helps industry to shift slowly but steadily to new ways of thinking about production and service. It inspires industry to create new ways of handling material, people, and ideas. The target is always one of bettering the process.

TQM amasses its gains from worker participation and knowing its current reality in real numbers. Better quality is declared a reality when the numbers are better. Consistent process improvement and statistical visualizing rule the TQM game.

TQM Does Help

There have been a number of comments from the popular press suggesting that quality management programs really don't work very well. But most of these comments have been based on casual observations.

In a more rigorous study looking at hard numbers, Sherry Jarrell of the University of Indiana and George Easton of the University of Chicago concluded that over a five-year period, firms were better than they would have been without TQM programs. The researchers looked at variables such 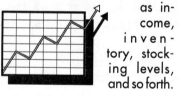 as income, inventory, stocking levels, and so forth.

Given enough time and money, TQM can convert an organization from inefficiency to profitability, from conflict to harmony. But merely implementing TQM does not automatically guarantee success.

Sometimes an organization will find quality too late, or it may push TQM hard and succeed, only to find that their goals of quality have been met better or sooner by a competitor. Or, as is too often the case, human fatigue sets in and the process that began with enthusiasm runs out of steam. For whatever reason, the company is out of business.

THE FOCUS IS PROCESS

One important reason for TQM's success is that it never blames a particular individual or department for production problems. Instead, both management and workers focus on improving the work process.

Continual process review and experimentation foment the search for ever-better work processes. As a bonus byproduct of this emphasis on processes, individuals are inspired to move toward greater quality in their personal lives as well.

Eliminating blame is genius because it enables all personnel to work on improving the process, rather than angrily and inefficiently pointing fingers at one another.

Blame, with its corollaries, shame, guilt, denial and turf protection, takes a lot of energy. Without blame, we no longer have to be defensive. Everyone is now working to reinvent new and more efficient processes.

Right Brain + Left Brain

TQM seems to require mostly left-brain characteristics, those which emphasize the analytical, statistical and sequential. This would be logical, given that Deming was a dedicated statistician. TQM has been seen as a godsend by the left-brain, or analytical employee.

But when an organization is desperately searching to renew processes and to better its culture, it

THIS IS THE RIGHT SIDE OF THE BRAIN CALLING THE LEFT SIDE OF THE BRAIN. COME IN, LEFT SIDE...

Yo!

needs creative vision throughout the organization. Lean production has discovered that the mind is the essential element in the search for quality. Thus the emphasis on quality circles and other worker participation tools.

Edward DeBono, author of many books on creativity, says, "Executives in the Western countries have come to realize that people are their most precious resources." Only the mind can think outside the present fad-box and initiate the new profit center, and that new health breakthrough.

TQM Needs Creativity

TQM knows that new ideas are necessary. However, TQM tools fit more naturally with some employees than with others. Theoretically, TQM can continually better itself, but the process may become too method-bound and slow-moving in today's nimble marketplace.

Edward DeBono cautions against a company's absolute reliance on lean production tools. In his book, *Sur/Petition*, he asks, "In all those things that have become obsolete, would a higher degree of quality have prevented their obsolescence?"

The answer is no. The quality of the rotary dial phone was very high, but it was rendered obsolete by the touch-tone phone. The telegraph was supplanted by the telephone; the grooved-record by tape, and tape in turn by digital CDs; sailing ships by steam; and steam by diesel; passenger ships by airplanes; manual typewriters by word processors; ad infinitum. In today's business world, quality is not the only game that must be played.

As good as lean production presently is, the next step includes everyone embracing the Inch Worm's persistence *and* the Kangaroo's leapability.

CREATIVE HINTS
"How many times it thundered before Franklin took the hint! How many apples fell on Newton's head before he took the hint! Nature is always hinting at us. It hints over and over again. And suddenly we take the hint."
—Robert Frost

HISTORY OF CREATIVE PROBLEM-SOLVING

In his 1926 classic book *The Art of Thought*, Graham Wallace describes the creative process as observed in a number of European scientists and poets. Wallace summarizes the creative process as "preparation, incubation, illumination, and verification." Recognizing that creativity *is a process* permits one to understand that *creativity can be learned*. The tools of creativity are process-oriented in the same way that the tools of quality are process oriented. Everyone can learn to be more creative about quality, or anything else.

Alex Osborn was an advertising man who invented tools such as brainstorming to increase creativity. He first wrote about them in his 1954 book *Applied Imagination*. His ground-breaking work continues at the Creativity Education Foundation in Buffalo, New York, which publishes the *Journal of Creative Behavior*.

Children Are Naturally Creative

My own interest in creativity began in the field of child development. I wanted to help children become more creative. It soon became evident to me that children are best helped to their creative potential by first helping their parents and teachers to become more creative themselves. (And to not *discourage* creativity in their children!). When adults are given tools to retrieve and advance their own creativity, they help everyone around them become more creative.

The best gift you can give children is to provide them with a dynamic, problem-solving human model. Likewise, management can do no better than to personally demonstrate a creative style to their employees.

"Innovation, Daisy, it's innovation."

Management Is A Role Model

Sadly the reverse is also true. When management does not demonstrate creative thinking, and worse, when they disapprove of it or resist new ideas, employees cannot become creative problem-solvers. When managers are open to new ideas, they possess a marvelously inexpensive tool of creativity. When they have an open attitude, managers are always surprised how creative their employees can be.

Employees who are in healthy organizations need very little leadership to optimize their creative abilities. What they do need are tools and an accepting atmosphere to generate and follow through on implementing their new ideas.

Thinking Outside The Box

As an example, let's take the familiar nine dot problem. Nine dots are arranged in a square of three rows and three columns. The goal is to connect all nine dots with four straight lines without lifting your pencil from the paper.

If you stay within the square formed by the nine dots, the problem can't be solved. The problem is only solved when you allow your lines to protrude outside the perceived boundaries. Try it and you will see the drama of the phrase, "thinking outside the box."

If we stop there, we will have learned something significant. However, these nine dots offer many more lessons.

The problem can also be solved with three straight lines, and even with two straight lines. And yes, even with just one straight line. In fact there are at least 12 perfectly logical ways to

Nine-Dot Puzzle

. . .

. . .

. . .

Connect all nine dots with four contiguous straight lines. (Turn the next page for one solution.)

solve the problem with one straight line. Here are two: Try drawing the line with a paint roller. No one said the line could not be as wide as the three columns of dots. You may also fold the paper on which the nine dots are placed so that all nine dots are adjacent to each other in a straight line. And there are other solutions that are even more clever. E. Glassman in his *Creativity Handbook* shares the others.

The one-straight-line solutions can be converted to metaphors which in turn may be applied to real work-related problems. Metaphors are a powerful tool of creative thought.

The point: Even when the process to attain quality is excellent, it can too soon become a box in which the boundaries become uncrossable mental limits. They become "the standard." There is little invention when this calcification occurs. Getting outside your self-determined box means finding ways to defy the old limits and think up new and better standards and solutions. Just as thought has no end, there is no end to possible improvements.

THE "RIGHT" CREATIVITY COURSE

My move from developing imagination in children to helping industry and government become more creative was easy. All these realms include people, thought, and the demand for solutions.

Right Attitude
Imagination
Goals
Health
Thought

My acronym for the tools of creative thought is RIGHT. I created the RIGHT Course emphasizing activities to *implement* creativity.

The acronym itself is also a tool. For example, when you have an unsolved problem, ask, "Is my Attitude holding me back, or is it my lack of Imagination? Do I have the right Goals? Is my Health up to the task, and is my Thought disciplined?" If one or more of these questions is answered negatively, you have a clue to why your problem has not been solved.

The tools of creative thought are tools of motivation, inspiration, discipline, mental flexibility, deferred judgeiment and, most of all, the ability to perceive the world with new eyes.

Painting with a broad brush, below is a brief outline of the RIGHT categories.

Right Attitude

Attitude creates mood. Call it your personal style, or your philosophy. A positive mental attitude is a tool to see more than is currently thought possible.

Attitude is a framework within which thought has its being. Basic to all attitudinal improvement is the use of affirmations such as; "At this very moment, I am becoming more creative." Inherent in the statement is the fact that *creativity can be learned,* which in turn fosters the attitude of being open to new possibilities.

Imagination

My four-word definition of imagination is, "Conceiving what isn't...yet." Imagination connects past, present and future. We are time-beings, and our creativity is enhanced when we give our imagination time to become reality.

Imagination is the power to "see" what can't be seen with your eyes. One grand imaginative tool is the powerful question, "What if?" The "What if" question activates the imagination to dream that impossible dream. Once the vision is "seen," it can be articulated into a goal. Intuition is also part of imagination. Intuition fills in the cracks when the facts are unclear, contradictory or absent.

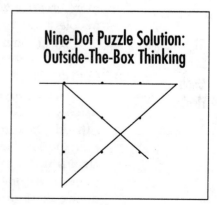

Nine-Dot Puzzle Solution: Outside-The-Box Thinking

Goals

Goal setting is now a science, whether for creative or other purposes. The fundamental goal is to continually improve your creative problem-solving ability. If you follow the carefully planned steps of goal formation, you are significantly more likely to reach your goals. Here are seven criteria of goal formation: Make your goals personal, positive, in the present tense, reachable, specific, written, and last, goals are only achieved when goal-makers are willing to change themselves.

Health

Exuberant mental and physical health is essential to creative thought. Good health will add immensely to the quality of one's life.

The tools for creative health are logical and scientific. They are nutrition, exercise, stress control, *and* the ability to give yourself away without becoming resentful about your giving.

Thought

Sometimes thought must be disciplined to a pinpoint focus. At other times, we must look broadly to see overall patterns. At quiet moments, we let thought bubble up out of nowhere. Self-control is a tool. Disciplined thought overcomes denial. The reality is that the mind is multifaceted. Find and use the thought tool that works best for your given purpose.

Imagine each of the five RIGHT elements as a box filled with practical tools for improving creativity. These tools may be categorized by thought, behavior, sequence, philosophy, and paper-and-pencil techniques. They may be used on the job, at home, or wherever creative thinking is done.

There is not space here to list all RIGHT course tools. However, I will discuss some general categories.

Expansive And Contractive Thought

There is a dynamic interplay between the free expansion of thought and the contraction or focus of thought. For example, the solutions that are offered near the end of the brainstorming (lateral thinking) list are generally the best. Then, in the process of prioritizing your list, you eliminate all that is unusable. The result is more creative possibilities than if you had acted on your first thoughts or inclinations.

Another expansion-contraction tool: When exactly right words are put on paper, the will is galvanized into action. *The pen is mightier than the sword.*

The best word can be more quickly found using a thesaurus with its vast spread of word-thoughts. A thesaurus offering an expanded choice helps you be more precise. A thesaurus search will expand your thought until you find the focus you require to think decisively and successfully.

> ### Rules Of Brainstorming: Alone Or In A Group
>
> Free associate ideas to the designated problem. There is no discussion or criticism—deferred judgment is the rule. Bounce off one idea, combine, do the opposite, etc. The idea is to generate as many ideas as possible. It's often the "zany" ideas that get us thinking in new directions.

The trick is to use tools of expansion when it is right to expand, and those of focus when focus is required.

The Two-Minute Think: TMT with its exacting time pressure focuses the mind. It forces you into a self-imposed, hyper-adrenaline focus on the problem. Sit quietly with a blank paper and pencil on your desk in front of you. Place your problem statement at the top of the sheet. For a brief 120 seconds, you extend your thought "reach" into creative possibilities. This exercise is like brainstorming, but is more intense and much more personal. Later you can unscramble your scribbles, expand your recorded words and images, and structure your thoughts into action.

Other Creativity Tools

The Short View Vs. The Long View. Briefly, you can't achieve a long-term goal without many short-term goals. A journey of 1,000 miles begins with one step. Of course, each of the following 999 steps are vital to reaching the goal.

Right-Brain, Intuitive, Metaphor-Oriented Tools And Left-Brain Analytic, Sequential Tools. We seem to have two distinct brains. If you find yourself predominately using one side or the other, you have probably become biased in your thought patterns. A narrow focus may be good for the specialist, but problems are better solved when both halves cooperate.

It is said that Einstein's greatest genius was his ability to use and coordinate his whole brain.

Usually employees first choose tools that are comfortable to their preferred sides. As confidence increases, they choose tools that must be learned by their less preferred side. This expands their abilities to solve problems. Now the possibility increases that the two sides can work together as never before.

Using History Vs. Futuristic "What If" Thinking. "Received wisdom" is too often calcified as doctrine. Its use becomes passive regurgitation. "Generated wisdom" is that which is created when past learning is synthesized with present perception, and both with future goals. Of course, we need to know history so we may avoid its mistakes.

Creative planning helps us avoid mistakes. "What if" thinking finds new victories and avoids problems. Doing it right the first time is a basic tenet of the quality movement. This point highlights the personal responsibility of us all to integrate past, present and future.

Promoting Creativity Through Tools. Creative problem-solving in general, and the RIGHT Course in particular, with its smorgasbord of right- and left-brain thought tools, has something for everyone. Your employees will usually enjoy creativity development programs. In addition, they can often use new creativity tools for more than work. Work is no longer work, rather, work becomes a way toward personal growth, at home and elsewhere.

TRUDGING *AND* HURDLING

Clearly, the message of this chapter is that you need both TQM and creativity. The marriage between the Inch Worm and the Kangaroo creates the possibility of new ideational forms. Their children represent a willingness to share each other's traits.

The Inch Worm and the Kangaroo each bring different talents to their partnership. TQM's tools are: employee involvement, measurement, goal orientation, teamworkn and the ever present continuous process improvement. The Creative Problem Solving tools include: imagination, innovation, and a revolutionary entrepreneurial attitude exercised by all employees. Like TQM, creativity also has a compulsive side. Discipline and perserverance are vital tools for innovation, as they are for increased quality production. The marriage described in this essay promotes both trudging and hurdling. Its proponents have available to them a vast array of thought tools.

Whereas TQM's thought tools are largely left-brain oriented, creativity tools tend to be right-brain oriented. The RIGHT Creativity Course makes use of both left- and right-brain characteristics, thus allowing every person to become more completely involved.

Lean production asks employees to use their minds and gives them specific tools to participate. Creative problem solving offers many "cookbooks" filled with practical creative problem-solving tools. One of the best is *Thinkertoys* by Michael Michalko. Bailey's *Disciplined Creativity* is a creative cookbook designed specifically for engineers.

"CLEANING UP" WITH TQM AND CREATIVITY

A large organization had kept its janitorial function within the company. As the entire organization caught the quality bug, the supervisor of the janitors vigorously lobbied for his people to participate. He reasoned that his group was privileged to work in every space in the plant and office. With TQM training, plus their special working view of the company, they would be in a position to see important relationships between place, function, people, and space which others with narrower vision might not see.

When he sensed raised eyebrows, meaning others were questioning the intelligence of the janitorial group, he would stand in their defense citing the difficulty of their assigned tasks and the inventive manner in which they had conducted themselves in the past. He countered, if his group had training in quality as everyone else, there was no reason his group could not uniquely enhance the quality of the company and thus become more a part of the overall effort.

The CEO grasped his reasoning and the janitors received the TQM training. They began to benchmark, record, and experiment with new work processes and equipment. They specifically redefined their customers, (both internal and external), and formed new relationships with their suppliers.

TQM And Creativity

Then they went further. The supervisor had read a great deal in the area of creative problem solving. He had some ideas for his group that went beyond TQM tools. Among the many tools of creativity, he encouraged the one tool most influential in their many successes. It was the individualization of the company mission statement.

He first dramatized the company's mission statement, insisting that all of his group memorize it. Then he asked, "Why don't we janitors have one of our own?" Through the collective effort of the entire group, they came up with a meaningful departmental mission statement that dovetailed with the mission statement of the company.

Personal Unique Missions

The next step in this process allowed them to eventually became a company legend. All janitors invented unique mission statements for themselves! Each had to be no more than fifteen words, different from all of the others.

Of course, in the process of their writing and editing, each had to compare theirs with all the others. This was quite a process. They had to find out just how their own work was unique among their colleagues. Several of the janitors did not read or write but they got help with their statements.

The janitors became the talk of the company. They surprised everyone (and themselves) with their inventiveness, commitment, and teamwork. They also documented magnificent savings, safety ideas, and created an array of company-wide ideas generated from their special view of the workspace. The supervisor moved up in the organization, the janitorial group continued to be innovative, and the company thrived.

There is more than one way to reach quality. Inch Worms and Kangaroos are both creative, each in their own way. The janitors in this story were the progeny of the two; working and thinking beyond their expected capacity and becoming an inspiration to the entire organization.

CONCLUSION

The TQM Inch Worm is a slow-moving, powerful force pushing forward, inexorably evolving better quality. But the Inch Worm is dangerously slow in this fast-moving world.

The Kangaroo represents the leaping and sprinting necessary to invent new products, discover fast-changing markets, and to

initiate better interpersonal relationships. But creative leaps alone can't overcome the discipline of competitors.

Their marriage more than doubles the possibilities of process improvement *and* innovation.

The RIGHT Course tools represent the marriage of the Inch Worm and the Kangaroo, because its tools are both evolutionary and revolutionary. Each person may now choose from a full array of thought tools for the purpose of planning, coordinating, and contributing.

This odd couple is dedicated to helping solve problems, generating more successes, and smoothing the roads to short- and long-term goals. This marriage is a viable next step in the continual search for ways to market, produce, and service.

Your Invitation:
All members of your organization are invited to the wedding.
The couple only asks that you bring awareness of your own historical realities,
A willingness to concentrate on present actualities,
And dedication to your creative possibilities.
The goal is unending personal and organizational quality.

By the way, our newlyweds are planning a trip to Sydney for the next Olympics. They will introduce a new event called "thought vaulting." Like all competitive-thought athletes, you may practice at anytime on your field of mind.

ACTION SUMMARY

▶ Measure how well your company uses lean production tools like TQM.

▶ Analyze how creative your company is based on whatever criteria are appropriate like adaptability, patents issued, or new product innovations.

▶ Set up a task force to explore the changes you will need to make over the next few years.

▶ Make a list of the TQM and creativity tools your company can use for change.

▶ Set up a pilot program of volunteers who want to combine detailed process with creativity.

▶ Develop a creativity change training program that fits your culture.

▶ Know that change will arrive with or without your involvement. Success requires your active commitment to creative thought.

Chapter 8

MANAGING CHANGE FOR ORGANIZATIONAL TRANSFORMATION

Phillip P. Andrews & Jerome A. Hahn

Phillip P. Andrews works for EDS's Manufacturing Industry Group as the vice president of Strategic Business Initiatives. Prior to that, Mr. Andrews was with EDS's Management Consulting Group in charge of the Reengineering, Benchmarking, and Change Management practices. His teams have performed over 100 reengineering projects around the world. Mr. Andrews' customers include 3M, Caterpillar, J.I. Case, Colgate-Palmolive, and General Motors. He is in the process of co-authoring a book on Enterprise Transformation. Mr. Andrews has delivered over 2,000 talks on a variety of topics, throughout the world.

Jerome A. Hahn is president of Hahn & Associates, a management and information technology consulting firm that helps companies improve business performance. Areas of consulting emphasis are performance metric improvements in sales, supply-chain management, manufacturing processes, and information technology implementation. He specializes in paradigm change strategies, and the development and implementation of aligned reeengineered processes and systems. Mr. Hahn has provided consulting services to GE, Ford, Ciba Geigy, FMC Corporatiion, and LTV. Mr. Hahn has delivered hundreds of speeches and seminars both nationally and internationally.

Phillip (Phil) Andrews, EDS, 5400 Legacy Drive, MS: H3-5C-45, Plano, TX 75024; phone (972) 605-5777; fax (972) 605-0287; e-mail laertis7@aol.com.

Jerome (Jerry) Hahn, Hahn & Associates, 5208 Lakeland Drive, Frisco, TX 75035; phone (972) 335-8593; fax (972) 335-8854; e-mail jhahn@dhc.net.

Chapter 8

MANAGING CHANGE FOR ORGANIZATIONAL TRANSFORMATION

Phillip P. Andrews & Jerome A. Hahn

"No company can escape the need to reskill its people, reshape its product portfolio, redesign its processes, and redirect resources."
—Gary Hamel & C.K. Prahalad,
Competing for the Future

Change management can be viewed both as a body of theory and a process. As a body of theory, it addresses the latest concepts in organizational transformation, organizational design, organization behavior, group and individual dynamics, and many other relevant subjects.

As a process, change management (CM) is the catalyst and a strategic tool for transforming people, organizations, value systems, behaviors, infrastructures, and whole enterprises. The CM process acts both as a framework for planning and implementing change, and as an ongoing mechanism for either taking corrective action at the right time, or preventing an ugly situation or problem from happening the first place.

A ROAD MAP

Regardless of how change management is viewed, it must include a master plan that describes the purpose of change, the desired end state, the approach, and the methods, tools, and techniques that will be deployed. It must also describe the teams to be used and their members, the rules of working with each other, the expectations and deliverables, and the change initiatives.

Change should also be viewed in conjunction with the organization's growth curve in order to design the proper actions that will result in the desired endings, transitions, and new beginnings.

New beginnings involve introducing a new growth curve that has its own paradigm set, guiding principles, and rules. These in turn must be documented and communicated to employees at all levels. The new growth curve represents the new era and business environment that embody the proposed vision of the organization, its products and services.

Change Skills Are Key

The ability to manage change has become critical for an organization to successfully undergo a transformation.

In environments where change has been associated with sudden downsizing and restructuring, the organization, as well as the individual, often adopts a form of protectionism where survival instincts take over. The result is that many individuals have come to view change negatively. This leads to resistance.

The Impact Of Resistance To Change

CURRENT SITUATION	BARRIER	FUTURE STATE (VISION)
Dysfunctional Organization	*Resistance to Change*	*Effective Organization*
• Distant from customers	• Why?	• Bonded with customers
• Cost driven	• What is in it for me?	• Value driven
• Structured jobs	• What problem?	• Virtual work
• Silo mentality	• Is this another program-	• Cross-functional teams
• Stand-alone systems	of-the-month?	• Integrated systems
• Islands of automation	• Didn't we try this before?	• Integrated enterprise
• IT viewed as a cost to be contained	• Who cares?	• IT is viewed as a strategic weapon
• People are treated as a commodity		• People are an important enterprise asset
• Multinational		• Global
• Self-sufficient enterprise		• Virtual enterprise

Dealing With Resistance

Resistance to change can cause an organization to lose its resiliency, even its willingness to achieve its goals. If left unchecked, it can paralyze a whole enterprise. Open or underground resistance will force a company to consistently miss its goals, while quality begins to suffer, and customer dissatisfaction skyrockets. At the end, resistance can cause entire operations to collapse.

The box above shows how resistance to change acts as a formidable barrier to achieving the new vision. The future state will be achieved when the organization has collectively invested the thought and energy needed to reduce the barrier.

MASTERING THE CHANGE

This chapter introduces a view of change focused on:

- Identifying both near and long term issues that must be resolved before a company can achieve the benefits of enterprise transformation
- Leveraging change management techniques to ensure smooth transition to the new growth curve

The body of information on change management related to enterprise transformation is so vast that one could write an encyclopedia on the topic. This chapter covers the important basics.

A Transformation Example: EDS

EDS, the leading professional services company, concluded in the early 1990s that it was time to re-invent itself once again. Just like many large enterprises, EDS came to the conclusion that "we have met the enemy and it is us." Thus, the starting point for re-inventing and transforming the enterprise was their own mindset. They coined the phrase "mindset reengineering," to emphasize the need to change their culture first, ahead of industry or enterprise reengineering.

To guide them, EDS hired Dr. Gary Hamel, to help them see themselves from a different perspective. To quote Dr. Hamel, "A new perspective is worth 50 IQ points." Dr. Hamel's strategy was to get away from the traditional strategic planning approach. This normally produces plans, not strategies. He focused on strategic thinking that is "subversive" in nature, promoting a new way to see the world.

EDS's approach was to have parallel thrusts in developing the components that they needed for mindset reengineering. The purpose of the parallel thrusts was to shorten the planning process, to involve as many key people as possible, and to separate the steps of the process that were to be handled internally versus the ones requiring external intervention (i.e., the help of Dr. Hamel and others).

Dr. Hamel wrote extensively about his experience with EDS, and his perspective on the approach taken in his book called *Competing for the Future.*

Here are the stages that EDS went through to reengineer its own mindset:

The EDS Planning Evolution

1970	Planning is an afterthought and a weakness
1980	Ready, Fire, Aim
1985	A teaspoon of planning and a cup of execution
1990	"It is time we steered by the stars and not by the lights of each passing ship"
1992	"A victorious army seeks its victories before seeking battle"—The Beginning of Mindset Reengineering

Stage #1

Stage one was focused on introspection (beyond a SWOT analysis) about the company's ability to handle change and the role of senior management.

SWOT =

Strengths

Weaknesses

Opportunities

Threats

The introspection yielded interesting results because it revealed how little EDS knew about the planning process, about itself, and about large-scale transformation. This is typical for companies that grew too fast to worry about planning and strategic thinking. In order to reinvent the company, the EDS leadership realized that they needed to develop the vision, create the environment, and inspire individuals and teams to pursue goals and achieve results substantially greater than they would on their own.

Next, they moved ahead with identifying their approach to "advantage creation" which is shown in the diagram below. The advantage creation starts with the company's strategic intent, which

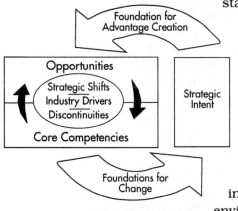

states that "EDS will be the global leader in shaping how information is created, distributed, shared, enjoyed, and applied for the benefit of enterprises and individuals worldwide." EDS then proceeded to identify the strategic shifts (which are the same as paradigm shifts) with the idea of understanding its role in an ever-changing environment and the opportunities that may be created as a result of these shifts (see box next page).

In order to better understand the process, and to gain a deeper understanding of the current environment as it pertains to EDS's business, the strategic shifts had to be tied to industry drivers (a convergence of trends and

EDS's Strategic Shifts	
Expanding from:	To:
IT Performance Improvement	Business Performance Improvement
Processing Data	Informationalizing
Solution-based Selling	Strategic Value Selling
Long-term Fixed Pricing	Value-based Pricing
Discrete Responsibility and View	Shared Responsibility and View

events that shape the structure and evolution of an industry).
The prevalent drivers were determined to be:

- data overload
- customization
- globalization of markets
- collapsing value chains
- information content is key
- ubiquitous information/knowledge
- rapid proliferation of technology
- computer power becomes free
- revolution in work
- individual services
- human interface

Stage #2

The second stage was done in "waves." These were intended to
represent a series of brainstorming and interview sessions aimed at
creating certain elements of the transformation vision and road
map. The Wave Concept had three objectives:

- create the deliverables that are asked of each team
- demonstrate that getting to the future is more about
  foresight, smart investing, preparation, and consistency,
  than the original strong culture (based on determina-
  tion, "can-do" attitudes, ambition and heroics)

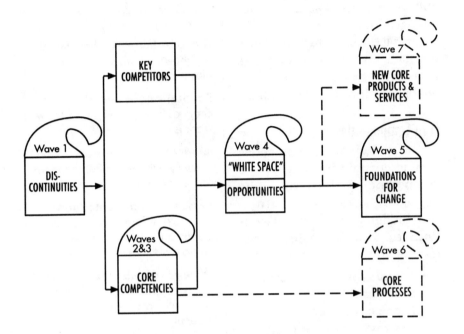

- instill a sense of concern and hope in the individuals involved in this process, that will allow them to behave as change agents once they return to their respective organizations

Initiating The Wave Movement

Each wave involved a discovery assignment starting with "discontinuities." (See figure above.) Discontinuities were tied to the already identified Strategic Shifts and Industry Drivers in order to create a more complete picture of the business opportunities available to the enterprise.

This represented a rare example of where top-down and bottom-up views were blended in one seamless effort. EDS realized that top-down or bottom-up views by themselves were not alternatives. Nearly 3,000 executives, middle- and first-line managers were involved in creating the deliverables for the first five waves. Waves 6 and 7 were not completed in Stage 2.

Collectively, discontinuities, industry drivers, and strategic shifts can be used as triggers for change. These are sources for inspiring the introduction of new products and services, as well as hints for organizing to meet the challenges in the market place.

Core Competencies

EDS then focused on determining current and future core competencies that would be needed to tackle the opportunities hidden inside the discontinuities. The EDS core competencies are:

- **Computing and communications**
- **Process and performance improvement and innovation** (methodologies, frameworks, etc., required to help customers with reengineering, and systems design-type projects)
- **Managing complexity**
- **Industry signature** (profound industry knowledge and expertise, required in dealing with customers in the vertical markets that EDS serves)
- **Relationship behaviors** (a set of behaviors and processes for developing, cultivating, and advancing relationships with customers)

Business Discontinuities

Here are the discontinuities that were identified in 1992:

Globalization—significantly alters the way nations and companies compete.

Revolution in work—major changes in where, when, and how work is done.

Information content, access, and delivery—the value components of the information industry.

Personal communications—untethered information access will create an explosion of services and capabilities.

Shifting IT architectures—exploitation of emerging IT Architectures will become a competitive necessity.

Virtual reality—changes the way users interact with computers, view, perform and manage processes, design and test products; even the way we communicate.

Education transformation—radical changes in teaching and learning methods, distribution channels, delivery mechanisms and funding.

Health care—access, funding, and administration will become increasingly critical as social and competitiveness issues increase.

Home services—the demand for services in the home will be unprecedented in variety and quantity.

Developing Opportunities

The information from discontinuities, core competencies, and competitive analysis (an on-going effort), was used to develop the areas in the "white space" of opportunities (see "wave" figure on page 157) that define the markets that the company is willing, but not necessarily ready, to tackle. This information is now the foundation for EDS change.

The opportunities were grouped into three "buckets:"

Horizontal leverage—opportunities to establish and enrich the foundation of products and services that provide horizontal leverage within EDS (supporting their strategic business units). An example would be an offering that allows customers to outsource their processes and functions to EDS. The new products and services are to be developed around three important criteria:

- Globalization: making products and services pervasive by thinking globally and acting locally

- Individualization: providing products and services perceived as selected, designed, and/or developed uniquely for the customer

- Informationalization: offering products and services capable of adding value by translating data into useful information, and translating information into knowledge and wisdom

Vertical marketplace—vertical markets that could be significantly impacted by EDS's presence. One such market is crime prevention.

Leveraging current core competencies—opportunities for leveraging current core competencies by pushing EDS's role deeper and wider. An example of this is to globalize EDS's competencies.

FOUNDATIONS FOR CHANGE

Strategic Initiatives

The result of Wave 5 was to create four strategic initiatives that put the company on the path of enterprise-wide, significant, and strategic change.

1 **Initiate and execute a global opportunity management network**—addressing portfolio management, shared sense of priorities, and the critical dimensions of the network

2 **Establish and maintain core competencies**—including mergers, acquisitions, and competence migration strategies.

3 **Refine corporate governance**—including a new balanced scorecard, redefinition of roles and responsibilities, and organizational realignment.

4 **Develop and execute a communication plan, which reaches all of EDS's constituents**—mobilizing the corporation around the new corporate direction.

One of the golden rules in change management is: communicate, communicate, communicate. EDS used the following framework to communicate how the pieces of the vision and direction came together for implementation.

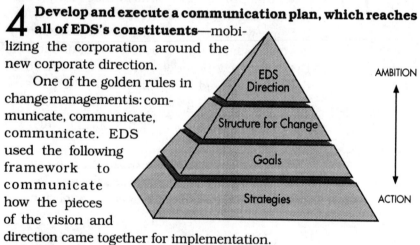

Stage #3

EDS proceeded to develop its goals, shared beliefs, and differentiating behaviors (the underpinning of core competencies, which manifest the enterprise's values, culture, and commitment to customers' success). The latter became the basis for a leadership development model.

At the end of Stage #3 EDS was ready to move ahead along two other paths (as the figure on the next page shows), in order to achieve global leadership, which was stated in its strategic intent.

The way EDS handled their transformation approach is almost

unique. They created a new process for planning, with many new components based on what they felt they needed to succeed in their enterprise transformation effort.

Of course, all of the transformation charts and wonderful concepts are meaningless without the organization having a sense of urgency to adopt and apply them in their daily work.

Creating Urgency

Dr. Hamel's greatest value may have been to teach EDS how to artificially induce a sense of urgency that rallied the troops behind the new vision and shared beliefs. The EDS employees responded extremely well to the need for change and the introduction of these new approaches and directions. They realized that all great companies could surrender their leadership if they fail to recognize the opportunities in front of them.

Starving for direction also helped the situation. Dr. Hamel very astutely pointed out that EDS's biggest trapdoors were:

- little sense of urgency, which was fueled by mistaking momentum for leadership, and a view that resources will win out, and
- inability to escape the past, which was strengthened by deep-down recipes and well-rooted dogmas, along with the lack of vision.

Interestingly enough, the introduction of a vision and the effort to think strategically helped the company in more ways than expected. It:

- increased appreciation for senior management and their efforts to finally get their arms around a chaotic environment;

"The competitive marketplace is strewn with good ideas whose time came and went because inadequate attention was given to moving rapidly and hitting an open window of opportunity."

—Constantine Nicandros, president, Conoco

- increased pride in the company that they worked for, by being a thought leader, not just a market leader;
- increased faith in the future and clarified a role for the company in its industry and society as a whole.

CHANGE IN THE ENTERPRISE

When a major change is necessary to realign a company with changes in markets, or any other trigger, companies and employees will often undergo significant individual, group, and organizational transformations. Transformation is primarily focused on providing a new beginning by positioning a company and its people anew. It also establishes and absorbs new cultural, organizational, structural, infrastructural, and process models.

Computers and robots can be easily reprogrammed with minimal disruptions or risks to the enterprise. But "reprogramming" people is difficult and poses major risks to the individuals and the enterprise itself. To cope with the professional and personal aspects of major changes, change management has developed tools, techniques, methodologies, and processes that minimize the risks and drastically improve the chances of a smooth transition to the new environment.

WHAT IS CHANGE MANAGEMENT?

Change management (CM) is a body of theory that provides a model that people and organizations can use to cope with major shifts in the workplace. CM is not only about changes to things we can see and touch. It is also about changing attitudes, views, mental models, and states of mind.

CM is more than a planned or unplanned response to a set of triggers and pressures. It is about changing the very foundation of a business. To deal with change, CM addresses basic business fundamentals such as how a business and its people are aligned with the marketplace, perform work, deal with partners, interact with each other, create products, delight customers, and enjoy work and life itself.

CM as a body of theory addresses questions such as:

- how to explain or create a case for action
- how to explain the future or end-state of the journey
- how to develop a process for CM, and staff it with the right people
- how not to overwhelm the organization

A Change Management Process

The overall thrust of the change management process can be captured in nine basic steps, shown in the figure on the followng page.

We have not found two transformation or reengineering projects alike. It is easy to see why, since the change management process is deeply grounded in the principles of continuous feedback and improvement. Every transformation team is empowered to tweak the process to achieve their goals, objectives, expectations, and skills development.

CHANGE APPROACHES

The greatest difficulty that most companies have is in creating the vision and "road map" to get there. The tendency is for executives to allow things to develop slowly over time and be created through the actions of formal and informal leaders. This attitude typically leads to a remedial approach of addressing only what is broken. It represents a reactive mentality looking for easy solutions and band-aid fixes. It also tends to perpetuate non-team behavior.

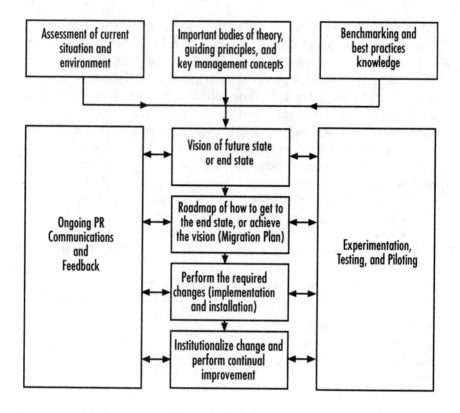

Executive Resistance To Change

Through the years we have found that most executives do not want to bother with the so-called soft aspects of change. By talking to executives and reengineering teams, we have found that there is a high level of frustration in the way proposed changes are presented and communicated. Three major shortcomings are:

- The proposed changes seem to be too theoretical and esoteric. Only certain individuals within the human relations development organization seem to understand them.
- The actions to achieve the proposed changes are either too superficial or too overwhelming, thus the work in this area always seems to be incomplete.
- Change management costs are difficult to quantify.

For Change To Succeed, We Must:

- demonstrate the connection and impact of the proposed changes to each other (there usually is a domino effect), and to the overall reengineering or transformation effort
- quantify beyond any reasonable doubt the benefits of the proposed changes
- outline an action plan that is integrated into the transformation, reengineering, and IT (information technology) strategy plans

Hard And Soft Change

To overcome these three shortcomings you need to integrate hard, "engineering-oriented" changes with the "soft," human aspects of change by addressing:

- culture, values, behaviors, and style of management
- skills, both organizational and individual
- structure, which addresses governance scheme, layers of management, organizational structure and modus operandi, decision making, span of control
- infrastructure, which addresses performance measures, policies, procedures, frameworks, methodologies, tools, compensation schemes

Remedial Change Management (RCM)

Remedial change management applies to changes that address an immediate problem or improvement opportunity. Examples of RCM include:

- introducing minor organizational changes, and/or changing the mission or scope of work of a functional organization
- performing narrowly-focused education and training
- implementing new or modified performance incentives

There is a better way to deal with the road map, which is based on the systems approach. We

Gestalt Change Management

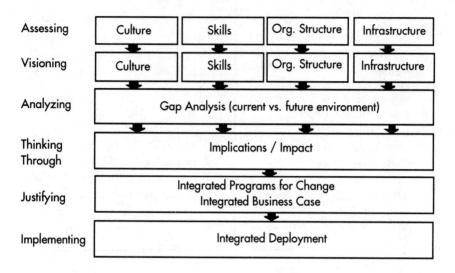

call it the Gestalt change management approach, and it is derived from the Gestalt theory of treating the whole.

Gestalt Change Management (GCM)

To deal with the human side of transformation, we like the Gestalt approach. Gestalt change management is systems-thinking oriented. It ensures that the planned change is consistent with the company's overall strategy and culture, is aligned with and supports expected behaviors, and is consistent with the company's values, beliefs and purpose.

Gestalt change management should not leave anything to guesswork or interpretation. The entire process is shown in the diagram above.

THE MACRO VIEW OF CHANGE

The Gestalt approach is holistic in nature because it looks at the big (macro) picture of change. One of the ways GCM helps an enterprise with the macro view of change is to put the genetic code of the enterprise under scrutiny.

The genetic code of the enterprise is formed by the enterprise's:

- values and beliefs of its founder(s) and/or current senior executives
- industry, and the markets that it serves
- current competitors
- customers and their needs and wants
- competencies, capabilities, and skills
- ways of organizing, growing, and making money
- management theories, style, and guiding principles
- practiced operational approaches, techniques, and tools
- policies, performance measures, and awards/rewards
- paradigms, dogmas, and orthodoxies that influence the societies where it does business

Your Growth Curve

Collectively, the genetic code elements represent more than just an enterprise's culture. They also represent a cycle, an S-curve or growth curve, in the life of the enterprise. The S-curve can be described in terms of a beginning, a main period of fast growth and expansion, and a plateau or ending.

It is extremely important for the change leaders to know as much as possible about the current cycle, and the enterprise's position on the growth curve, prior to proposing any major transformation activities. The reason for needing this knowledge is to avoid making serious mistakes about ending a current growth curve and starting a new one before its time.

For instance, at GM, Mr. Jose Ignacio Lopez de Arriortua pushed to put aside the TQM (total quality management) and JIT (just in time) efforts in favor of his PICOS (Purchased Input Concept Optimization with Suppliers) approach. Despite the fact that Mr. Lopez saved GM billions of dollars, the resentment that he caused, externally with the automotive suppliers, and also internally with the TQM and JIT stakeholders, is historic. Mr. Lopez was forced to hire bodyguards to protect himself from physical harm, and eventually felt totally unwelcome in North America. To this day he is remembered unfavorably for his lack of sensitivity to the changes he forced on the supplier community and on GM culture.

Changing Curves Is Complex

The lesson learned is that he tried to derail TQM and JIT at the height of their acceptance as the prevalent manufacturing paradigm in American industries. This clash reached war-like proportions when he tried to replace JIT/TQM with a "cost is everything" paradigm that had already been rejected by the supplier community.

It is obvious that each cycle or growth curve has its own sponsors, champions, disciples, agents, and fans (fanatics). These people will take action to defend and preserve their status quo, especially if they feel threatened by the introduction of a new cycle. Naturally, the further away the stakeholders feel they are from the end of their current S-curve, the higher their level of resentment and resistance towards the new growth curve. Thus, timing of a change introduction is crucial.

When Is The Best Time To Transform/Reengineer An Organization?

The right time to transform an organization depends on the stage that the enterprise is at on its growth curve. The best times to perform transformation/reengineering in order of preference are:
- at Point A (end of entrepreneurial stage), as it becomes necessary for the enterprise or organization to change its management style, build up its infrastructure, and introduce new processes and technologies to cope with fast growth

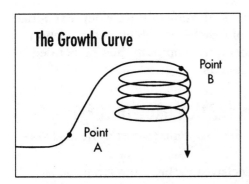

The Growth Curve

Point B

Point A

• at Point B, shown in the diagram, at the end of the growth curve, when it becomes obvious that the current business set of paradigms have served their purpose, and it is time to move on with a new set of guiding principles, or as the company fails to rejuvenate itself in the mature stage of the growth curve, but instead it finds itself in a downward spiral fighting for its survival

Motivate The Organization While Enjoying Success

So what happens if one finds it necessary to change in the middle of a paradigm or growth curve? There are three acceptable options:

1 **Create a "perceived crisis" that will force the end of the current paradigm.** The crisis takes many forms, from mergers and acquisitions to "severe fiscal fitness programs."

2 **Create a case for action based on the new paradigm that clearly demonstrates the benefits and the need to change.** This is where benchmarking and competitive analysis play a very important role.

3 **Allow "revolutionary strategies" to emerge within the organization.** Every company has its revolutionaries who are waiting for the opportunity to change the world. Most revolutionaries are thought leaders.

Gap Analysis

The migration or transition from one growth curve to the next is heavily dependent on the organizational gap analysis between the existing and future environments. The gap analysis itself is extremely important—it is the source of knowledge for designing a series of actions to support the migration.

The gap analysis and change can be a breeze for those organizations that have been through the change process before. But it can be very difficult for those organizations that are going through it for first time (or in a long while). Organizations that are new to change will demonstrate a high level of resistance, which is a reflection of existing paradigms, and the way the company has responded to "out-of-the-box thinking" in the past.

MOVING AHEAD ON THE NEW GROWTH CURVE

In order to move ahead with the second curve one needs to take the following steps:

- Introduce a crisp and decisive new beginning that mobilizes and energizes the troops.
- Migrate quickly from the old to the new growth curve.
- Avoid the "never ending scenario" of the old curve being promoted by its stakeholders, or lack of leadership commitment to change.
- Ensure that everyone understands and can defend the "right side" of the new paradigms, values, and beliefs that are being introduced.

Once a new growth curve is established, the best way to move ahead is to have continuous feedback, reinforcement, and communications in all directions, lots of empathy, and sustained coaching and mentoring.

Changing Individual Values

The "After" column in the table on the next page represents a new mental model that requires time for an individual to accept, internalize, and eventually externalize in his or her everyday work. That's where coaching and mentoring is most useful and productive. People are not automatically able to translate this new set of values and beliefs in terms of new behaviors, business etiquette, and collective experiences.

Changing personal values and beliefs is an area that requires special attention. Most individuals go into a defensive posture when they believe that someone else is trying to change their value system. Yet, individual change is necessary if a company is going to move forward with its new culture.

Changing Personal Values And Beliefs In A Reengineered Organization	
Before	*After*
Pass the buck	I am responsible
I succeed by building empires	I succeed by performing
Work the hierarchy	Work the network
My boss pays my salary	Customers pay my salary
My work/opinion does not matter	I make the difference
Look out for number one	We are all in this together
I am not in position to change anything	I will start the ball rolling
I don't need help	It is OK to ask for help; I need help
I am afraid to express my opinion	I am not afraid to express my opinion because it is important

No Magic Wand

The big misunderstanding we see in change situations is that many company executives believe that once the new culture is spelled out, the people somehow will find their way to the promised land on their own! This totally underestimates the difficulties that are caused by "throwing the ball into the employees' court."

Some employees choose the easy way by quitting the company. Others stay on and feel stressed out. Others are either tuned out or resort to guerrilla warfare, especially if they feel that they were wronged. It is not easy to migrate from the left side to the right side of the changing personal values chart without help.

Introducing A New Value Set

Models such as the one shown on the next page help in comprehending the proposed changes. It is important to realize that change will invoke a negative reaction in most cases because it is simply natural for people to view change with some fear and skepticism.

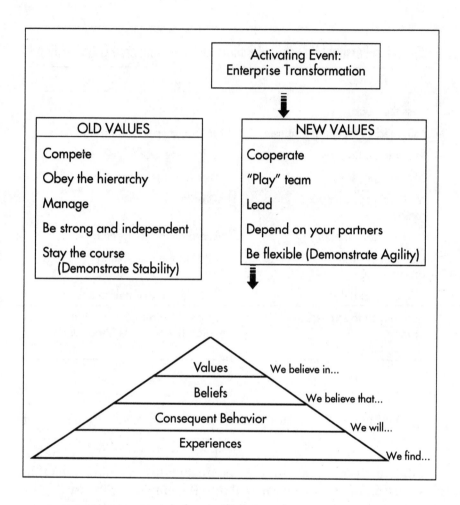

Reactions To Change

The chart on the next page shows the four organizational behaviors and postures towards change. In a changing environment, the positive vision is counterbalanced by the forces of fear and perceived pain. Each quadrant of the chart has barriers that are built on an individual and collective basis, aided by memories of pain experienced from previous attempts. Other common barriers include:

- different perspectives within/across management
- insufficient involvement within the organization itself
- lack of executive commitment

Assessing Current Culture

	High	**Experimentation** (short journeys)	**Renewal** (ready for the long journey)
FORCES OF OPPORTUNITY	Low	**Denial** (holding on)	**Status Quo** (contentment)
		High	Low

FORCES OF FEAR

Source: Adapted from Tony Petrellas's Change Cycle and Claes Janssen's Four Room Apartment.

These barriers can foretell the company's ability to change from the current environment to the desired state.

Systemic Issues Handcuffing Change

As is mentioned several times in this book, most companies struggle to perform enterprise transformations. The primary reasons for this struggle appear to be:

- Organizations are designed for execution, not for change.
- Most organizations are designed to contain changes in their "silos." They strive for stability by monitoring variances to forewarn themselves of drastic changes in performance, which leads to a culture of stability, not one of resilience.
- Change is not an explicit issue or activity on anyone's agenda.
- Many companies have outsourced their strategic planning and reengineering expertise to consulting firms, thus finding themselves unable to do it right on their own.
- The senior executives' plates are full, making it very hard to worry about massive changes which may require full time attention.

The Value Of The Teaching Organization®

The greater the memory of pain, the higher the fear and resistance to change. It is no surprise that for years, attempts by many companies to make great changes were met with skepticism and resistance. Employees need to see and accept the "win-win" scenario as it applies to them as individuals as well as at the organization level.

The greatest pain and fear is associated with layoffs and firings. Many senior executives view downsizing as good since they believe it produces a more efficient operation.

This view is typically not shared by employees who view downsizing as a series of layoffs, spinoffs and divestitures, which is all negative from their perspective. This has resulted in a perception among low-level employees that most changes are bad. Unfortunately, the employee view is not too far from the truth as indicated in this A.T. Kearney 1995 survey on company performance following major restructuring efforts.

This does not imply that executives should avoid downsizing and restructuring. It does imply, however, that paying attention to the way change is handled can affect the result consistent with the new value set shown on page 171. There are some approaches to downsizing that are acceptable, such as reskilling and redeploying, early retirement programs, "silver bullets," and attrition, versus the adversarial pink-slip approach.

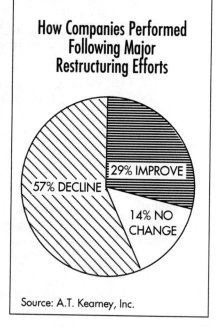

How Companies Performed Following Major Restructuring Efforts

57% DECLINE

29% IMPROVE

14% NO CHANGE

Source: A.T. Kearney, Inc.

When employees are "burned" after a poorly handled restructuring effort, even survivors mistrust their management team. They develop a

The Learning Organization	The Teaching Organization®
Passive mode	Active mode
Internalize message	Externalize message
Focus on knowledge	Focus on wisdom
Ability to learn	Ability to learn and communicate

level of indifference and apathy that acts not only as a barrier for future changes, but also as a trigger for low productivity. Much of their energy is devoted to:

- digging fox-holes for sniping at the new ideas
- defending their interests, whatever they may be
- politicking
- preparing for a career change
- agonizing, and coping with stress

It is easy to detect organizations that were "burned" by change from the levels of cynicism, sarcasm, and free-floating hostility that are encountered in the workplace.

One of the ways to overcome these negative reactions to change is to accept the culture of The Learning Organization, which is saturated with mechanisms, techniques, approaches, and processes about learning from others that are successful at dealing, coping, and managing change. Better than a Learning Organization for dealing with change is the Teaching Organization®. The difference between the two is shown in the chart above.

CONCLUSION

Your current growth curve provides hints as to when to start or avoid major changes. However, techniques have been developed to provide a new start even in the middle of expansionary growth periods because there are times and instances where it is necessary.

It is important for enterprise leaders to review growth curves on a regular basis and make intelligent decisions regarding the death of one growth curve and the introduction of another. This way an executive team has the chance to manage its own change, rather than being forced into it by outside forces.

Companies that anticipate and plan for change (Gestalt approach) have a chance of gaining a strategic advantage over their competitors. At the same time, they can minimize the pain and trauma caused internally.

The bad news is that resistance to change will always be present is a natural reaction to change. The good news is that proven techniques have been developed to reduce its impact on organizations and individuals, enabling an enterprise to think on change.

The most enlightened companies recognize that the reinvention of their companies is a continuous process requiring long-term leadership. Organizing for change should be incorporated in the enterprise's overall plan for restructuring and creating new business and technical infrastructures (including the organizational structure).

Poorly managed change affects more than its components;

Dealing With Resistance To Change

Here are some of the proven ways to deal with resistance to change:

- Recruit a sponsor of change who has high integrity, commands instant respect, and enjoys a solid reputation as a change master.

- Perform a risk assessment to identify the location and types of resistance that may be encountered.

- Initiate good two-way communications and PR.

- Ensure that issues have ownership and a plan to resolve them.

- Develop a critical mass of supporters and assign change agents and change champions who will work as influencers and mentors for change.

- Explain the win-win scenario as it applies not only at the enterprise level, but as it applies to the organizational/departmental level and the individual level.

- Engage in benchmarking and best practices studies that will support the vision and advance the current thinking.

- Instill a culture based on a teaching organization.

Companies that are reactive to the forces of change, end up playing Russian roulette with their futures, their employees' careers, and the well being of all stakeholders.

it affects the whole transformation effort. Change management requires true experts who have learned what tools and techniques to apply in a given situation. Such expertise is rarely found inside the enterprise. For this reason, it is appropriate for company executives to seek outside professionals who can guide an organization through the complex web of changes involved in enterprise transformation.

ACTION SUMMARY

► Base your change plan on where your organization is on the growth curve. If you're currently successful, extra justification for change must be created.

► Use your core competencies as the basis for change.

► People cannot be easily "reprogrammed" to accept change. Therefore, so-called soft aspects of change are crucial to success.

► Change needs to come from a Gestalt, or holistic approach that takes the entire organizational system into account.

► Resistance to change is natural. Show those involved how they'll win, individually, from the change.

► Instill a mindset that change must be an ongoing process in the successful organization, not an isolated event.

Part Three
THE PERSON-ORGANIZATION LINK

Chapter 9
MANAGING PEOPLE DURING ORGANIZATIONAL CHANGE
Charles Milofsky & Carl E. Huffman, Jr.

Chapter 10
PERSONAL TRANSFORMATION GUIDES ORGANIZATIONAL TRANSFORMATION
Pat Gill

Chapter 9

MANAGING PEOPLE DURING ORGANIZATIONAL CHANGE

Charles Milofsky & Carl E. Huffman, Jr.

Charles Milofsky, EdD, (left) has been a licensed clinical psychologist and human resource consultant for over 20 years. Dr. Milofsky specializes in stress management and developing a change process for individuals and organizations. He has practiced as an individual and group psychotherapist and has facilitated executive-board retreats and team-building sessions for many businesses and agencies. Dr. Milofsky has presented workshops on change, making relationships work, stress management, critical incident stress debriefing, and disaster mental health services.

Carl E. Huffman, Jr., (right) is a professional speaker, corporate trainer, and management consultant. He founded Huffman Enterprises in 1981 and has worked with such companies as DuPont, Siemens, Ameritech, 3M, IGA, IBM, Graybar, and many others. Mr. Huffman has conducted seminars for almost 15,000 people during his 15 years as a full-time management trainer. He also has been a keynote speaker for MAC Tools, Society of American Florists, ASUG, and other organizations. Before founding Huffman Enterprises, Mr. Huffman was CEO of two major health care corporations. He is a graduate of Indiana University with a BA degree in speech and theater.

Charles Milofsky, EdD, 1749 Golf Rd. #151, Mount Prospect, IL 60056; phone (847) 632-9655; fax (847) 593-0625.

Carl E. Huffman, Jr., Huffman Enterprises, Inc.; P.O. Box 8357, Bartlett, IL 60103; phone (630) 483-8997; fax (630) 483-8931; e-mail CarlH007@aol.com.

Chapter 9

MANAGING PEOPLE DURING ORGANIZATIONAL CHANGE

Charles Milofsky & Carl E. Huffman, Jr.

"If the rate of change within your organization is less than the rate of change of your environment, then your end is in sight."
—Jack Welch, CEO, General Electric

"Change or Die" is the motto for American business today. Organizations have two choices: they can ignore change and become its victims, or they can accept and manage change. Businesses must be flexible enough to take advantage of all opportunities—failing to do so shifts the advantage to the competition. And in today's global market that competition can be in Ohio, Taiwan, or points in between.

AN "AVERAGE" COMPANY

Apex Manufacturing Company has been in business for 25 years. The founder and owner retired to Florida and his two sons now run the business. The company employs 500 people and has a ten-person sales staff, with sales of about $1 million.

In the last three years, sales have dropped off by 10% while costs have remained about the same. Major new competition from overseas has emerged and Apex is facing further threats to their market share.

In order to stay in business, three things must happen at Apex:

- First is a reduction in force, with more employees reporting to fewer managers.
- Second is product improvement. There haven't been any important changes in their products in over eight years.
- Third is product development in new areas to decrease their reliance on their aging main product line.

Apex is an all too familiar story. Change in corporate America includes downsizing, product innovation, and fewer managers supervising more people. All this is a direct result of global competition and other factors. How this affects people and their lives is the topic of this chapter.

FORCES OF GLOBAL CHANGE

Successful organizations choose to make change work for them, but often at workers' expense. In the past ten years, reorganization has dislocated over 30 mil-

"What the heck is this the age of?"

How Technology Is Changing Our World

Within companies, tremendous change has taken place. Since 1983, 25 million computers have been added to the workforce. Intranets and e-mail are sweeping most industries. Cellular phone usage has jumped from zero in 1983 to over 16 million today; over 19 million people carry pagers, and over 12 billion voice messages are left each year.

lion American workers. *Fortune* 500 companies have eliminated 3.2 million jobs since 1980. Over 2,000 U.S. companies and corporate divisions have changed hands—just since 1990. It's predicted that an additional 15% cut in the U.S. workforce will occur in the near-term.

The weekday edition of a major newspaper contains more information than most people learned in a lifetime in 17th century England, making information processing a key field of our time.

The cost of computing power drops approximately 30% each year and microchips are doubling in performance power every 18 months. The home video camera has more computing power than an old IBM 360, and the video game Saturn runs on a higher performance processor than the original 1976 Cray super computer, which was only available to the most elite physicists of that time.

WORKERS ARE UNPREPARED

How can corporations prepare their employees for constant change? How does this new technology affect workers? What is the employee state of mind during all this, and most importantly, how can an executive manager manage people in a time of rapid change? These are the questions we will answer in this chapter.

To date, organizations have performed poorly when it comes to preparing their workers for change. Upper management sees its role as innovators responding to changing market trends and spearheading new and better ways of doing business. The resulting directives are passed down to the workforce for implementation. Their focus is solely on improving the bottom line.

Management often fails to realize that there are two critical elements involved in getting people to change—time and communication. Corporations can't control the speed with which they must react, but they can control how they communicate with the people expected to carry out the directives.

HELP EMPLOYEES DEAL WITH CHANGE

Let's look at a typical scenario. Carol, a supervisor, has come into her manager's office disturbed about the effect of a new directive that completely changes the way the department is run. She has 20 people reporting to her on two first-shift production lines.

Carol: Marty, this job is impossible. If I didn't need the extra money, I'd go back to being on the line in a heart beat.

Marty: Hey, slow down Carol, it can't be that bad.

Carol: Oh no? Then you go out there and put up with their guff. All I've heard since we were told to switch over is, "I hate it," "It won't work," or "Get a new life." I'm telling you these people just don't want to change and I don't know what to do about it.

Marty: Well, let's see if we can help you put this together. Just how big a problem is it? All you said was "these people."

Carol: Well, a few don't complain about anything and they're easy to manage. But there are some vocal ones who almost scream in your face. And then there are the rest.

Marty: What kind of numbers?

Carol: Four or five are okay—even looking forward to the new way. Then there are the "four musketeers" who are doing all the ranting and raving. The rest seem unsure. I'm afraid the four rebellious ones will gain support from the rest, and I'll have a mutiny on my hands.

"I'm telling you these people just don't want to change and I don't know what to do about it."

Marty: Carol, let me share with you what I've learned about leading people through the change process. This can help you go out there and get the situation turned around.

Carol: Hey, if you can help me change the "four musketeers" and get this process going, I'm all ears.

Marty: *I can help you get the process going, but I can't make any promises about your "four musketeers." You see, we have found that about 20% of any group or workforce accept change with no problem, 20% resist, and the rest have to be convinced. Of the 20% who resist, we sometimes lose a few because they just refuse to go along with the new procedures.*

Carol: You mean I may have to let someone go?

Marty: *I'm not saying that. I'm just telling you what we've learned. Let's not worry about possible casualties. We need to talk about how you can get your group on track and maybe— just maybe—everyone will fall into line. Okay?*

Carol: Okay. Where do I begin?

Help Employees Overcome Fear

Marty: *First, understand that your people are uncomfortable and even afraid of the new process. They are unsure. They were used to doing the process the old way for so long, it has almost become a habit. Now we're asking them to do it differently. You need to be patient, and reassure them that everything will be okay.*

Have you explained why we are making the change?

Carol: No, not really.

Marty: *Do you remember how we presented the change to you and the other supervisors?"*

Carol: Yes, you called us in and went over the new process, how it would help produce more products, and the time frame you expected—which according to my people is totally unreal.

Marty: *We'll see what we can do about the time frame, but did you do the same for your people—I mean, explain what was going to happen and why we did it?*

"The first rule of getting people to change is to explain what will happen."

Carol: I didn't get a chance to. As soon as I said change, they started screaming and moaning. A couple of them even walked out in disgust. I had to go calm them down. So I just said we'd work it all out.

Communicate The Benefits

Marty: *Carol, the first rule in getting people to change is to communicate the benefits. You need to get them together and go over it the same way we did in our meeting. Let them see how this will benefit the company and them.*

"But why should they cooperate with the change?"

Carol: How can it help them?

Marty: *Explain that when we become better at producing our products, customer loyalty increases which gives us an edge on our competition. If we can produce a better quality product and keep our price down, we can sell more, and that's job security for them.*

Next, form some small groups to help plan the change-over and be sure to include people who are positive about this. Try to get as many of the majority involved as you can. Then, your job is to work on the "four musketeers."

Carol: Okay, so far, but what do I use on my musketeers—a whip and chair?

Marty: *My advice is to be firm. Tell them up front that this is going to happen and you expect them to cooperate. Also, tell them you understand their feelings. Show them you care. I know it's easy to become defensive with these types of people, but don't let them get to you.*

Carol: You're right. I did let them get to me.

Overcoming Resistance

Marty: *Next, you "divide and conquer." Call them aside one by one. Ask them to share their concerns and try to work through each issue. Give them reassurance about what will happen. Above all show them you have confidence that they can do it. Are these your older workers who are rebelling?*

Carol: Just a couple. The other two have been here for three to four years.

Marty: *Well, age isn't always a factor in resisting change, but older people are often more afraid of something new. You just have to point out how this change will help the company and, subsequently, help them.*

Carol: You know they were talking the other day about a

"They'll buy the change if you just explain what we're doing and why."

company across town that closed down because their major contractor stopped doing business with them. They had friends who worked there. These people said the company hadn't kept up with new technology and that's why they went under. I could use that to convince them to buy into this.

Marty: Now you're beginning to think the way you need to. That 60% majority of yours will need time to come around, but they'll buy it if you just explain what we're doing and why. Give them the support they need right now and tell them you have faith in their efforts. If you can convert any or all of the "four musketeers," then use them to champion your cause—so to speak.

Carol: This is great, Marty. Do you think they will fall into place if I do this?

Marty: Yes I do, Carol. But I can't guarantee everyone will just fall into line. Some may take more time than others. We may even have to think about transfers if they refuse to buy in. But, come and talk to me before you make any rash decisions. Your main job now is to go out there and encourage them, communicate why we're doing this, and keep them on track. People go through the change process at their own speed.

The Change Process

Carol: What change process?

Marty: There are three phases. Phase #1 is called unfreeze. This is where we stop doing things the old way and begin to do them the new way. Phase #2 is called the neutral or perform stage. This is where they are carrying it out the new way. And, then phase #3 is called refreeze. Now the new way becomes the only way. A good supervisor has to be aware of these phases and help people through them.

Carol: Boy, I can't wait for the refreeze. Thanks, Marty, you've been a big help. Now I'm going out there to take charge and turn this around. As they start going through the rest of the phases, can I come in and talk to you again?

Marty: Sure, Carol, anytime. Remember, I've always said your success is my success. I know you'll get this back on track.

LESSONS FOR HANDLING CHANGE

What we saw in our scene is a typical story in today's workplace. What lessons can be learned? First, there are basic phases of change. In her book, *The Essence of Change*, Liz Clarke calls these phases Ending, Transition, and Beginning of the Future. Scott and Jaffe in *Managing Change at Work* and *Managing Personal Change* talk about four phases: Denial, Resistance, Exploration, and Commitment. We see the phases of change as Unfreeze, Neutral, and Refreeze.

1 Unfreeze. This is probably the most critical and difficult stage for most people. People are being asked to stop their old ways of doing things and start a new process.

Giving up the old familiar way of doing something is hard in the best of circumstances. Our old familiar ways are habits and represent our comfort zone. Few people willingly leave their comfort zones.

Unfreezing includes some observable behaviors. First— refusing to accept change. Some typical phrases are, "Don't pay any attention to it—it'll go away," or, "Why do we need to change, it's working okay the way it is," "Who's dumb idea was this?" and "It'll never work," but the geniuses will learn that the hard way and then we can go back to doing things the old way. These reactions represent a fear of failure. No one can predict if the change will work.

Even if it is successful, how much pain and agony must be endured in the process? The essence of the fear is uncertainty.

Another aspect is that people often feel that change implies criticism—that what they were doing was wrong. So they take the change very personally. Finally, resistance comes from the fear of the unknown. In the unfreeze stage, people are exposed. They feel inadequate or

WAIT A MINUTE. INSTEAD OF TRYING TO ADAPT, MAYBE I'M JUST UNSUITED FOR LIFE ON THIS PLANET.

How Should Managers Handle Their People During This First Critical Phase?

Don't make change a surprise. Let people know in advance that something will change. This allows them to become mentally prepared.

Don't let people stay rooted in the past. The more they cling to old ways, the harder the transition will be. It pays to connect the new way with the old way, but move quickly to the new method.

Realize that the greatest concern about change is that it's being done *to* the person rather than *by* them. Since they feel they have no control over the situation, offer help by allowing employees some "ownership." Consult with staff about what the change means to them, ask for ways to implement the change, and involve them in the planning.

Help employees set personal goals for making the transition to the new method.

Throughout this process, you must be a positive leader. This means you must accept change and be a strong proponent of the new method or system. Your encouragement and high expectations are most critical in the first phase of change.

dumb. Their self-esteem is threatened, and they feel incompetent and that they must start all over again.

In addition, people are insecure. They may say, "What if I can't perform under the new process? What if I can't learn to do it?" As a result of this fear, performance will surely drop, and stress becomes an issue. Change involves greater effort, energy, and time than the status quo. The new way adds more work and responsibilities, which causes even more stress.

2 The Neutral Phase. People are now in the process of doing the new job or action. While they may have left the old way behind, this doesn't mean they have achieved a new comfort zone. Observable behaviors still include insecurity and fear. During this time, statements include: "This is so hard," "I really don't think I can do this," and "I just can't seem to get it."

Managers need to give close supervision during this phase because people don't want to leave their old comfort zone. Some people may drift toward their old way of doing things. For example, typing a document on a manual typewriter instead of using a computer word processing program. The manager's job is to give them a subtle reminder, some refresher training, and get them using the new process.

Who To Help?

Next comes the question of with whom to begin working: the "encouragers," "resistors," or "non-committals"? Researchers tell us that about 20% of people in a group readily accept change, so we call this group the "encouragers." Another group fights change, so we call them "resistors." The remaining 60% are neutral and need to be convinced. We label this group the "non-committals." The non-committals are typical, in that most people do not want to change, but they can be persuaded to accept it.

Conventional wisdom advises us to begin with the encouragers and begin to build a larger and larger base of acceptance. However, managers need to spend the majority of their time with the non-committals, but can't risk ignoring the encouragers, who also need support to continue their positive attitudes. If possible, team up the encouragers with the non-committals.

Unfortunately, the critical few—the resistors—demand the most attention. It is easy for a manager to either ignore the resistors or give them full attention. The best advice is to do neither. Keep the resistors busy and somewhat isolated because they usually start to work on the non-committals to build support for their views.

Expect Mistakes During The Neutral Phase

Mistakes are common during this period and productivity will be low. Insecurity and fear of loss of jobs could be driven even higher, depending on management's attitude and how they handle employees during this phase.

It's easy to fall prey to corporate demands for increasing productivity and higher quality as the relentless push to change overnight continues.

SOLUTION: Be patient and show support. A successful, caring manager will keep this stage in focus. By showing a caring attitude, patiently working through mistakes, and helping employees learn from errors, this phase can move smoothly. Realize that errors will occur. Keeping them to a minimum, both from the company's standpoint and for the employees' self-esteem, is the manager's key responsibility.

Managers must take the time to provide training and feedback. An important step is to set short-term objectives. Once you and the employees have a plan for the change, sit down with each person to get individual buy-in.

How To Work With Different Behavioral Styles To Build Support For Change		
	Behavioral responses	*How to build support for change*
Encouragers	Readily accept change	Support them to keep their morale high; team them with non-committals
Resistors	Fight change	Keep busy; keep isolated from non-committals
Non-committals	Neutral; need to be convinced	Self-esteem is low, need nurturing

During the perform stage, non-committals can easily be swayed. Their self-esteem is low because mistakes and uncertainty are high. Be alert to this and offer assurance and support. Adapt a special nurturing attitude with the non-committals and they will come along.

Keep A Clear Vision

During this phase, it's important that a manager have a clear set of goals and a vision about how the change will evolve. The goal or outcome should be ever present in your mind. Employees should be reminded of where they are and where they are going. Hold frequent planning sessions and meetings to discuss progress. Be careful, however, that meetings don't turn into gripe sessions and become negative.

Managers must stay focused on their goals and persevere. An important way to build a positive environment, especially during this period, is to set short-term goals or objectives and celebrate their achievement. The greatest difficulty during this and the first phase is that the managers are also going through their own personal transition.

Finally, realize the paradox of change: during a time when everyone needs more structure, they are given the least because no one can predict the outcome. Some comfort should come from the fact that managers and employees are sharing the experience and working through it together. Managers, too, have personal concerns about the change process and should tell employees about their experiences. Workers appreciate managers who let their guards down and come across as human and personable.

3 **Refreeze: The New Standard Operating Procedure.** The managers probably thought this would never happen. Now the new procedure has become the accepted way.

Now, workers' attitudes are positive and philosophical. We hear statements like: "This is great—we should've done this a long time ago," or, "I knew all along it would work." People like to forget the unpleasantness of the past and move forward.

> "This is great—we should've done this a long time ago."

Change Continues

Here is a caveat. Those who have been through previous changes are concerned that it will happen again. Management may say they won't have to go through this again, but many people won't believe it.

Given the premise that change is constant, other changes are almost certain. Now managers must manage worker skepticism. To do this, accept, even celebrate, the fact that the change has been so successful. Let employees enjoy their triumph—continue to praise them for their efforts. But, don't hide the fact that they may need to begin to prepare for the next change, planned or unplanned. This may not be good news, but it must be addressed. Just as in phase

How To Handle Resistance

Every manager must face the fact that approximately 20% of the workforce will fight change. These resistors are individuals who just refuse to change. A few will quit rather than deal with the new situation.

Solution: Resistors must be moved, transferred, or gotten out of the mainstream.

If resistors are left within the team or department, they can become the proverbial "rotten apple that spoils the barrel." However, many resistors can be changed. If they continue to fight, and removing them is not possible, we can learn to cope with them.

Resistors may fight just by saying no and walking away. Comments like: "I've never been good at that," or, "You can't teach an old dog new tricks," and, "What for? I've done it this way for years," are tactics meant to make managers give up.

Resistors are manipulators. They have trained you to leave them alone and to look the other way in order to avoid a confrontation. Some resistors stay stuck in their ineffective behavior patterns because they are scared to change and would even leave rather than shift their attitudes.

one, no surprises is the rule.

Actually, talking about future change may not be at all bad. Employees already feel good about the results of the change effort. There's every reason to believe that other changes can also result in improved methods and performance.

Managers should reinforce the way difficulties were handled and compliment employees on their perseverance, all the while suggesting that this could prepare them for any future change. Then, when change is in the air again, review the phases and difficulties and determine what lessons were learned and how they can be applied to the new situation.

MOTIVATING BUY-IN

Research supports the premise that people will change if they believe there is significant reason to. Here are some ways to effect the change for those resistors and non-committals who can be persuaded to change.

Hold Group Sessions

Begin with focus group meetings that allow people to express their feelings and give their input. The key is finding reasons and getting workers to buy into the new way of doing business. Mixed groups work best. Be sure to include those people for and against the reorganization, as well as those with attitudes in between. If only one person is leading the group, limit the size to no more than 20 people. If two leaders are present, limit the group to 30.

Expect these meetings to get heated, so pair a manager with a human resource specialist, who has extensive experience in facilitating groups. This should prevent meetings from becoming just gripe sessions.

Ask For Buy-In

The next step is to obtain buy-in for the outcome. This is best done in small group formats.

The first-line supervisor is often the management person with the most credibility from the workers' viewpoint. One strategic approach is to have this person disseminate some of the general effects the new operations will have on the business and then work down to the personal level—for example, "I'm sure you realize that if we don't change our process, we cannot remain competitive in the marketplace," translates, "And if that occurs, our production will be reduced and that may mean more layoffs."

Dealing With Resistance

In some cases, the above approach could create even more disbelief and resistance. One way to counteract this development is to use a compare and contrast method. You begin by noting—even writing down—the current activities and show that outcome. The conclusion that failure will follow should be obvious.

Tips For Effective Group Sessions

- Don't hold these meetings if the organization is not planning to incorporate worker suggestions and recommendations into the overall change process. Otherwise, workers will think their input is not important and that management has set them up.

- During the meeting, assign participants to take notes. After the meeting is over, summarize what was said, and send a copy to every participant with their recommendations clearly listed.

Another approach is the direct approach. Here a manager ignores refusal and acts as if employees will do what you want. Begin by being positive, not defensive. Be pleasant and mention that some changes are coming and that you are counting on their expertise. Specifically, ask for their support and help during the process. Next, state your request and lay out a plan. Be specific about what you want and the desired outcome.

You most certainly will hear an objection. You then decide whether it's reasonable or just a smoke screen. If the objection is legitimate, handle it right away.

The final approach to handling resistors is the trade-off. The two most important words to use here are "if" and "then." The "if" describes the action and the "then" describes the consequences of the action.

Begin with a very specific request, complete with detail about what you want. Then, find something you can offer in exchange. Don't make the "then" benefit a benefit for you, but rather for them. There must be some personal thing in it for them. "If you'll do x, then you can have y." The trade-off technique is versatile, because you can use many things as personal benefits.

Warning

Pay attention to a couple of hazards. First, it could appear that you are offering a reward to resistors for their poor performance. Second, others may see this as giving resistors preferred treatment and may try the same approach.

The trade-off approach should be used selectively, with really tough cases. The perk or trade-off shouldn't be too significant, and observers who voice their disapproval can be told, "Hey, it worked, didn't it?" In difficult cases, everyone will be dissatisfied with the resistors behavior and accept—even welcome—anything that changes the person.

These aren't guaranteed approaches for handling resistors, but they have been tried and worked in many cases. Remember, too, there will be some cases that end up hopeless. But don't give up too soon. Give your best efforts to the task of changing these employees. Failing that, be decisive enough to remove the problem.

Another tactic the resistors take is to throw up another smoke screen, but you can just ignore it and proceed. For example, " I understand your point, but what I'm asking you to do is this."

"Selling" Change

Here's a sales technique for handling objections that may help in change situations. The five-step technique is:

1. Respond with an empathy statement: "I understand how you can feel that way."
2. Turn the objection into a question: "So, what you're saying is...."
3. Get agreement—"Do I have that right?"
4. Give an "if we can" statement: "If we can overcome this, then you would go along with...."
5. Answer the objection: "Here is the way we can do this," or, "this is the way this will work." Be factual and specific.

CONCLUSION

We know that change isn't easy, but there are principles organizations can follow to facilitate the process.

FEEL, FELT, FOUND: Here is another way objections are handled in sales that can be applied to change. Say, "I understand how you feel. Others have felt the same way, until they found that..."

First, understand that change in today's business environment has a new focus. In the past, organizations could change products, markets, even processes, without greatly affecting their workforce. Now, the emphasis has shifted to reorganization, reengineering, total quality, empowerment, and self-directed work teams. These mean changing employees' skills and behaviors. As a result, organizations need to address this in a much different fashion. Upper management cannot just announce the change and expect everyone to fall in line.

Transforming workers to perform in different ways is not an easy process. It takes planning, commitment, and an understanding by management that change will take longer than anticipated. Problems are inevitable. Confusion often precedes change and provides the opportunity to clarify issues. Workers require training and direction to learn new procedures. It is bad business practice not to provide this instruction—as frequently happens.

Change can be managed, even during the most difficult times. Just remember these principles. Keep focused on the needed change. Never start a second fire while trying to put out the first one.

ACTION SUMMARY

▶ Be a role model. Accept change yourself before you expect others to change.

▶ Put policies and systems in place to support the change process. Provide training, encourage risks, and accept mistakes.

▶ Communicate, communicate, communicate—not only about the change, but why it's necessary and what the result will be. Continue to provide feedback about how it is going.

▶ Concentrate your change efforts on the work being done, not on decision-making authority.

▶ Make sure that company initiatives are in harmony with expected results.

▶ Use a team approach to help drive expected change.

▶ Don't adhere to rigid management plans during the change process. Encourage initiative and creativity.

▶ Put people in a position to learn by doing and give them the support to accomplish what you ask.

▶ Keep reminding people that their efforts matter and will improve the whole organization.

▶ Practice leadership by continuing to support the new approach. Don't move on to the next "program" until the change is accepted as the new status quo.

Chapter 10

PERSONAL TRANSFORMATION GUIDES ORGANIZATIONAL TRANSFORMATION

Pat Gill

Pat Gill
is a speaker, facilitator, and consultant who stresses personal responsibility and contribution. For over 20 years, Ms. Gill has helped individuals develop the skills to operate successfully in the business world. She is president of Alexis-Gill Inc., a human resource consulting firm that specializes in the identification and development of new behavioral and mind-set skills for the changing workplace.

Ms. Gill is also a motivational speaker on personal development, learning strategies for success, and specific organization transformation strategies. An experienced facilitator and trainer, she has conducted hundreds of sessions on consulting, management, internal partnership, and setting vision and developing strategies for quality and other organizational change implementations. Some of her current clients include Johnson & Johnson, Pennsylvania Blue Shield, and the World Gold Council.

A published author, Ms. Gill has Masters degrees in Business and Counseling Psychology, and is pursuing her doctorate in adult learning at Columbia University.

Pat Gill, Alexis-Gill, Inc., 222 Manaroneck Ave. #207A, White Plains, NY 10605; phone (914) 683-5300; fax (914) 683-5346; e-mail 73164.3721@ compuserve.com.

Chapter 10

PERSONAL TRANSFORMATION GUIDES ORGANIZATIONAL TRANSFORMATION

Pat Gill

"Management is about coping with complexity.
Leadership is about coping with change."
—John Kotter, Harvard University

CHANGE VS. TRANSFORMATION

Change is a given. Change exists, like death and taxes. The big problem for organizations is not change itself. The problem (if it can be called that— change is also an opportunity) is how to develop the ability to cope effectively with the increased demands brought about by rapid change.

To put it another way, the problem is how to learn to help workers and organizations meet the demands of relentless change, while successfully minimizing its negative aspects and maximizing its benefits to the greatest number of people. Transformation of organizations involves providing lower cost, higher quality products and services, while simultaneously providing meaningful work for workers, and increased shareholder value. Certainly a tall order. Transformation implies not just reacting to change, or even just changing in some way, but evolving to a "higher" level to meet the challenge of change. Transformation implies *better*, not just different.

PERSONAL CHANGE VS. PERSONAL TRANSFORMATION

Let's start by discussing personal change versus personal transformation to clarify the concept. People age. This is a biological fact. It is a classic example of change.

It is possible that as you age, you could learn from experience, reflect on life's events, and evolve to a more mature level of functioning and reasoning. This is transformation—a possibility, not an inevitability. There are many old people who have not evolved, are not more mature—just changed, just older. On the other hand, we all know one or more older people who, over time, became wiser, more integrated, and more mature in their dealings with life and people. Some developmental psychologists suggest that wisdom is inevitable. But, common sense and observation tell us otherwise. The potential for transformation is there, but not the guarantee.

In the literature on adult education, transformative learning is defined as learning that leads to a more mature and developed perspective on life. Transformative learning means someone has learned to *be* different, not just to *act* differently.

You don't go anywhere when personal transformation is put on hold.

Transformation means growth and progress. It means being more evolved and enlightened, and more able to successfully handle new information and new situations as they present themselves.

ORGANIZATIONAL TRANSFORMATION

Transformation is often so difficult and problematic because it implies creating new ways of operating and new ways of being. Many practitioners of transformation attempt to create higher-level, or more evolved, ways of functioning without adequately trying to change the individual levels of people in the organization, especially the leaders themselves. Their efforts are inevitably going to be disappointing. You wouldn't try to create a more sophisticated product with the same old tools—why would you try to transform an organization to a higher way of functioning using the same levels of leadership?

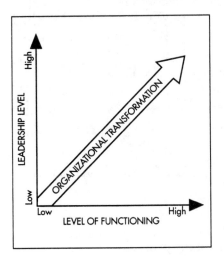

The issue of organizational transformation is on the minds of countless scholars, business practitioners, and organizational leaders. In a report on leading business transformation, jointly published in 1994 by the International Consortium for Executive Development Research and Gemini Consulting, over 1,400 worldwide business leaders indicated that leading ongoing, continuous organizational transformation was the number one business challenge for the foreseeable future. This report also indicated that leaders, formal and informal, do not appear to be ready for this challenge.

Ready For Transformation?

Let's consider a practical example to clarify further. One of the my client organizations was attempting to use quality as a strategy to create organizational transformation. Quality was selected for a variety of reasons, but primarily because management felt quality initiatives could create the types of changes to processes that would result in greater customer satisfaction and lower costs. Two leaders from two different departments within this company saw the challenge differently and achieved dramatically different results.

In both cases, the individuals were clear about what needed to be done, and the premises of the quality paradigm. Both wanted and felt their organizations needed to be different and to work differently to be successful. But Leader A (in Finance) and Leader B (in the Human Resources Department [HRD]) saw the need for personal transformation differently.

Leader A started the process with himself. He worked on changing and evolving himself and his ways of working. During every step of the process, he was open to changing and was able to transform into a different type of leader.

Leader B understood the process conceptually, but was not as committed to personal change. He believed, correctly, that his superiors were not at all interested in his personal change and growth, and that change and growth were not going to be rewarded.

The attempted transformations of Finance and HRD were operationalized in exactly the same way. Finance, under Leader A, changed and is still making a concrete bottom-line difference with reduced costs and improved customer satisfaction with services. Finance continues to use the processes to stay focused and bring together various parts of the organization.

The HRD implementation never took hold. HRD changed briefly, but returned to its previous level of operation. I believe that HRD's failure boiled down to the lack of personal transformation on the part of Leader B. He was willing to give the process a try, but he was not open to deep personal transformation because it might have threatened his role in the organization.

Because Leader B was unwilling to take personal risks, his team was not willing to risk much either. No one really wanted to change. No one really wanted to examine underlying assumptions about work and work processes. Therefore change was very superficial and there was no significant transformation.

```
┌──────────────┐     ┌──────────────┐     ┌──────────────┐
│   Personal   │  ╋  │ Transformed  │  ═  │     REAL     │
│Transformation│     │Organizational│     │TRANSFORMATION│
│              │     │   Processes  │     │              │
└──────────────┘     └──────────────┘     └──────────────┘
```

No End In Sight

It seems clear that the need for organizational transformation will remain unabated as long as international competition, and the need for higher quality products at lower costs continue to exist. During the last twenty-plus years, strategies have been introduced to help achieve transformation in organizations. From quality to process reengineering, downsizing to innovation, empowerment to teamwork, and the creation of a learning organization—all have been used to reorganize and revitalize organizations. Each of these approaches, singly or in combination, can improve and transform organizations. Sustained and thoughtful efforts do yield some positive results. But most efforts fail to achieve their full promise of organizational transformation.

WHY TRANSFORMATION FAILS

John Kotter, Harvard Business School professor, writes most eloquently about these failures and what he sees as the reasons for them. His *Harvard Business Review* article (1995) on why transformations fail was, and continues to be, widely read and cited. His book *Leading Change* elaborates on why change approaches are less than successful in creating organizational transformation. Kotter outlines what he considers to be the eight stages necessary for a company to achieve its goals for transformation (see box).

My experience with organizational transformation efforts agrees with Dr. Kotter's concepts and his prescription. But, in order to accomplish these things, leaders must demonstrate transformational behaviors and changes in themselves. Yet many leaders who are formally and informally attempting these types of transformations do not currently have the ability, the skills, or the mindsets to accomplish these tasks, even when they theoretically understand the need. Leaders need to develop to higher leadership levels if they are going to be able to achieve the stages outlined by Dr. Kotter and other proponents of organizational transformation.

Kotter's 8 Steps To Transformation

1 Establish a sense of urgency.

2 Create the guiding coalition.

3 Develop a vision and strategy.

4 Communicate the change vision (about what I call the new transformed state).

5 Empower broad-based action.

6 Generate short-term wins.

7 Consolidate gains and produce more change.

8 Anchor new approaches in the culture.

START WITH THE LEADER, NOT THE ORGANIZATION

In order to achieve transformation, people have to change as individuals. Individual transformation must precede, or at least occur simultaneously with, organizational transformation.

Don't Focus On Blame

Most transformation efforts begin with the assumption that something is wrong with the current state. This probably is true in

Examples Of Change Vs. Transformation

I was involved with an example of transformation using technology at Wal-Mart. Wal-Mart recognizes that training of their "associates" is key to their success. The question became how to do it most effectively. Marrying technology and know-how, Wal-Mart is changing the nature of how people are trained. They are not just changing, but rather transforming the culture to a learning organization, and transforming people's expectations and power to learn.

* * * * *

Another example of the difference between organizational change and transformation is the recent crisis at Texaco where senior executives were found to be less than sensitive to minorities within the organization. Diversity is a fact of life. This is change. Companies have been forced through demographics and the law to hire more minorities and women. But numerical diversity does not imply a changed mindset and evolved attitudes and values—real transformation. Nor does the fact that diversity training programs and policies state that all employees are valued and that diversity is an important element of the company's success mean the company is transformed. Change, yes; transformation, less likely.

light of the changing conditions noted. But, a strong focus on what is wrong quickly leads to finger-pointing at who is wrong, especially in organizations where the people have not experienced personal transformation.

This emphasis on who and what is wrong proceeds quickly to fixing those, or firing those, who are doing it wrong.

Instead, transformational programs need to begin with the assumption that leaders at every level must start the process by examining themselves. Leaders need to evolve and change themselves to a higher, more developed plane. Then they can institute the necessary stages or steps to create the organizational transformation process.

Many more transformational efforts would succeed if the change effort started with the change leaders themselves. The lack of personal change and growth, is a big reason why change efforts often fail to reach their full promise. The leader is not sufficiently changed, not sufficiently in the process of ongoing personal change and growth, to have the power to lead others, and help employees to lead themselves. The change effort does succeed partially. But, it stops short because others do not see the change efforts embraced by those leading the change.

Growth Leads To Growth

These concepts have been nurtured by my years of consulting experience, as well as by the ideas of authors such as Bill Torbert and Robert Kegan who also suggest that personal growth and transformation can impact the ability to change and lead change. The idea of being an agent of change by changing oneself is not entirely new, but is rarely stressed or commonly understood.

Part of this problem is caused by we practitioners and consultants who act as support for the change efforts taking place. In our efforts to facilitate and encourage change, we suggest and then implement various approaches and strategies. This reinforces the idea that some set of carefully applied approaches and strategies will lead the organization to change and improvements. In listening to us, and taking our advice, leaders of organizations have come to rely less on themselves and their own learning processes, than on the advice and counsel of "experts." And, with unrelenting pressures for quick results, when one "formula" failed, there was always room for the next "silver bullet."

This is not to suggest that consultants have duped leaders. Nor does it suggest that all of the advice given was harmful or wrong. But too much emphasis has been placed on using strategies and processes, without integrating personal change and growth strategies of the leaders.

"My son, I have the secret to organizational change if you follow my approaches and strategies."

More emphasis needs to be put on helping leaders reflect, learn, and develop as people and as leaders. Little or no effort is usually made to suggest that it will be through leaders' ongoing personal learning and development that greater change will occur in the organization.

LEADERSHIP AS TECHNIQUES VS. DEVELOPMENT

It is interesting to consider the leadership literature, and the emphasis of that literature over the years. Much of it suggests what leaders need to do to lead—to set vision, to empower others, to show compassion, to demonstrate commitment to goals, to show and be worthy of loyalty and honesty, to give and receive feedback, and to act with urgency.

These ideas and concepts fit very easily with the ideas of what is needed for successful transformation as suggested by Kotter. In other words, the authors of works on strategies (like Kotter, Hammer, Drucker, Deming, Juran, and Crosby) stress setting a clear vision and mission. But what if the people in leadership roles cannot do these things? What if just teaching them *how* to do these things is not enough? Leaders have to not only know how, but to *be different leaders*. They need to be evolved, and transformed into higher-level thinkers and higher-level practitioners of the art of leadership. They have to have evolved to a place where they can practice leadership strategies because they are truly different leaders.

An Example

Let me illustrate. I've spent a number of years working with an organization that is attempting to transform its technology organization into one completely aligned with its diverse business units.

Thousands of people are involved and many millions of dollars are being spent in myriad ways to create a transformed organization able to meet ferocious worldwide competition.

Management and leadership of this organization is sophisticated and highly educated. The messages about what has to change, and how it has to change, are clear, articulate, and fit all the models of leadership and organizational transformation. Change efforts involve a number of other vendors including MIT Sloan School. The range and scope is wide and deep. The commitment absolute. But, the evolution goes slowly, and many wonder what is happening and why the changes—the transformation—is not happening faster.

There are some groups where the change is taking hold and people are feeling quite aligned. There are others where the efforts seems forced, or are stalled.

The difference? Leaders in the former are part of the process of change and are transforming themselves into different types of leaders. These leaders are communicating and doing all the right things. But most of all, they are starting the process by looking at, and changing, the most important person they need to influence— themselves. This self-change leads naturally to ease with the processes that lead to transformation in others.

Conversely, the leaders in the less-transformed groups tend to be those who may attend training sessions and "get" all the learning, but who are not willing to fundamentally change themselves and the way they are currently operating. They are in favor of change, but not personally.

What Have You Seen?

Let me illustrate, using your own experience. Think of a major change initiative, well conceived and implemented, that has failed. By failure, I mean that it did not significantly change the fundamental nature of the organization and how it works, nor did it improve the products and services your company offers to customers. Now, continue to think about this situation and visualize the key players in the change effort. Who were they? What were they like? What was their approach to the change? Inevitably, the answers to these questions lead to a description of someone "doing to others"— someone, or someones, carrying out the strategy upon others and to others. Almost never does the description of a failed initiative

Living With Change

by Peter F. Drucker

The most probable assumption today is the unique event.... Unique events cannot be "planned." They can, however, be foreseen, or rather, one can prepare to take advantage of them. One can have strategies for tomorrow that anticipate the areas in which the greatest changes are likely to occur, strategies that enable a business or public service institution to take advantage of the unforeseen and unforeseeable. Planning tries to optimize tomorrow the trends of today. Strategy aims to exploit the new and different opportunities of tomorrow.

Any institution needs to think strategically what its business doing and what it should be doing. It needs to think through what its customers pay it for. What is "value" for our customers?...Every institution needs to think through what its strengths are. Are they the right strengths for its specific business? Are they adequate? Are they deployed where they will produce results? And what specifically is the "market" for this particular business, both at the present time and in the years immediately ahead?

Typically, businesses—but even more, no-profit public service institutions—believe that a strategy that aims at "a happy medium" is most comfortable, least risky, and adequately profitable. They are wrong. In many markets one prospers only at the extremes: either as one of the few market leaders who set the standard, or as a specialist supplying a narrow range of products or services, but with such advantage in knowledge, service, and adaptation to specific needs as to be in a class of one's own. The in-between position is rarely desirable or even viable.

include the description of a leader, formal or informal, who was actively engaged simultaneously in the process self-transformation with the organizational changes they were creating.

Conversely, if you think of successful transformational initiatives, and reflect upon those involved, you begin to visualize one or more leaders who were in the process of change and growth themselves. They embodied the changes they were leading others to. Ghandi, Mother Teresa, and Sam Walton come to mind.

These evolved leaders did not "do unto others," but rather recognized a need to transform, and modeled a way to achieve it. This is in direct contrast to the downsizing and other simpleminded approaches that may create short-term shareholder value but fail to build organizations that can sustain competitive advantage. Downsizing is not a sufficient strategy for organizational transformation.

WALK THE TALK

Some descriptions of how to lead change efforts suggest that leaders need to act consistently to make the change happen. This is not the same type of personal change that I am suggesting, although on the surface it might appear similar.

Modeling change for others is part of an approach that essentially remains "doing unto others" rather than being part of the change. It is part of what I like to call the "school of techniques leadership and management." This school told leaders and managers how to act a certain way, but it did not help them to *be* a certain way. And being a certain way is what personal change and ongoing growth is all about.

The type of people who are lifelong learners, or who are at least willing to change themselves in order to lead change, are those willing to handle feedback, to reflect and grow based on experiences. They are willing to let go and move on based on new input and challenges. The role of consultants and change agents should be to help people do that. We consultants have often failed to understand the importance of this effort, or to create the appropriate conditions for this type of change. We often buy into the "changing others" model. Yes, we were for reengineering and quality—but for others out there—not for ourselves and the leaders who are paying us.

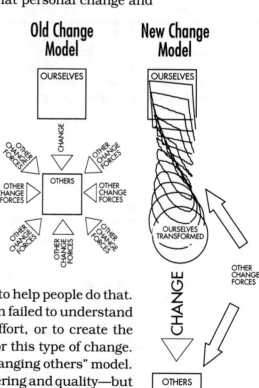

An Example

A recent example in my practice comes to mind. Company management wanted to become a learning organization and decided to create a team of consultants to support the effort. But the consultants themselves did not want to share and question assumptions about their own ways of working and being rewarded. The experiment fizzled before it got off the ground—not the first example of the shoemaker's children having no shoes.

There are, unfortunately, many leaders who want consultants with all of the answers. The idea of growing and developing jointly is such a paradigm change that only the bravest can practice it. Change and transform others? A snap!! Change and transform ourselves—a struggle. Chris Agryris talks about this concept directly in his well-known article, "Why Smart People Can't Learn."

Peter Senge and his colleagues have been talking about the importance of creating a learning organization for years. But this is not the same thing as suggesting that there is a need for concerted personal change efforts critical to the implementation of every strategy change effort.

It is doubtful that all leaders want to initiate change by initiating change within themselves. It is also doubtful that they would necessarily be able to do it successfully. But, the first step in creating this possibility is starting an intelligent conversation in leadership and business circles to the effect that learning and personal development is going to be the prerequisite for leading change. This conversation has in some senses been going on continually. Kotter, in his new book, suggests that the issue of lifelong learning is becoming essential, and more so as business change requires even deeper changes on a continual basis.

> "Leaders' actions rather than their words are the barometer by which employees measure commitment. It is substantive behavior, not the gloss of slogans and t-shirts, that is needed to engage hearts and minds."
> —Gemini Consulting

ONGOING PERSONAL EFFORTS

If your organization wants to be the market leader in meeting customer needs, then your leaders are going to have to continually work on their own development and understanding of what meeting others' needs is about. They cannot do it by finding the world's leading authority on meeting customer needs and using those ideas to transform the organization.

Organizations are trying to create change by identifying the best practices developed by other organizations and then trying to force those strategies on their own organization. This idea is not all bad—using what others have done as a starting place makes perfect sense.

We all use models to be successful. But we still have to work on ourselves, even as we work to emulate others. And working on ourselves is the part that many organizational leaders forget or minimize in importance. They understand it intellectually, but they resist it practically. They think that by understanding what needs to be done, and getting others to do it, they can achieve organizational change. This is like trying to change your marriage by changing your spouse. It won't happen.

Ideas For Integrating Personal and Organizational Transformation

You may still be wondering exactly how to begin, even if you are convinced that the argument to tie personal and organizational development together makes sense. How do I need to transform? How do I get to really *be different?* Good questions, tough answers.

Reflect for a moment on your own growth and development. Assume that a more developed person is more open and more willing to question his or her existing assumptions about life. You are more accepting of diversity, and generally, socially and emotionally in control while being spontaneous and comfortable in your own skin. This is not an exhaustive list, of course, but most working professionals might list these as qualities of a more mature person. Now, reflecting on your own life, think about those situations that helped you to learn, grow, and develop as a person. What events in your life helped you develop in these directions? What were the greatest learning experiences of your life?

If you answer the way most people do, your defining event or events were relatively dramatic or traumatic—the death of a loved one, your divorce, the illness of a child, becoming a parent, losing a parent, getting married, getting fired, or moving to a new place. These types of events help us focus on our existing assumptions about life and move and expand them. We either tend to learn and grow, or become narrow and bitter. The event (or change) doesn't cause transformation to a higher level, but it gives you the opportunity to develop.

Now, back to changing or transforming at work. You may have already figured out the challenge. We do tend to grow and develop through traumatic change—or, at least the possibility exists. The road is rocky, and the journey to higher levels of understanding and maturity often bumpy. Sometimes we fall back, and sometimes we do not evolve at all.

I am asking you to transform yourself *on purpose*! Do you fire yourself and see how you handle it? Of course not! You have to simultaneously set direction, and allow yourself to question that direction, and work toward higher levels of reasoning and inclusion. It's a tall order.

An Example Of Personal Change From An Organizational Model

Authors and scholars Bill Torbert and Robert Kegan were mentioned earlier. Their ideas on personal development and the struggles that help us evolve are particularly helpful for leaders. In *Personal and Organizational Transformation*, Torbert, with his co-author Fisher, offer the concept of *action inquiry* as a viable approach to personal and organizational development. They suggest that leaders combine action and strategies like quality and process engineering. Then reflect and question as a vehicle to create and lead transformation, and develop themselves.

Recipe for Change
1. A base of ideas you respect.
2. A dash of personal challenge and urgency.
3. Mix and apply well to self!

Here is an example using the steps needed for organizational transformation suggested by Kotter. The first step is to establish a sense of urgency. Apply that to yourself as a person. Ask yourself: Do I have a sense of urgency about changing myself to a higher level of functioning as a leader? Do I read and reflect on qualities of highly effective leaders? Do I attempt to evaluate myself against them and feel an urgency to change myself to meet those models? Or, do I have a sense of urgency but that sense is always focused on what needs to change *outside of myself?*

Kotter's next suggestion is to create a guiding coalition. Using this step one might ask: Do I have a group of leaders in this company where we work together to change ourselves and each other by offering and receiving solid feedback and acting

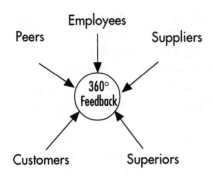

upon it? Do I agree that others need 360-degree feedback, but resist this idea for myself? Am I willing to work with others to change myself, or do I resist sharing those parts of me that need changing with others?

You get the idea. The lists of ways to change are not as important as the focus of change and development being on yourself. Always search for ways to be better at the art of leading. Learn to *be* better, not just to *do* better.

SUMMARY

Change continues its relentless pace. Organizational transformation to meet these changes is an imperative. Yet, for the most part, we are not collectively or individually up to the challenge according to researchers, practitioners, and business people themselves.

We can and should continue to try to use strategies proven useful. We should continue to search for and use strategies in new and combined approaches to affect our organizations in ways that will lead to higher quality goods and services, lower costs, and higher levels of worker satisfaction. But, we should not do this without starting from the assumption that the change efforts we want to create must begin with a focus on changing *ourselves* in the direction we want and need others to change.

Many scholars have suggested this concept of personal change leading to organizational change. Certainly the idea of modeling the way is ingrained in Western thinking. Most popularized by the Tom Peters' imperative to "walk the talk," leadership books and transformational-strategy books continue to suggest that leaders need to be open to continuous learning, and personal change.

But the practice of continual self-reflection, development to higher levels of personal excellence, and focusing on leading organizational change by starting with self-change is an idea whose time has not yet come. These ideas are far from universally understood or practiced. Although to some extent common sense, this approach continues to be resisted for the reason most personal transformational efforts are resisted: They are difficult, require self-analysis and reflection, and imply that leaders need to be different.

Transformational efforts are continuing to proliferate. They will not cease. Organizations are being forced to consider more effective ways of dealing with pressing change. The only question is how will they do it.

Transformational efforts must, and should, start with personal transformation to higher levels of development. I hope this chapter and your reflections on change will stimulate further conversations for you and others interested in organizational transformation.

Your individual transformation will facilitate the process of leading change in others, and creating transformed organizations. Your improved results will repay your efforts.

ACTION AGENDA

▶ Don't just react to change. Decide how you want to transform your organization.

▶ Examine the real underlying assumptions about your work processes.

▶ To motivate change, create a sense of urgency and communicate your vision.

▶ Involve the group to drive change.

▶ Generate short-term wins to anchor support and move forward.

▶ Leaders who succeed with organizational transformation, first transform themselves. Decide how you'll change yourself.

Part Four
THE HUMAN SIDE OF CHANGE

Chapter 11

CHANGE AND HARDY PERSONALITIES

Susan Stephani

Susan Stephani, CSP (Certified Speaking Professional) earned undergraduate and graduate degrees in clinical social work and psychology from the University of Wisconsin. She spent 10 years working for the State of Wisconsin's Division of Family Services.

In 1990, she earned the CSP designation from the National Speakers Association. In that year, less than 6% of the 3200 membership had done so. Ms. Stephani was the first woman in the state of Wisconsin to earn the CSP.

Ms. Stephani's topics include: Change, Stress, Time, Motivation, Creativity, and Rapport. Some of her clients include Alcoa, American College of Emergency Physicians, Eastman Kodak, General Mills, Harvard University, IBM, the U.S. Army, Westbend Company, Blue Cross/Blue Shield, and Northwestern Mutual Life.

Ms. Stephani has authored several learning cassettes including *Meeting the Challenge of Change,* a two-tape album focusing on dealing with the stress of change and on building the skills necessary to make change work for you.

Susan Stephani, S.A. Stephani Associates, P.O. Box 497, Hartland, WI 53029; phone (414) 538-4270; fax (414) 538-4290; e-mail SusanSpkr@aol.com.

Chapter 11

CHANGE AND HARDY PERSONALITIES

Susan Stephani

"Any fact facing us is not as important as our attitude
toward it, for that determines our success or failure."
—Norman Vincent Peale

The visiting pastor talked about a study he
had come across on the Internet. Interviews with
people who had reached the age of 100 years old
had revealed that almost all of them had something
in common.

What did these centurions have in common?
It wasn't diet. It wasn't exercise. It wasn't heredity.
It was the ability to adapt and deal with life changes.

Let's face it, most of us don't like change. We
would rather have things in our lives be predictable. Change creates stress.

CHANGE IS EVERYWHERE

Change is all around us. The majority of
speeches and seminars that I have been invited to
deliver over the last five years have been related to

change. Companies are changing rapidly, yet many of the people in the companies do not have the skills to deal with all the changes that confront them.

Change Is Normal

There seem to be two basic truths about change. The first truth is that change is a normal part of every person's life. There is no way that you could be here today without having gone through change. Life is filled with changes: your first day at school, getting married or divorced, getting a job, changing jobs, having children, losing someone you love, and on and on.

Resistance Is Normal

The second truth about change is that resistance to change is normal—at least for most of us. Change is frightening—even terrifying—for many.

Change involves shifting a paradigm. Whenever a paradigm is shifted, there is room for fear. Why? Because now you have to learn how to be successful in the new paradigm. This often means learning something new or doing something in a different way. This opens us to the possibility of failure. Fear of failure is so strong for many of us that we resist change.

We also resist change because we like things the way they are—predictable and *our* way. We have strong feelings about the *right* way to do something and the way it "ought to be."

Change The Toilet Paper

Here is a silly yet illustrative example of people's penchant for predictability.

It is amazing how many people hold strong feelings about *the right way for the toilet paper to come off the roll.* When I ask the "toilet paper question" in seminars, hands shoot up almost instantly and

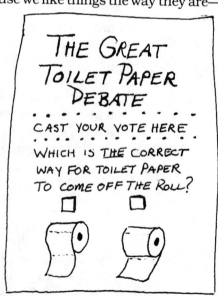

THE GREAT
TOILET PAPER
DEBATE
· · · · · · · · · ·
CAST YOUR VOTE HERE
· · · · · · · · · ·
WHICH IS THE CORRECT
WAY FOR TOILET PAPER
TO COME OFF THE ROLL?
☐   ☐

people argue their point with all sorts of interesting reasons—and plenty of passion.

In fact, one day I was in a friend's bathroom and I noticed that she had her toilet paper on the holder "the wrong way," so I switched it. Suddenly, a flash of insight struck me: "Susan, you are out teaching Corporate America how to deal with change and you can't live with the toilet paper on the 'wrong' way for 60 seconds?!?"

If having the toilet paper roll on the "wrong" way can generate such discomfort, we should not be surprised that we are experiencing anxiety in our business and personal lives with all of the much larger and significant changes affecting us.

YOUR OUTLOOK AFFECTS YOUR HEALTH

We know that change has a more or less permanent position in our lives. Having some evidence that the ability to adapt to change may give us longer and probably healthier lives, it will be of real benefit for us to learn to deal with change in positive ways.

A study done at the University of Chicago in 1985 provides some answers for teaching people how to handle change successfully. A group of social scientists conducted a study to determine why some people could work under stressful conditions and remain well. Their findings established that these healthy people shared a set of personality traits and attitudes. This set of attitudes was collectively termed "hardiness." Hardiness manifests itself in three principal ways:

> Stress is not always bad—stress can have stimulating, positive effects. Scientists call the positive effects of stress *eustress.*

Control. Hardy people feel *in control* in all situations. They are not control freaks. They simply know they always have options. They are flexible and understand choice. They don't feel like victims.

Commitment. Hardy people see the big

picture. They believe in themselves and in their work.

Challenge. Hardy people view change as a challenge, *not* as a stress.

Let's take a look at each one of these hardy personality attitudes and find ways to make them work for you in dealing with the changes you are experiencing at work and at home.

HARDINESS TRAIT #1: CONTROL

The University of Chicago scientists give the following excellent example of the hardy attitude of control. An employee is told by her employer that she will be transferred to another city. The employee is not happy about the change—she likes the city in which she currently lives. The city that the employee is being asked to relocate to is not desirable to her.

What might an "unhardy" person's reaction be? Probably to passively acquiesce to the move. Unhardy thoughts or "self-talk" may go something like this: "How can they do this to me—this is not fair! I've worked hard for this company and now they are insisting I go where I don't want to." This person would most likely feel distressed, anguished, and unhappy for an extended time.

Now, what might the hardy person do to establish control? Remember, having the ability to deal with and adapt to life changes does not mean that one just always passively accept whatever happens. It means being aware of, and being wise about, all of your options.

As our hardy person reflects on the options available, those options would most likely fall into the following three categories:

- change the environment
- change the situation (quit the job)
- change your mind

Change The Environment

In the case of the job transfer, the hardy person would begin to review available options. Can the

> "Proactive people focus their efforts...on the things they can do something about. This causes their circle of influence to increase."
>
> —Stephen R. Covey,
> *The 7 Habits of Highly Effective People*

environment be changed? In other words: Can the change be changed? Can our hardy person convince the company to change its mind about the transfer? This option would require approaching management and laying out a good case as to why the company might be better served if this employee stayed put.

Our hardy person approaches management and, in a most convincing way, establishes that staying in the current city would be a better benefit to the company than the transfer. It is possible that management will say, "Hey, you're right—you have a point." Trip canceled!

Most of us have learned by now that we can be totally right in a situation and still lose! The company could also tell our person, "You have a point but we still want you to move." Changing the environment has just been eliminated as an option—for now. (See page 237 for a detailed example of changing your environment.)

THEIR PERSPECTIVE
When you attempt to influence your bosses to change their minds, present your favored alternative, and state the benefits to *them*, not you.

Change The Situation

Our hardy person now needs to consider another option. What about changing jobs? The pros and cons of such a decision would be carefully considered. For now, let us assume that the negative aspects of changing jobs far outweigh the positives, even though choosing to stay at the current job means the reality of moving to another city.

Change Your Mind

So, our hardy person has attempted to change the environment, and has considered the option of changing jobs. Neither of these is a good option. Now, it is time for the third possibility. The hardy person would then work on embracing the change, looking for the positives in it, and figuring out ways to make it work.

Please understand that I am not implying that hardy personalities do not have "negative" feelings or attitudes in the process of reviewing their options. They have feelings of anger, fear, and all of the rest of the normal human emotions that go with an undesirable life event.

The difference between the unhardy and the hardy personality is that eventually the hardy personality will *take control of* the situation. The unhardy person will *be controlled by* the situation. The hardy person knows that continuing to resist ultimately causes more stress and wastes a lot more energy.

HARDINESS TRAIT #2: COMMITMENT

Hardy people are committed to something more than just the day-to-day duties of work and life. They believe in themselves and the work that they are doing.

Believing in themselves means that they trust their ultimate ability to deal with a situation. Their self-talk might be something like: "I don't see the answer to this now, but I will."

"I don't see the answer to this now... but I will."

THE HARDY PERSON

"I'll never figure out this problem."

THE UNHARDY PERSON

People who do not believe in their ultimate ability to figure things out have very different self-talk. It tends to put that person into a victim position rather than a position of strength and confidence. The self-talk may go something like this: "How can this be happening to me; this is not fair. I'll never get out of this." Again, remember that hardy people may have some of those thoughts initially, but they move on to a more hopeful attitude.

Along with a belief in themselves, hardy people also have a belief in their work. They believe their work is important and necessary. There is an altruistic type of feeling about whatever it is they do out in the marketplace or in their homes.

The Bigger Picture

You need a big picture of your life and your work. If you are working just for the paycheck, it won't be enough. Money is great, but you need another reason for doing what you do.

Why? Because in the day-to-day experience of living your life, you will need to deal with quite a few "turkeys"—those big and little irritations that are part of everyone's days.

Don't Focus On Turkeys

Turkeys come in the form of angry customers, procrastinating coworkers, rush hour traffic, arguing children, and the like. If we focus on those parts of our day, we won't be happy campers to say the least—and we will not enjoy our stay on this planet to say the most.

I remember a time in my life when I was totally focused on the turkeys of my career: delayed flights, driving in snowstorms to get to a program, hot seminar rooms, AV breakdowns, long hours, etc. After one particularly frustrating series of mishaps while out on a speaking tour, I called my husband from my hotel room to "share" my misery. I had actually planned to practice the age-old technique of "taking it out on the one you love!"

Control Your Focus

- Keep the big picture.
- Don't let "turkeys" get you down.
- Don't blame others.

Reverse Psychology

My husband Jerry spotted the real reason for my attempt to get him involved in a little marital spat to relieve my frustration. (Now, don't be so smug—I'll bet some of you have finessed a nice argument to relieve your stress, too.)

Instead of taking the bait, Jerry challenged me. He asked why it was that I continued to do what I did for a living if it were so awful. He en-

couraged me to quit such a frustrating and
cruel existence.

Of course, I went to work defending my reasons for continuing. I
mentioned the fact that we had goals
to reach and I wanted to do my part. I
told him that I loved the fact that I actually
helped people see that having a better life
was possible. I emphasized our belief that everyone is uniquely created. Everyone has talents and
abilities. We had made a commitment to use the talents
and abilities with which we were gifted. Miraculously, I instantly felt
better.

My clever husband had reminded me that when the turkeys
take over, you must look up. When you do, you will see eagles. The
eagles are gorgeous, majestic, and inspiring. Focusing on eagles
makes turkeys smaller and less significant. What are the eagles in
your life? Why do you do what you do? If you don't know or if you
forget to focus on those "higher" reasons, the turkeys will get you
every time!

That's commitment. It takes many forms. Believing in yourself,
in the importance of your work, and in a higher power can be some
of the forms that it takes. Whatever it is, it needs to be compelling
and motivating for you. It needs to be your Eagle defending you from
a Turkey Takeover!

HARDINESS TRAIT #3: CHALLENGE

Hardy people view change as a challenge, *not* as a stress. Is this
easy? Not for most of us. It isn't for me. But, have you ever noticed
that you don't improve without problems (challenges)?

We find talents we never knew we had, learn new things, and
discover improved ways of doing things through challenges. Challenges include solving a problem, dealing with a change, and
striving for a goal.

Even if we don't solve the problem, deal totally with the change,
or reach the goal, we can still be successful.

How?—If the experience taught us something.

Experience can only teach us something if we are willing to look
at all of life's tough times as challenges, not as continual stresses.

"Just when you think you've graduated from the school of hard knocks, someone thinks up a new course."
—Anonymous

So, what is in it for you if you learn to do this? Let me show you. Let's say that you deal with a change. In the process, you discover an attitude shift that really served you well in the situation. You put that new attitude in your "Life Bag of Tricks." (This is what I call that part of ourselves that we keep adding to as we grow wiser in our walk through life.) Then, we go for a goal and in the process we find a talent we never knew we had— into the "Life Bag of Tricks" it goes. If we keep adding to our learning, we are better and better equipped to handle later experiences.

Problems = New Options

It happens something like this: Life presents us a nice big problem. We take out that attitude we learned sometime ago. Oops, it didn't work. OK. Let's try that talent we unearthed while reaching that goal last year. In other words, the more "stuff" you've got in your "Bag of Tricks," the higher the chances that you will successfully handle the current problem that you are experiencing.

Some people have refused to take on challenges in their lives or they play "victim" whenever they can. There isn't much that they have in their "Bag of Tricks." When life delivers a problem, they take out the one little attitude they have or the one little skill. If those don't work, they don't have any other options.

"A problem is a chance for you to do your best."
—Duke Ellington

Get it? The more options we have, the more likely we are to have more fun and more successes in life. The intention here is not to minimize the difficulty of life's problems, stresses, etc. It is simply that the more choices you have for dealing with them, the better your chances are of eventually dealing *successfully* with them. That is why learning to develop the habit of viewing change as a challenge and not a stress will serve you well.

It's time for another story to illustrate this point.

Business BC (Before Computers)

Some years ago, before computers had made their way to the top of desks, I worked with the support staff of a company. We would meet about once a month to discuss handling stress, time, and change. At one of these meetings, I could tell the minute I walked in that some- thing was not right. The entire group looked angry.

I asked them what had happened. They were delighted to tell me. I soon learned that they had all walked into their office the month before and had discovered computers sitting on their desks. The company had given them no forewarning. The only training given to them was the manual sitting next to the computers.

Life Can Be Unfair

Was this a smart way for their company to handle this change? NO! (Especially for a company that believed in "soft skill" training.)

Did these people have a right to be upset? Yes! Was this unfair? Yes! I told them they were right on all counts.

Here is how they handled this unfair, difficult situation. After complaining to each other and expressing their anger (a very healthy first step), they got down to the business of figuring things out. They learned how to boot up the computers. They discovered that one of them could even understand the manual.

This creative, impressive group pulled to- gether and solved the problem. They met the challenge of that change.

Yes, they were right to be upset about how their company implemented this change. It is most certainly true that many organizations have a lot of work to do in learning to introduce and handle change correctly. But, this group of employees also received a gift from their willingness to rise to the occasion. They earned two things that no one could take away from them: new computer implementation skills and, more importantly, the knowledge that they can survive!

See The Good Side

Viewing change as a challenge and not as a stress is not easy. But, what are your options in a situation like this? Life is just plain not always fair. You can try to make something fairer. That is a good idea sometimes. Other times it is a big waste of your time and energy.

I know of people who cannot *not* fight what happens to them. They have spent years of their precious lives complaining to anyone and everyone who will listen. To those sad folks, I would like to make this suggestion: Write up a petition stating how unfair the incident was, and I will sign it. I will even help you get 5,000 other people to agree with you and sign your petition.

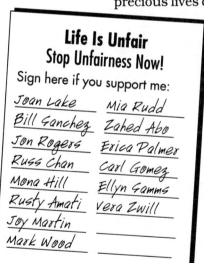

Life Is Unfair
Stop Unfairness Now!
Sign here if you support me:

Joan Lake	Mia Rudd
Bill Sanchez	Zahed Abo
Jon Rogers	Erica Palmer
Russ Chan	Carl Gomez
Mona Hill	Ellyn Samms
Rusty Amati	Vera Zwill
Joy Martin	
Mark Wood	

Then what? What good does it do you if you cannot change what happened? Do what you can to make sure it doesn't happen to anyone else. (The support staff in the previous story did manage to convince the company to offer training in computer skills and to introduce future changes in a better way.) It is now time to move on to the next stage: change the environment, change jobs or change your mind. In the process of the work that you do next, you will build your character, your skills, your attitude choices, and much more.

A COMPANY THAT MADE A DIFFICULT AND NEGATIVE CHANGE IN A HEALTHY AND POSITIVE WAY

Several years ago, a medium-sized company asked me to advise them on the best way to announce that a difficult time was ahead and to help employees through the changes. I was impressed by their request. A smart step to take for a company or individual is to ask for advice if you're unsure of the best option to use.

This company had made a decision two years before that had taken the company in a direction that proved to be erroneous. In the process, they lost money and some of their positive image. They felt they had some good ideas on how to regroup and go forward, but their past mistake would mean layoffs, budget cuts, reduction in benefits, and a wage freeze. They knew their employees would be angry. The fear of dealing with that fallout had kept them from making the announcement and moving forward. We planned and accomplished the steps in the box below.

A Plan To Inform Employees Of Major Changes

1. Understand that the employees will be angry and afraid. The best way to get past these emotions will be to let them be expressed and to deal with them.

2. Bring all the employees together in a meeting and make an announcement.
   A. Explain why the direction was taken, how it proved to be wrong, and apologize—tell the truth.
   B. Tell the truth regarding exactly what the fallout will be for all concerned.
   C. Answer employees' questions and concerns, and deal with their anger and fears.
   D. Discuss the new direction. Tell them their input will be asked for in the future.
   E. Hand out the above in written form.
   F. Tell employees exactly (as far as known) what will happen next, especially how laid-off employees will be helped.
   G. Give a time line.

3. Ask direct managers to get feedback and suggestions from their employees on how to implement the changes and the new direction.

4. Ask direct managers to involve everyone in the problem-solving skills and the new direction.

5. Continually update the employees, and continue to get feedback—communicate a lot!

OPTIONS AND PRIORITIES: AN EXAMPLE OF HOW TO TAKE CONTROL OF YOUR TIME BY CHANGING THE ENVIRONMENT

Your choices in life relate closely to your priorities.

Remember that the attitude of control means being aware of options. And, remember that we were looking at options as being in three categories: the environment, the situations, and your mind.

My time spent helping people in companies and organizations meet the challenge of change has convinced me that changing the *environment* is a viable option that needs to be considered in more instances. For example, how one organizes the work is clearly related to the perception of control.

Meet The Challenge

It is rare to go into a company where people are *not* complaining about having too much work to do and not enough time to do it. Often, part of the problem is that these people are continuing to do what they have always done even though the company has changed or their own job focus has changed.

The unhardy types assume a victim's stance. These people tend to see only their personal chaos. Hardy people mesh with the corporate rhythm and flow and make changes and choices in their work accordingly. Hardy people are more likely to understand that when corporate goals or their own jobs have changed, they have to adjust their priorities. This helps them remain in control of their work and their stress levels.

Change The Environment With Priorities

Priorities are an important way to change the environment and begin to experience more control. There are three compelling reasons for setting priorities to deal with a work environment where you suddenly find yourself with too much to do and not enough time:

1 **If we don't have priorities, how do we know what to do first?** Finding a starting point is imperative. When we do not know where to start, we tend to feel overwhelmed. Feeling overwhelmed can be immobilizing and often causes procrastination.

Perhaps you are familiar with the cycle—we feel overwhelmed so we procrastinate. We now accomplish even less; get more overwhelmed; procrastinate some more; get more immobilized. Now, we feel guilty, distressed, angry, beaten— definitely not in control of our environment!

2 **If we don't have priorities, how do we know what NOT to do?** When our companies, our jobs, or our lives change, we frequently keep doing the things we have always done even when they are no longer important at all!

Don't Love Your Problems. At one of my seminars, a young man raised his hand, stood up and said, "Do you know what my time and stress problem is? It's those girls in my office. They are always having problems with their computers. I spend most of my day fixing this and that, and showing them how to do things. I am a new manager and I never seem to get time for the things that I need to be doing because I'm always dealing with their stuff."

My suggestion to that nice, young new manager was to establish a block of time with these young women and provide them with a quick computer 101 class, explaining the basics as they related to the recurring problems. Then, he would be freed up to do his real job.

After some additional discussion, it became clear that he would not be following that advice

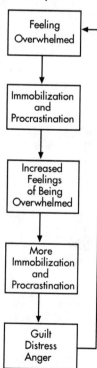

The Overwhelmed-Immobilization-Procrastination Cycle

Feeling Overwhelmed

Immobilization and Procrastination

Increased Feelings of Being Overwhelmed

More Immobilization and Procrastination

Guilt Distress Anger

because he liked his problem. Some of us fall in love with our problems. If we don't have them, we may have to face something that we find less familiar than The Problem. We know The Problem—it is familiar—it provides a comfort zone.

Look at this young manager. Having his problem gave him a wonderful excuse for not having time for his new job. The Problem gave him an excuse to spend his day doing the things that he did well, providing instant gratification with little room for failure. The new job was scary. It was a change, so there was the possibility of delayed gratification and failure.

Do What Counts. How often do we spend our days doing the things that we can check off quickly, leave little room for failure, and give us instant gratification? In reality, we are avoiding the things that are priorities because they are new, there is room for failure, and we might well experience discomfort. Then, we complain that we have too much to do. If our companies and jobs have changed, we need to learn to reprioritize. Let go of doing the things that are no longer important in order to take on the new and feel less overwhelmed. It is part of the answer for many of us in the "too much to do department." (This is a difficult one—I know from personal experience.)

3 If we don't have priorities, then we believe that it is possible to get everything done.
I love to ask my audiences this question: "How many of you would get everything done (at work and at home) if you had 25 hours in the day? (no hands) —26 hours? (no hands) —30 hours? (again, rarely any hands). In fact, I don't get many hands at even 40-hour days.

Why? Because there will always be more to do. I promise you that when you die, the possibility is high that you will be clutching a "to-do" list! When we don't have priorities, we somehow carry

> "Time is an equal opportunity employer. Each human being has exactly the same number of hours and minutes in a day."
> —Denis Waitley

> "When a man does not know what harbor he is making for, no wind is the right wind."
> —Seneca

around the belief that we can get it all done. When we can't, we feel bad, depressed, or stressed.

In this era of change, it is important to understand how important priorities are to feeling in control. This can only happen when we perceive choice in every circumstance and then take a look at all of our options in that situation including changing the environment. To gain relief from too much to do, clearly establish priorities.

10 WAYS TO PROMOTE HARDINESS IN YOUR EMPLOYEES

Employees who possesses hardiness traits will be happier and more valuable to your organization.

1 Model the traits of a hardy personality by being one yourself: Think control, commitment, and challenge.

2 Learn technology. Computer-literate employees have difficulty respecting or being motivated by a boss who knows nothing about computers—that's why the cartoon *"Dilbert"* is so popular.

3 Continually communicate with your employees during times of change. Keep them up to date and tell them the truth.

4 Be a coach by helping people solve their own problems. Instead of always giving them the answers, help them to review their options.

5 Encourage them to add to their knowledge and skills by taking seminars, classes, reading, etc. to add to their "Life Bags of Tricks."

6 Point out their strengths and remind the employees of them when they are faced with a scary change on the job.

7 Communicate the big picture frequently; i.e., we will treat our customers exactly the way we want to be treated when we are the customer.

8 You are the liaison between top-level management and your employees. Be proactive in asking for information from the top and in updating them on your department's needs and progress.

9 Be open to and encourage feedback. And don't take negative feedback personally.

10 Keep learning and building yourself to add to your own "Life Bag of Tricks."

USING HARDINESS TRAITS

Taking Control

The first attitude of hardy personalities is that of control. The way we begin to feel in control is to realize our options. In this chapter, I concentrated on the option of changing the environment with the specific example of establishing priorities in order to deal with the "too much to do" problem. Let me try to provide some insight into the other two options—changing jobs and changing your mind—for dealing with a change or stress or problem.

Changing Your Mind, Changing Jobs

It is important to remember that with every job certain things "come with the territory." We must be willing to accept those things if they cannot be changed (i.e., change our minds).

If you work in the complaint department and get massively stressed out by complaints—and can't change your perceptions of the job—you are in the wrong job!

People may need to look to the option of changing jobs for many reasons. One of those reasons can be a poor job fit, as in the above example. Sometimes changing jobs may simply mean moving to another department in the same company, or another company but keeping the same career.

Let me also add this: If you are looking to go

to another company or another profession to avoid experiencing changes, call me when you find a company or profession that is not experiencing change! I have a long list of people looking for that, too. No one has called me yet!

SUMMARY

One of the things we do have to change our minds about is that we can avoid change! There is just no question about the fact that change is a constant in the world. We can be assured that change has happened, is happening, and will always happen!

Hardy personalities embody these attitudes:

- **Control** (change the environment (e.g., reestablish priorities); change the situation (job); change your mind

- **Commitment** (focus on eagles and not turkeys)

- **Challenge** (add to your "Life Bag of Tricks")

I don't know if these hardy attitudes will ensure that you will live to be 100. But, I think I can pretty much guarantee that learning and practicing hardy attitudes will give you a less stressful, more enjoyable, more fun, less frustrating life.

The attitude of control takes away the victim mode that many of us fall into during times of change. The attitude of commitment helps us to

A Poem To Live By

I like to end my presentations on change with this poem. Someone gave it to me years ago after a seminar. The author is unknown.

I came to the swift, raging river,
  And, the roar held the echo of fear.
"Oh, Lord, give me wings to fly over,
  If you are, as you promised, quite near."
But He said: "Trust the grace I am giving.
"It is all pervasive and sufficient for you.
"Take My hand, we will face this together,
"But, My plan is not over, it is through!"

focus on what is really important instead of the difficulties that are part of life. And, the attitude of challenge reminds us that even though this is a difficult time, we will put some new "tools" in our "Life Bag of Tricks" when we face change and deal with it.

ACTION SUMMARY

▶ Accept the fact that change will be a constant in your life. Then list the three areas where change is affecting you the most.

▶ Write down all your reasons for disliking each change. If you can do something to change the environment or your situation, write down an action plan.

▶ Focus your energy on areas where you have some control.

▶ Work with other people in your situation who are taking realistic, constructive action about the situation.

▶ If you can't do anything about the change, file your list of reasons why you dislike it away. Now is the time to work on changing your attitude.

▶ Make a list of the good things that can result for each change. Add ideas from other people.

▶ Decide to look at the bright side in your situation. Then take the actions that will make a positive outcome more likely.

Chapter 12

MANAGING HUMAN TRANSITIONS

Wayne A. Fogel & Lance H. Arrington

Wayne Fogel (left) is a founding partner and creative director of The Arrington Group. Mr. Fogel previously served as president and chief executive officer of The Creative Factory, Inc., an international education and consulting firm.

Lance Arrington (right) is a founding partner and chief executive of The Arrington Group (TAG), headquartered in Winter Park, Florida. Prior to founding TAG, Mr. Arrington previously served as president and chief operating officer of Philip Crosby Associates.

The Arrington Group is a national management education consulting firm that works with a select group of clients engaged in creating outcome-focused, process-based organizations. A significant part of TAG's work is focused on the human issues associated with helping the people of the organization transition through change.

Lance Arrington and Wayne Fogel, The Arrington Group, 1245 W. Fairbanks Ave. #200, Winter Park, FL 32789; phone (407) 647-5516; fax (407) 647-2901.

Chapter 12

MANAGING HUMAN TRANSITIONS

Wayne A. Fogel & Lance H. Arrington

"A change is a shift in the world around us. A transition is the internal process we go through in response to that shift."
—William Bridges, *Job Shift*

Today, more organizations than ever are involved in mergers, acquisitions, partnerships, and strategic alliances as part of their responses to marketplace change. In every case, these actions require organizational change, and when executives talk about what makes these needed changes work or not work, it always comes down to people.

The issue of getting people through the changes is the single greatest determinant of success or failure. Yet, this human side of change is the subject most often ignored when it comes to action. Even worse, when action is taken on the human side of change, it is often the wrong action.

Executives want to focus on hard assets, operating efficiencies, and synergies. Yet the most critical assets are the "soft" assets that ride down the elevator at night. It is not steel, concrete, and wire that determine the future success of an organization. It is the *people* of that organization. People are the critical element that makes strategic changes like partnering and alliance actions successful.

HELPING PEOPLE HANDLE CHANGE

How do executives deal with this human side of change? When pressed, most executives describe their efforts in one of the following three ways.

- Do nothing
- Provide change management training
- Manage both change and transition concurrently

Let's explore each of these options further.

Do Nothing

Many companies tend to ignore the problems of change and let people muddle through on their own. This method is a formula for disaster. It guarantees that 90 percent of change efforts will fail to work as intended.

How many managers does it take to change a light bulb?

None. Managers don't like to change!

For example, consider an organization that is acquired by a significantly larger company. In one case that came to our attention, the acquisition looked like a match made in heaven. Each firm had complementary geographic strengths, products, marketing forces, and delivery teams. Both were highly profitable and growing rapidly. The plan was to keep each organization independent, but to work together in a strategic alliance to the benefit of both. Five years later, the acquired company is essentially out of business with sales less than five percent of what they were at the time of acquisition.

The acquiring organization, in this case, fared somewhat better. Its sales dropped by only 50 percent. Needless to say, profits have vanished entirely. This alliance, perfect on paper, came apart not because of technical reasons or a poor design, but because the people were never able to let go of the old and embrace the new. And the people were the real asset of both organizations.

Unfortunately, this approach of letting people muddle through remains the most "popular" method for managing the human side of change. This is not because most executives believe it to be the right way, but because most know of no other way.

> "The pace of events is moving so fast that unless we can find some way to keep our sights on tomorrow, we cannot expect to be in touch with today."
> —Dean Rusk

Provide Change Management Training

The second method commonly used over the past 10 years is an approach frequently referred to as *change management*. This is significantly better than the do-nothing approach, and change management enjoyed a high degree of success in simpler times.

Virtually all change management programs are based on the seminal work of Dr. Kurt Lewin and his "unfreeze, move, refreeze" model. This model was highly appropriate in the 1940s when Dr. Lewin did his work. The model is based upon Gestalt theory (the whole is greater than the sum of the parts), and manages change through groups rather than individuals. This is absolutely correct, since change is experienced by more than one person at a time.

Change management programs can help

groups implement any single change, once the members of the group are ready. However, today this approach has two problems:

- The nature of change it-self has changed. Rather than discrete changes, we face almost continuous changes at unprecedented levels and frequency. If we use Lewin's idea, then the model becomes not "un-freeze, move, refreeze," but "unfreeze, move, move, move, and never refreeze."

- The second problem is that change management is a group process. But while change is experienced as a group, the response to it—the psychological ad-justment if you will—is different for each indi-vidual. This individual response to change is termed "transition" and is very different from change.

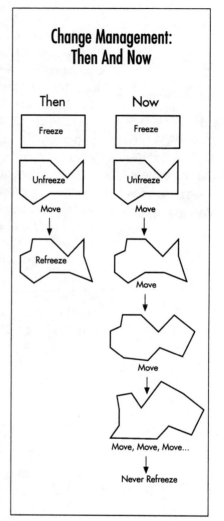

**Change Management:
Then And Now**

Then

Now

Freeze

Freeze

Unfreeze

Unfreeze

Move

Move

Refreeze

Move

Move

Move

Move

Move, Move, Move...

Never Refreeze

Manage Change AND Transition Concurrently

The third method is to manage change and transition together. It is important to look at these in a holistic manner. The roots of change exist in the marketplace success that every organization enjoys to one degree or another today.

This is good news, but also bad news. Why? Because marketplace success breeds marketplace change.

THE CYCLE OF CHANGE

Marketplace change is caused by a number of driving forces: competition, technology, demographics, regulatory issues, economics, and so on.

Every organization must decide how it will respond to changes in its marketplace. It must craft an organizational response that will allow it to remain competitive and successful in the newly emerging markets. Mergers, acquisitions, partnering, outsourcing, and strategic alliances are all both key sources of change *and* parts of organizational responses. They deserve your serious attention and consideration.

The Cycle Of Change

Marketplace Success

Marketplace Change

Organizational Response

Once an organization has crafted its response to the emerging market changes, many people believe that they can implement it immediately, thereby quickly regaining marketplace success (see diagram at left). Nothing could be further from the truth. There is one critical ingredient missing.

CHANGE *AND* TRANSITION

While an organizational response is made up of changes that affect groups of people, the missing ingredient is how to get the *individual* from the old to the new. Only then can the new way of doing things result in the marketplace success you need (see diagram of the *full* cycle of change on the next page).

Change is situational, but the transition that individuals must make as a result of change is an entirely different, and psychological, process.

A few years ago, Dr. William Bridges recog-

nized this dif-
ference and
focused a ma-
jor part of his
life's work on it.
He has had
three books on
the *New York
Times* best-
seller list on
the subject of
transitions
(*Transitions,
Surviving Cor-
porate Trans-
itions,* and *Man-
aging Transitions).*

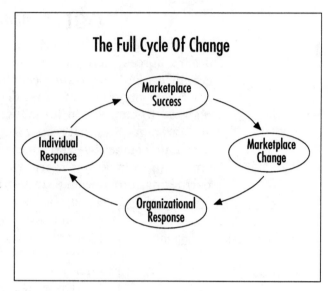

The Full Cycle Of Change

In his work, Dr. Bridges found that change
and transition are entirely different issues. And
each requires its own unique way of dealing with
the situation.

Change does not equal transition. Change is
situational. It occurs at a specific time, and it
usually affects groups of people, rather than
individuals. In other words, change is external.

Transition, on the other hand, is internal. It is
a psychological process that occurs over a period
of time. Each person's response is different.

PHASES OF TRANSITION

At the core of Dr. Bridges' work is a model that
describes the three phases individuals go through
as they move from the old to the new—as they
transition through change. The transition process
is diagrammed on the next page.

The psychological process for an individual
dealing with change begins with the endings. You
must end before you can begin. Yet, endings can

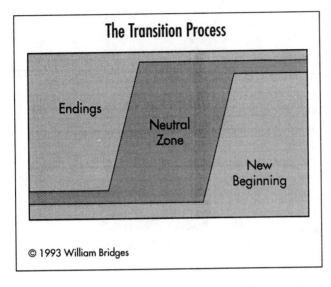

The Transition Process

Endings

Neutral Zone

New Beginning

© 1993 William Bridges

be messy, uncomfortable times.

Change, whether perceived as good or bad, creates losses. Individuals tend to magnify these losses. But the tendency of management is to minimize or ignore losses, particularly when the change is perceived as "good."

We all resist change. And given half a chance, we all want to go back to the way things were before.

Think about this in the context of your professional environment. Most of us want to hold onto the way things are done today, or go back to the way things used to be done—to the "good old days."

Dealing With Endings And Losses

To deal with endings and losses, individuals must first identify the specific endings they perceive, and the losses associated with each of these endings. Next, individuals need to look at these endings and losses and decide what they mean.

In most cases, the long list of perceived endings and losses turns out to be a relatively short list that can be defined and dealt with proactively.

Many individuals are still trying to deal with endings of the past—they are experiencing a *transition deficit*. This accumulation of unresolved endings can cause future change efforts to fail. To fully manage new transitions, you must help people resolve their past endings as well.

The Neutral Zone And New Beginnings

As individuals deal with endings and losses—and before they personally define the new beginnings associated with change—they go through a confusing time. We call this the *neutral zone.*

An analogy to describe the neutral zone might be this: When the circus trapeze artist lets go of the first bar and before grasping the second bar, the artist is in a neutral zone. The security of the old has been lost, and the security of the new is not yet here. We

In The Neutral Zone

have all experienced this feeling at one time or another in our lives.

The down side of the neutral zone is that it takes time and can cause people to become dysfunctional. It does not occur as quickly as the trapeze artist's switch from one bar to another. And its impact can be devastating.

Creative Transitions. The up side is that, when these feelings are channeled, the neutral zone can become an individual's time of greatest creativity and personal development.

At this time, it is important to encourage people to take actions that will facilitate their smooth transitions from the neutral zone to the new beginning:

- First, help people learn to experiment. You can set an example by experimenting with the way things are being done at your level. Encourage them to try a work-related idea that they have had.

- Next, encourage people to study their recent experiences for clues to new possibilities to explore. Suggest that they look closely at things that worked better than they expected, as well as things that did not work as well as they expected.

- Finally, help people generate a lot of new ideas. Introduce methods such as brainstorming, lateral thinking; and analogies, and help people learn how to use them effectively.

When people are rushed through their time in the neutral zone, they do not receive the full benefit of this stage. You need to understand and accept the need for this stage for the greatest benefit.

EMOTIONAL CHARACTERISTICS OF TRANSITION

Guilt
Resentment
Anxiety
Self-Absorption
Stress

People in transition deal with many emotional issues. To describe them, Dr. Bridges developed the acronym GRASS.

Guilt is frequently felt by those who watch others leave the organization or who see others in the organization take on different, perhaps less important, roles. It is certainly felt by the survivors of a downsizing, whether they were the carriers of the bad news or simply those who "were not directly affected."

Resentment goes from the extremes of violence and sabotage to passive resistance. Resentment is fostered by a feeling of injustice. And people who feel resentful strike back in some way, either actively or passively. This can vary from not stepping up to do what needs to be done, to not being willing to work late when needed, to becoming extremely cynical, snapping at coworkers, etc.

Anxiety is a fear or deep concern about what is going to happen. Anxious people are not focused on the up-side potential of what lies ahead, but on the down side. Anxiety often leads to "awfulizing"—

developing in one's mind the most disastrous of outcomes and then dwelling upon them. This can lead to dysfunctional behavior and become a self-fulfilling prophecy for the individual.

Self-absorption involves focusing on ourselves rather than what is happening around us. Self-absorbed people are often withdrawn, indifferent to the worries of others or the needs of the organization, absentminded, and looking out strictly for "Number One." They feel they have little or no control over their own destinies.

Stress manifests itself in many ways. The dictionary defines it as "a physical, mental, or emotional strain or tension." People under stress get upset by little things, get tired easily, have increased health problems, have trouble focusing on the job at hand, go through the motions without producing results, etc.

The five emotional states described above are characteristic of people in transition, whether they perceive the change that brought about the transition to be good or bad. It is important to remember that not every individual will exhibit all of these behaviors, but every organization will see all of these behaviors exhibited by some of its people.

MANAGING TRANSITION

When external change *or the perception of coming change* occurs, psychological transition follows. Individuals start at different times and go through transition at different speeds. It is much like a large marathon. People start at different times, run at different speeds, and finish at markedly different times.

Top management often knows far ahead of everyone else that major change is going to occur. They "start" then on their race of transition. Others follow as knowledge of the change unfolds. The last ones to get the word get the latest start. By the time they start, top management may be reaching the finish line and wondering what the confusion is all about. This is why top management is often surprised by the impact of change down deep in the organization. The question we often hear is, "Why should this change bother the workers? It doesn't impact what they do every day."

The 4 Ps Of Individual Requirements For Beginnings

For individuals, the change isn't finished until they complete their personal transitions. In order to make a new beginning, individuals require four things:

Purpose. People need a clear sense of purpose.

- Why is the organization making this change?
- Why did they have to leave the old ways behind?
- What is the organization trying to accomplish?

Picture. They need an understanding of the whole.

- Create a vision people can use to keep them going and assure them that there is a clear destination.
- What will the end result be?

Part. Individuals need to know what roles they will fill in the new way of doing things.

- Let them develop a role in planning the implementation where possible.
- Help them transform *the* change into *their* change.
- Get them involved in the change—for most, it is not "what is in it for me," but "how much of me is in it."

Plan. People need a step-by-step understanding of how this change is going to unfold.

- What are the key steps?
- When will they have to change?

Helping Individuals Change

The organization, in order to fulfill individuals' needs (see box at left), and to help the individuals (and thereby itself) deal effectively with their transitions needs to do the following:

1 **Make clear what has ended and what is going forward in the organization.** Honor the past and give each individual a symbolic part of it to take forward.

2 **Educate management, and then all the individuals** of an organization in transition, and provide the tools necessary to deal with change constructively. If we understand how people can be expected to feel and act during transition, then we have the opportunity to deal constructively with the issues that arise.

3 **Establish and train a group of senior managers** to handle communications during this critical period. The guiding words have to be "communicate continuously and honestly." At certain points in their transition, people will only internalize the concern and care being voiced, but the communications must go on or the people affected will invent what they believe is happening in the absence of other information.

4 **Establish and train a cross-sectional group of the organization** to monitor the impact of communications and other inputs people are receiving, and provide feedback to help the communications team. This feedback loop is essential for the communications to achieve their intended purpose.

5 **At all times remember:**
   - People go through transition at different speeds.
   - Transition presents an opportunity for individual and organizational renewal.
   - Organizational change is not the only source of stress—most people in the organization are simultaneously dealing with other changes in their lives. In fact, many of them are suffering from transitional deficits resulting from the accumulated impact of these changes.

CONCLUSION

Marketplace change is with us today as it never has been before. We all know that the pace of change will only continue to increase as we go forward. The work of meeting that change is our never-ending job.

Meeting marketplace change requires both an organizational response and an individual response. These must be done in a concurrent and coordinated manner. Crafting and implementing organizational change is something with which most organizations are familiar. Picking the right response is the main difficulty. Crafting and implementing a transition program for the people of the organization is not as easy, but there are a few rules to guide us in this effort.

"The hard part of implementing change is communicating to the people affected why you're doing it. You must make clear that the changes are not punitive. They are strictly a shift to use people's talents in the best way."
—Ed Rohner, Director of Public Services, City of Longview, Texas

1. Identify where people are in the transition process.
2. Develop and implement strategies for
   - managing endings and losses
   - leading people through and profiting from the neutral zone
   - helping people make a new beginning.
3. Communicate in as many ways as possible, on a continuous basis.

It is important to remember that we cannot force transition to occur in individuals who are going through change. Each person must do it on his or her own. But we can provide individuals with a process to guide them in this journey and a tool kit to make it easier for them. This is our role as management.

Marketplace change drives much of what your organization will do in the future. An old, but true, saying is, "Those who fail to plan, plan to fail." When planning your organizational response, remember that your critical assets go home at night. Include them in your plans.

ACTION SUMMARY

▶ Understand the difference between external change and the psychological transitions people go through when reacting to change.

▶ If your people assets are more important to success than your "hard" assets, you should be spending more time on people during change.

▶ For successful change, you need to manage both change *and* transition concurrently.

▶ Remember that for success in the marketplace, organizational responses to change must be operationalized through individual responses.

▶ Responses to change go through stages of dealing with endings, caught in the neutral zone, and new beginnings.

▶ People in transition feel many emotions such as guilt, resentment, anxiety, self-absorption, and stress.

▶ To help people through transitions, help them see the purpose of the change, give them a picture of where they are going, help them understand their part in the new status, and tell them how the change will unfold.

▶ In managing people through their transitions: communicate, communicate, communicate!

Chapter 13

ENTREPRENEURIAL CHANGE
An Individual Perspective

Eloise Calhoun

Eloise Calhoun
is a speaker, workshop leader, attitude trainer, and consultant.

As you'll read, Ms. Calhoun experienced the chaos of change firsthand. Change opened up new opportunities. Among other endeavors, she is now a Carlson Learning Company trainer, giving workshops on Achieving Life Balance, Adventures in Attitudes, DiSC, Time Is Money, Dimensions of Leadership, and Innovate with C.A.R.E. In addition, she gives seminars on building creative and productive work teams, turning chaos into opportunity, stress- and time-management, self-empowerment, and customer service.

Ms. Calhoun has worked with the Grain & Feed Dealers Association, Bell Canada, Federations of Agriculture, various Chambers of Commerce, and many other organizations.

A member of the National Speakers Association, Ms. Calhoun is also involved with several local community groups.

Eloise Calhoun, RR#2, Chesley, Ontario N0G 1L0, Canada; phone (519) 363-3037; fax (519) 363-2354.

Chapter 13

ENTREPRENEURIAL CHANGE
An Individual Perspective

Eloise Calhoun

*"It's all the same somehow, the bitter and the sweet;
if you've never tried the bitter, how will you ever know
the sweet?"*

These words of wisdom came from a cattle buyer in Medicine Hat, Alberta, Canada. His name was "Big" Bill Larson. Picture yourself standing on a step talking to John Wayne who is standing on the ground—and still having to look up to look him in the eye. That will give you some idea of the size of "Big" Bill!

Why are his words important? They summarize the effects of change—we often have to experience the bitter before we can appreciate the sweet. Change is a process we go through after experiencing the "bitter," and then moving on to turn it into something sweet. His saying identifies the beginning and the end of the process.

THRIVING ON CHANGE

Our world is rife with uncertainty: uncertainty about our jobs, our marriages, the weather, the food we eat, the environment—the list goes on. Uncertainty is a constant. To deal with the uncertainty, we need to become "change-skilled"—we must learn to manage our stress and our time so we don't become victims of change.

Creating choices and alternatives is an important change skill. Reading, listening to informational and educational tapes, and visiting other countries and other communities all help keep us aware of changes happening around us, as well as giving us fresh perspectives on old problems. This is how we can turn change into a winner for us personally, professionally, and organizationally. Management guru Tom Peters calls this process "thriving on chaos."

CHANGE, CHALLENGE, CHOICE

Losing a big client. Getting downsized out of a job. Your company being overtaken by a competitor. Your bank calling in a loan you can't repay.

Events such as these are usually the beginnings of change. Call it a crisis, problem, challenge, or opportunity. Change is never easy.

Many of us fear change, and avoid it as long as we can. Instead, we need to learn to accept the challenge of change, and turn crises into opportunities for ourselves and others.

DEALING WITH CHALLENGES

Most of us look at change as a crisis: the company owes me my job; the government must look after me; we can't survive without benefit packages, etc. We have forgotten that these so-called benefits were not always there and people survived without them. No one owes us anything.

The banks call your

ON THE OTHER HAND IF THE WORLD WERE PERFECT WHERE WOULD I FIT IN?

© 1994 CHARLES BARSOTTI

company's notes and put you into financial ruin or bankruptcy. Your boss tells you your job no longer exists and here is your pink slip. You are now an associate with no benefits and no security....

What do you do now? The first step is to face a challenge head on. For years you have taken for granted that the company would employ you, your union would protect you, and you would always have all of these benefits. How can *they* take it all away just like that?

If we have never experienced a crisis or been taught how to be "change-skilled," how can we create or even see the new opportunities in change?

"In every crisis is the seed of an equal or greater opportunity."
—Napoleon Hill,
Think and Grow Rich

An Example Of Hard Growth

A group called Concerned Farm Women, based in Ontario, once argued with a radio announcer on a live call-in program that if the government, the banks, and the community did not support local farmers, the country would not be able to feed itself. The group wanted to see some action taken to protect the clean air, fresh water, and wholesome home-grown food supply.

Because of the economic conditions in agriculture at the time, what had been sound financial decision-making when the interest rate was at 12 percent, had become financial suicide when the interest rate climbed to 24 percent in less than one year. Many in the group felt that the government owed them protection from the banks to whom they owed a lot of money. After all, without farmers, who was going to feed the people?

It was a shock to them to realize that not all people felt as strongly as they did. One listener phoned in to the program and said, "It's not your God-given right to be farmers, and if you don't like the heat, stay out of the kitchen." As she reminded them, no one had forced them to take up the business of farming, no one forced them to borrow money to expand their operations so they could feed the people in the coming century. No one forced them to listen to the government advisors who told them there would be a food shortage by the year 2000.

The farmers had made these choices themselves and now they were going to be forced to live with them. For many of the farmers, it meant declaring bankruptcy and walking away from a lifetime of work on their farms and small businesses. Not only were they going to lose their farms, they would lose their homes, their pension funds, their livelihood and, most of all, their self-esteem along the way.

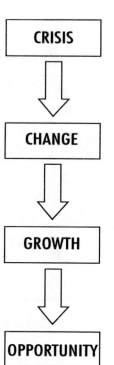

Crises Precipitate Change...And Growth

Change begins with a crisis or challenge. Circumstances and crises teach people how to change—their occupations, their livelihoods, their environment and, for many, their communities.

When we step back and look at the bigger picture of a crisis, we can usually see an opportunity that would not have been there had it not been for the challenge. In this case, a group of individual women joined together to begin a support group. They found other people who felt the same as they did, and were willing to take things into their own hands. They looked at what they could do; they didn't concentrate on things they knew they couldn't change.

They knew they couldn't change the weather, government policies, bank policies, or the fact that people did not see the need to save their small businesses. The only thing they had total control over was their attitudes.

ATTITUDE & ACTION

"It's not what happens to you that makes the difference, it's what you do with what happens to you that makes the difference."
—Wayne Dyer

When faced with a challenge—not a problem, a challenge—step back and look at the bigger picture. Ask yourself, "What can I do to make a difference?" Then start doing something—anything. As

Wayne Dyer says in his book, *The Sky is the Limit*, action is the single most effective antidote to fear, hostility, anger, anxiety, and depression. We need to learn how to take control of the situation, take some action and move on. Stop blaming, finding fault, or looking for excuses—just do it!!

Do something. Revamp your résumé; write a business plan; empower your employees. Do *something*. Our attitudes, combined with action, can make us mentally tough and teach us how to be resilient and bounce back from adversity.

Action is what the farm women took. They formed a group of like-minded people and began writing letters. They wrote a book, made a video-tape, and gave speeches about the crisis in Canadian agriculture. They even surveyed six hundred women to see if any of the rest of them saw the situation as they did.

None of these steps made any real difference to the situation in agriculture. But the women learned that by taking action they had many things to offer to each other, to their community, and to the world.

I was one of those women. From our experiences, most of us have gone on to opportunities that were not available when we complained about our ordeal on that radio program so many years ago. One works for the Ontario Heart and Stroke Foundation, another writes books and articles for a well-known magazine, another teaches adults "survival skills for the '90s and beyond." Many have gone on to be self-employed in small, home-based businesses. What began as a crisis in the early 1980s has turned into hundreds of opportunities in the 1990s.

> "The winds of change that can lead to a crisis or opportunity are classified as 'strategic inflection points.'"
> —Dr. Andrew Grove, president, INTEL

NETWORKING FOR CHANGE

Change is a process, not a destination. We tend to think that change happens overnight, but it doesn't. The precipitating factors that cause the change may happen overnight, but it takes us much longer to accept the fact that we need to change, and then to actually begin the process.

Networking was one of the tools we used to promote our changes. When faced with a challenge, a support group can help buffer the rocky road of change. It can be a network of fellow employees who have been laid off; a network of former employees who are now being hired back as associates with no benefits; a network of people who share the same interests or disease.

When confronted with change-precipitating events, most of us are temporarily thrown into a state of shock. When you pull your head up "out of the sand" and begin to look around, you will no doubt discover that you are not the only one facing a challenge. There will be at least one other person in the same—or worse—circumstances as you. Once you discover each other and begin to take action—any action—things begin to happen. People and situations that you would normally disregard present themselves in a new light. You stop and talk to people who you would ordinarily pass right by.

AN EXAMPLE OF JOB CHANGES

Creative Career Systems, a private vocational training school in Owen Sound, Ontario, works with people who are faced with change. They work with Canada Employment Services, Social Services, and private companies. Their courses consist of computer skills, self-employment skills, self-esteem building, team building, crisis management, stress and time management, "Adventures in Attitudes," and others.

Many of their clients come into the programs because they have been forced to change due to layoffs (downsizing). They have moved from unemployment benefits onto social services or welfare programs after their benefits have run out. Their feelings of low self-esteem confirm the damage done to them by "someone else." They had been oblivious to the changes going on around them locally and globally. Most felt that "life owed them a living" and they were going to collect. However, when reality set in and the economic crunch began to hit, change became a necessity and they finally started to look around.

> READY, FIRE, AIM
> "Action, action, action. That's how we learn and improve."
> —Tom Peters

The Courage To Change

The role of Creative Career Systems has been to challenge people to change and help them gain the courage to change. In one of their training classes, a student was redoing a résumé after being laid off from 21 years of employment with the same company. Devastated by the notice she had just received, she found it hard to find anything good she had done over those 21 years. After all she had done the "same" thing all that time, what else could she do? Her learning group peers questioned her about responsibilities and duties. She soon discovered that she had a lot to offer a new employer, and her self-esteem began to soar.

While at lunch that day, she bragged to a friend about her new résumé. Her friend asked if she had an extra copy with her that she could take back to her boss. Within 24 hours, this woman had a new job, with a company that she would never have considered because she didn't think she had the skills to handle the job.

We, as individuals, often get so caught up in our crises that we fail to see the opportunities all around us. If we only open our eyes and our ears, wonderful things can happen.

LOOK FOR THE GOOD, GO FOR IT, GROW WITH IT, GAIN FROM IT

As the woman in the prior example discovered, it is difficult to look for the good in the situation when faced with a crisis.

Putting ourselves down has become a way of life for many of us. We have been taught, or programmed, to "don't let it go to your head," "don't get a swelled head over your success," "you're not as good as you think you are," etc. If we are not proud of what we have accomplished in life, how can we expect other people to be proud of us or want to hire us?

"Your *attitude*, not you *aptitude*, will determine your *altitude*."
—Zig Ziglar

When we begin to look for the good qualities and strengths we possess, our attitudes begin to change. Learning to be enthusiastic about our achievements is important. No two of us are exactly the same. We don't have the same life experiences, backgrounds, genes, physical shape, ethnicity, or cultural backgrounds.

Creative Career Systems asks their clients to write a list of strengths and weaknesses, and then to summarize the "fruits of their labours."

It is sad to see how many people have lengthy lists of weaknesses and need the help of others to identify their strengths. In uncovering your uniqueness and your value, you need to learn to take pride in yourself and your accomplishments, no matter how small. Success does build upon success. If we don't feel we've had any successes, it is pretty hard to build on them to move forward.

Make Your Own Attitude

We must approach change with enthusiasm in order to succeed. It is like any twelve-step program—if you don't want to change, no circumstances, no experiences, no person, no relationship in the world can make you. Change must come from within to be effective. If we are not enthused about the change, chances are it will never happen. Enthusiasm for change creates new opportunities.

The Carlson Learning Centres' program, "Adventures in Attitudes," points out that changing one's attitudes is risky. Changing your attitudes means leaving the familiar for the unfamiliar—stepping out of the comfort zone and experiencing discomfort. Change requires mental and physical stamina, courage, and even some distress.

How we perceive and respond to events around us is our choice. This awareness is the first step in changing negative attitudes to positive ones. It's key to establishing personal responsibility and accountability in the midst of change—and it helps turn passive resistance into high-energy performance.

It's easier to say "no" to changing our attitudes than it is to say "yes." But the nos are simply ways of repeating the past. Saying yes opens up all sorts of new opportunities. Learn to choose your attitudes. Then you will really have the power and freedom to be your own person, capable of determining and achieving your goals and dreams.

FAILURE OR LEARNING EXPERIENCE?

It would be very simple to change the word "failure" to "learning experience" and begin early in life to prepare our citizenry to use crises to learn skills to create new successes. When you learn what you don't know, you improve your knowledge for the next attempt to take advantage of opportunities.

Change is an opportunity to look at things from a new perspective, to reassess where we are, and where we want to be. If we never experience any negative events, how will we ever learn how to change, or what we need to change?

SELF-RESPONSIBILITY

Of all the skills needed to become change-skilled, the most important is self-responsibility. You can't change what happens to you most of the time, but you can take responsibility for your own situation.

We can change our attitudes and take responsibility for our own actions. When we move away from blaming, finding fault, and looking for excuses, we can begin to see things from a new perspective. Accepting responsibility does not mean always apologizing for things. It means accepting the situation and moving on.

Moving Onward And Upward

We farm women found ourselves losing our farms, our homes, our livelihood, and our pension plans. We took action. Today most of us still live on our farms. However, we farm much differently. We have learned to work smarter, not harder. We have become computer literate, taken off-farm jobs using our skills in new areas of employment, or become entrepreneurs.

Many of the clients from the training courses go on to new and better jobs, or create their own jobs.

The biggest hurdle for all of us was to take responsibility for our own situations and "do" something about them. No one owes us a living; it's no person's right to be anything—we have to earn that right. When we begin to take self-responsibility great things happen. People look to us as leaders because we can challenge change and turn it into an opportunity. In these times of leadership crisis, we become the new wave of the future.

> "Man is condemned to be free; because once thrown into the world, he is responsible for everything he does."
> —Jean-Paul Sartre

Dr. Michael Durst, author of *Managing By Responsibility*, reminds us that you do not find the word "blame" or "fault" in the word responsibility. Instead you find the *ability* to *respond* to every situation. Our response to the situation can make the difference in our ability to see the opportunities in the crisis—or the sweet in the bitter.

We can't change what happens to us, but we can control our responses and our attitudes. Accepting responsibility for ourselves and our situations, learning all we can about our alternatives, and taking action to implement those alternatives forces us to look at the opportunities that a crisis presents.

Take A Break

At times, the most effective way to make a change is to give yourself permission to take some "time just for me." Go away to a quiet spot, do some relaxation exercises. Decide, when your mind is free of worries and fear, what it is you really want to happen as a result of an impending change. When your mind is quiet and relaxed, new perspectives present themselves for your business, your personal life, and your social life.

CHANGE, GROWTH, ENTREPRENEURSHIP

What begins as a personal change can quickly turn into a community, and even global, change. My family's company, Calhoun Agri Services Ltd., is a case in point. It began as a small one-person operation run out of the basement of a house six years ago.

Today we are an international company doing business across Canada, from Nova Scotia to British Columbia, in all of the United States east of the Mississippi River, and seeking expansion in new frontiers. The company now employs six families and is located on two hundred acres overlooking some of the most beautiful scenery in the area.

The location has helped provide the employees with the inspiration for creativity and innovation. When we all get together as a "think tank" to create new business products or ideas, we have only to look out the windows in any direction to be inspired.

The Unity Of Opposites

"Big" Bill Larson also says that "when everyone else is walking, that's when you should run; when everyone else is running that's when you should walk." A frequently-used technique in our meetings is to look at what everyone else is doing in the industry. Then we take a look at what the opposite of that would be, and try to create a different, unique way to market that product or idea.

Applying this technique can save money and expense. Every business, product, or idea that people run away from needs to be considered in a new light, or changed to meet the needs of today's "vigilante consumers."

Looking at what others are doing, and then doing the opposite can open up whole new markets or market segments not previously considered. Walking into places, jobs, relationships, companies, or businesses that others are running away from, looking for the opportunities to be different, faster, better, more unique, and still meet the demands of the consumer, can turn the bitter into the sweet.

> ### Definition Of "Vigilante Consumers"
>
> Vigilante consumers abide by the philosophy: "What we want, we get, right now, or we go somewhere else to spend our disposable income."
>
> —Faith Popcorn, *The Popcorn Report*

Be A Leader In Entrepreneurial Niches

When your idea, business or job becomes successful, everyone else will begin to run your way wanting a piece of the action. As this process accelerates, it is time for you to sell out, move on, change, or find a new challenge. Don't follow. Create change. The more changes you create in your business, your job, or your relationship, the more choices you will have.

"When you're not the lead sled dog, the view is the same no matter what your position."

THE CHANGE PROCESS

When faced with change, we go through a series of reactions. They may not happen in exactly this order but they will be a combination of the following elements.

How people change can be summarized using the letters of the word CHANGES.

C stands for *Challenge* or *Crisis* which usually precipitates a change.

H means *Holistic.* We need to stand back and take a broad view of the situation, instead of getting caught up in the immediate crisis.

A means reexamine our *Attitudes* because they determine 90 percent of our altitude.

N is for *Networking* with friends, family, or a support group of like-minded people to help us through the immediate situation.

G means to look for the *Good. Go* for it, *Grow* with it, and *Gain* from it.

E means *Enthusiasm* and *Education,* or lifelong learning, which will be a must for the information age and the new millennium.

S *Self-responsibility* is the most important of all the keys to change. You must take responsibility for your situation, rather than blame outside forces.

Changes are a challenge. But if you can implement this formula when faced with your challenges, you will have positive outcomes. Learn to have fun with change. Use the thrill of it and leave the threat behind.

Challenge your future, turn your ugly ducklings, (negative experiences, bad relationships, wrong job, place to live, etc.) into beautiful swans. This can be applied to your personal, professional or social life.

"It's all the same somehow, the bitter and the sweet; if you've never tried the bitter, how will you ever know the sweet?"

ACTION SUMMARY

▶ Look for the seed of new success in every negative change.

▶ Look for the broad, holistic picture beyond specific problems.

▶ When everyone else is running from a situation, seek the undiscovered opportunities.

▶ Take responsibility for your own situation, even if it is "caused" by outside factors.

▶ When in doubt, take action.

▶ Build a network of supportive people.

▶ Have a positive attitude. Be enthusiastic.

▶ Consider self-employment for maximum opportunity, flexibility, and control.

Part Five
IMPLEMENTING CHANGE

Chapter 14
SHIFT HAPPENS
A Customer Service Example
James Feldman

Chapter 15
HOW TO IMPLEMENT CHANGE
A Linchpin Model
Rick Crandall

Chapter 14

SHIFT HAPPENS
A Customer Service Example

James Feldman

James Feldman,
MIP, CITE is a Certified Facilitator and professional motivator. He is recognized internationally as a knowledgeable speaker and author with a proven track record for excellence. He has a twenty-year record for high energy presentations to the hospitality industry, entertainment, and Fortune 1000 clients including Toyota, Apple Computer, Hyatt Hotels and Resorts, Queensland Tourist Commission, San Juan Convention Bureau, Frito-Lay, MGM/UA, The Coca-Cola Company, Del Monte, and dozens of trade associations including NAMA, SITE, AIM, PMAA, DSA, etc. As president of Shift Happens! Seminars, Inc. with over twenty-five years of experience with corporations dealing with millions of customers and thousand of employees, he is not a speaker who just talks, but a "practitioner who speaks."

James Feldman, Shift Happens!® Seminars, Inc., 505 North Lake Shore Drive #6601, Chicago, IL 60611; phone (312) 527-9111; fax (312) 527-9112; e-mail Shift Hpns@aol.com; Internet http://www.shifthappens.com.

Chapter 14

SHIFT HAPPENS
A Customer Service Example

James Feldman

"We must obey the great law of change. It is the most powerful law of nature."
—Edmund Burke

In today's world, the only constant is change. With rare exception, it is difficult to participate in life without being touched by change; it permeates our personal lives, our business world, our government, and beyond.

Think for a moment of products and services that were not in common use a mere decade ago and how they have affected our lives. Cellular phones, personal pagers, modems, fax machines, CD-ROMs, personal computers, the Internet, e-mail, voice mail, and satellite dishes have revolutionized the way we transmit and receive information. Microwave ovens have altered the speed with which we can prepare food, and the food service industry has responded with new packaging and portions.

No sector of our lives has gone untouched by

change—there's NO ESCAPE!

Accepting Inertia

Many of us resist the idea of change—or the implementation of change. We desperately hang on to the ways we've always done things...even if we don't know why we're doing it that way!

We do things "the same old way" because it gives us a feeling of control over our lives and some measure of comfort or security. But just like the proverbial ostrich burying its head in the sand, ignoring or resisting change isn't going to stop it!

Instead, we must embrace change and manage it the best ways we can. That means having an open mind, learning new skills and behaviors, and having the willingness to change ourselves.

MANAGING CHANGE

As a microcosm of the world, corporate America is as vulnerable to change as any individual. We witness it in the form of restructuring, reengineering, total quality management initiatives, downsizing, resizing, acquisitions, and mergers. And, many of these change efforts fail. So, too, do many attempts to make personal changes. How many of us have failed to quit smoking or drinking, exercise regularly, follow healthier diets, lower our blood pressure, spend more quality time with our families, or end a bad marriage or job?

The Ham Theory Of Inertia

People's easy acceptance of inertia reminds me of the story about the ham.

At a family holiday dinner, the hostess cut off a third of the ham before she placed it in the oven to bake. Her new husband observed this and asked, "Why did you remove part of the ham before cooking it?"

His wife replied, "Because that's the way my family has always prepared ham."

Not satisfied with her answer, he approached his young wife's mother, and asked, "What's the secret behind cutting off the end of the ham before you cook it?"

His mother-in-law shook her head and replied, "I don't know. That's just how my mother did it. Why don't you ask her?"

Still curious, the young husband turned to his wife's grandmother and repeated the question. She responded, "That's the way my mother did it. Back then, the hams were too big to fit in our oven."

Why Is It Hard To Change?

In part, failures to change stem from mistakenly viewing change as an end result rather than a process. It's seen as all or nothing, now or never. By approaching it this way, we invariably fail. Rather, we must view change as a *process.*

Consider an example provided by a well known celebrity. Oprah Winfrey has waged a battle against her weight for many years: At a high she weighed 237 pounds, at a low 142. But even though she reached her goal of "x" pounds, she couldn't sustain the change, and ultimately regained the weight. She failed.

Then she met a man whose approach to making this change was totally different: Bob Greene helped Oprah to understand and focus on the reasons *why* she ate the way she did, not just *how* and *what* she ate. Once she truly understood the role of food in her life—a comfort, a way to avoid feelings, a reaction to stress, something she could control, etc.—she began to change her behavior. In addition to eating carefully, she incorporated regular exercise and other means of rebalancing and renewal.

"I like north by northwest better."

Oprah didn't do everything all at once; it was a process, a step at a time. As Oprah gained awareness and confidence, she attempted the next step. Finally she succeeded in making the complete change she had so desperately wanted to make for so many years. Shift Happens!

Team Play

Line up 10 people in a straight line, and ask them to pretend that they are a production line or a sports team. Give them 12 balls of different colors. *Explain that each ball has to be touched by everyone before being tossed in a bin.* The object is to do it in the least amount of time possible.

The game proceeds as follows: The first person to touch the ball hands it to the next person, who hands it to the next person, and so on. The last person to touch the ball hands it back to the first person who then places it in a container in the middle of the line. When all 12 balls are in the bin, the clock stops and the time is recorded.

Next, ask the "team" to come up with their own method of moving the balls, with the goal to cut their time by 50%. Then, give them two tries. Typically, they will repeat the exact same process and shave a bit off their time in their second and third attempts.

Team Resistance

After the third attempt, mix up the order in which the team members are standing, and without any discussion, ask them to try again. It's very likely that this fourth attempt will be chaos, and the team won't be able to reach their best times.

The only thing that's changed is the order in which the people are standing; yet the perception is one of total disruption which markedly affects performance outcome. The exercise reflects what happens in the real world: Just when we think things are going well, management—or the government, or family—changes the rules, and we don't know how to cope!

This same phenomenon occurs in the workplace: A change in one department may have absolutely no real impact on the rest of the organization but may be *perceived as affecting operations.* This is a key distinction. Often times things haven't really changed significantly. Only our perception of reality has changed.

In the exercise, one brave soul may suggest that the group change the physical structure from

CHANGE REQUIRES:

Courage
Heart
Adaptability
Nurturing
Grace
Energy

a line to a circle tight enough that everyone can touch the ball simultaneously instead of one at a time. This individual goes on to explain that since the ball never leaves the hands of the first person, she or he is automatically last to touch it and can immediately drop it in the container. This improves the performance time dramatically, which is the stated goal, while still adhering to the original rules.

> "Creativity requires the freedom to consider unthinkable alternatives, to doubt the worth of cherished practices."
> —John W. Gardner

While it may seem obvious that every group would immediately see the wisdom in the suggestion and adopt the change, that's not the case! Members of the team will come up with all sorts of reasons why it won't work, why they can't do it, etc.

This happens in the workplace all the time. The long-range performance goal or the short-term strategy hasn't changed; the only thing that's changed is the means of reaching it! Rather than panicking or resisting change, we need to assess what is perception and what is reality and adapt accordingly. Sometimes, as demonstrated in the game, that means mastering new skills, behavior, and working relationships. It isn't easy. But remember, Shift Happens!

Shift Happens

Managing during periods of change often requires changing yourself. Your old managerial skills and behaviors may no longer prove effective in a changed work environment—the "ham-in-the-oven syndrome."

If you want to be successful in getting others to take risks and learn new skills and behaviors, you must be willing to change the way you work and deal with others. You must learn skills to manage performance and change. You must have the courage to find new ground and establish your authority. Once attained, you can then help lead others and help them be responsible for their own changes, just as Bob Greene was a catalyst for Oprah

Winfrey. However, it is important to remember that people decide to change when they decide to change themselves. Only then does Shift Happen!

It is important to create an environment in which people feel safe to change. Mistakes should be viewed as learning opportunities. If employees are not allowed any creativity or imagination, or if they are denied training, they will have less incentive to change. Your job will be made that much more difficult.

CUSTOMER SERVICE CHANGES

One change impacting companies in all sectors is the level of satisfaction expected by today's consumers. Customers are more aware, more sophisticated, more assertive, and more discerning than they've ever been.

Companies that do not see the marketplace from their customers' point of view run the risk of losing those customers to their competitors who do. When this happens, they are not only losing revenues, but they're incurring costs to attract new customers. That price is high: It costs 91% more to attract a new customer than to retain an existing one! Put another way, repeat business creates higher profit margins.

Repeat Business Is King

The wise company focuses on creating long-lasting relationships with its customers. When faced with a business decision,

The Value Of Loyal Customers

"The average company today loses half its customers in five years. You can't grow when customers are defecting out the back door faster than the sales force can pull new ones in the front door...A five percentage point increase in customer retention in a typical company will increase profits by more than 25%, and growth by more than 100%! Most companies are feeling the dark side of these loyalty economics today. That is, their profits and growth are being devastated by declining customer retention."

—Frederick F. Reichheld, *The Loyalty Effect*

How Do You Become Customer Driven?

Being customer driven is easier when the "center of gravity" of your business is kept as close as possible to the point where the action is—the place where the business meets its customers. Here's how to become customer driven:

- Be your own customer on a regular basis.
- Ask your customers what they want.
- Listen to those on the front lines.
- Experience your company from the customer's perspective.
- See your customers as individual people with needs, wants, and feelings.
- Experience the marketplace firsthand.

the question becomes not "what do I think is good for the company," but rather, "How will this be perceived by our customers?" The main task is bringing customers back again and again, and having them refer new customers. This will only happen if your company is "customer driven."

Customer driven means that you're committed to narrowing your knowledge gaps about your customers. Companies that are customer driven realize that if they don't run their businesses to suit their customers, their customers will suit themselves—somewhere else.

Listening To Customers

The most important skill you can develop in the pursuit of customer satisfaction is listening! It's why God gave us two ears and only one mouth. Customers who complain are customers who care (or they wouldn't bother complaining!).

The customer-driven company views complaints as opportunities. They're an opportunity for valuable market research. They're an opportunity to discover problems and remedy them before they become damaging.

Complaints are an opportunity to interface with the customer and improve your relationship. In short, how your company handles complaints may make the difference between a satisfied and an unsatisfied customer, with far reaching consequences.

Remember the one bad apple that ruined all the good apples in the barrel? Well, customers are just like apples. If five dissatisfied customers complain to 20 people about a negative experience with your company that means 100 existing or prospective customers have been put at risk. It

Customers' Response To Poor Service

would take 100 satisfied customers telling one person how wonderful their experience was to neutralize the impact. And any media watcher knows that bad news is far more sensational and intriguing than good news! This reality underscores why *your company has a problem if your customer has a problem* and why it is so critical to settle problems quickly and positively.

Be Customer-centered

Another effective way to achieve customer satisfaction is to bring the customer into the center of the organization. This is the premise of Richard Whitely and Diane Hessan, authors of the book *Customer-Centered Growth*. They contend that customer-centered companies have satisfied employees who focus attentively and exclusively on the long-term relationship with the customer. The bottom line is secondary. Their recommendations:

- Focus like a laser beam on a specific group for whom you create top-of-the-line products or services.
- Make sure that each employee and manager can hear and respond to the voice of the customer.

- Have every employee engaged in the process of collaboration on behalf of the customer.
- Create hands-on, contact leaders who inspire and mobilize employees to provide quality service to their customers.

CUSTOMER-CENTERED COMPANIES

Lexus Amazes Customers

In the 100-year-old automobile industry, customers have rarely been in the driver's seat when it came to purchasing a car at their local dealership. Traditionally, they found themselves at the mercy of smooth-talking, highly polished salespeople armed with arsenals of special deals, closeouts, and demos. That was the case until Lexus revolutionized the sales process and gained legions of enthusiastic fans in the process.

What was their secret weapon? They simply started over. Without any preconceived notions, Lexus developed a new way of dealing with car buyers that was so distinctive and superior that it flabbergasted customers.

That way was treating the customer with respect: Sales personnel were trained to treat their customers as their customers wished to be treated—as intelligent consumers looking for a car that best met their needs. Even their titles reflect this philosophy: Customers are referred to as guests and salespeople are referred to as consultants. Guests aren't sold—they're "educated" about the benefits derived from owning a Lexus. The company's approach is exemplified by its motto: "the relentless pursuit of perfection."

> **The Lexus Motto:**
>
> *"The relentless pursuit of perfection."*

In less than five years, Lexus has positioned itself at the top of the luxury car market and has stayed there due to the support and loyalty of its customers. The company has become known for its near-perfect product and landmark customer interaction process described by many as "the ultimate customer satisfaction experience." Efficient and reliable communication links connecting employees at all levels characterize the corporate culture.

To talk to Lexus owners is to hear them speak of their car as a valued and beloved family member. While other companies, such as Saturn, have been able to encourage customer enthusiasm, it is Lexus which has maintained high levels of customer amazement through its quality product and continual process of refinement in the pursuit of perfection.

The Value Of Knowing Your Customers

Lexus paid attention to its customers. The company realized that less than 15% of contemporary households were a traditional, nuclear family. It understood that people are value oriented and that today's key values are quality, education, entertainment, and time.

Lexus also recognized that women, as wage earners in dual income families, are in many cases the decision makers—even for purchase decisions historically dominated by males (i.e., cars.)

This realization was incorporated in the guest interaction process. Consultants were trained to present the Lexus story to those who affect decisions; they targeted each member of the family as opposed to the traditional male buyer. To complete the customer amazement circle, the interaction process involves not only the sales force but those behind the front lines as well.

Apple Introduces Friendly Computers

As customers become more sophisticated, they no longer merely buy a product, they buy the benefits they get from using the product. Apple computers are a case in point. People who own Apple computers exhibit a loyalty that is extraordinary, especially in an industry known for planned obsolescence. Even with Apple's current difficulties, their customers hang on, hoping their beloved computer will once again emerge at the forefront of technology.

User-oriented Design. These consumers have the relationship they do now because early on Apple offered them a hassle-free, reliable way to enter the technological age. With Apple they didn't have to worry about whether the lighting was right or remember what keyboard configuration or interface went with what software. Apple's user-friendly design took the intimidation out of computing and made it fast, easy, and fun. Until the departure of John Scully, there existed a passionate connectedness between Apple and its customers—so much so that customers were probably the greatest sales force the company had. Management focused on its employees, promoted talent, and encouraged the individual mind to create within the collective spirit. Input was sought from customers, distributors, engineers, software writers—virtually anyone who could help improve the way the products were manufactured and serviced. This contributed greatly to the high level of customer satisfaction experienced in an industry where technological failures and customer frustration were all too common.

New Leaders

In customer-centered companies such as Lexus and Apple, gone are the old models of leadership—sitting back, giving directions, and having everyone else to do the work.

The customer-oriented leader comes in regular contact with his or her center of gravity: where the customer buys or uses the product or service being sold. The net result is that these companies get employees and end users excited about their products or services, and confident in the companies' abilities to perform beyond expectations.

Unfortunately, Apple lost sight of its customer, and the company is now practically nonexistent in the business sector and may soon lose the education market as well. It's a sad reversal for a company that was on the cutting edge. In contrast, Lexus continually tries to improve its relationship with customers. The result? Lexus has successfully introduced additional models into the marketplace and enjoys the highest resale value on its used models.

Nordstrom Department Store

Who can profile customer-centered companies without acknowledging Nordstrom, a retailer that has become a national model for outstanding customer service? This family-run business includes its customers as extended family and communicates with them one-to-one. Designer Donna Karan says, "The Nordstrom Way is what the 1990s are all about!"

R. Spector, in the book *The Nordstrom Way*, proposes three keys to Nordstrom's success:

Key #1. The first key revolves around the merchandise. Buyers work closely with manufacturers to obtain the best selection, value, and quality of goods. Salespeople are expected to have a complete understanding of the merchandise and its features.

Key #2. The second factor is the workforce. Nordstrom would rather hire nice people and teach them to sell than hire salespeople and teach them to be nice! Through extraordinary rates of expansion, Nordstrom has created a fast career track for energetic, highly entrepreneurial people who are rewarded for their performance through sales commissions.

Store managers have the freedom to hire a huge sales staff and are responsible for training, coaching, nurturing, and evaluating their sales team. Buying is decentralized: Managers are encouraged to buy as much inventory as their shelves will hold, and to solicit input on fashion direction, styles, colors, quantities, and sizes from their salespeople—because they know best what the customer wants. Decisions get made closest to the point of sale, the business's "center of gravity."

A Place At The Top For Women

Like Lexus, Nordstrom recognized the changing role of women and demonstrated it by establishing an open-ended career path: 40% of company officers and 66% of store managers are female.
—R. Spector, *The Nordstrom Way*

Nordstrom: Tales Of Incredible Customer Service

A customer, who was on her way to catch a flight at SeaTac airport in Seattle, inadvertently left her airline ticket on the counter in one of Nordstrom's women's apparel departments. Discovering the ticket, her sales associate immediately phoned the airline and asked the service representative if he could track down the customer at the airport and write another ticket. The answer was no. (That airline should take lessons from Nordstrom!) Having no time to get her car out of the garage, the Nordstrom salesperson jumped into a cab, rode out to the airport, located the customer and delivered the ticket herself in time for the woman to make her flight!

* * * *

A woman purchased a pair of jeans at Nordstrom and was advised by the sales associate to wear them, wash them multiple times, and then bring them back to be shortened—free of charge. Following this advice, she returned, and the alteration person pinned the hem. She picked the jeans up a week later, but didn't have time to try them on.

At home, when she took them out of the bag, she discovered that they had never been altered! The customer went back to the store and explained what had happened to the senior salesperson in the department. With abject embarrassment, the salesperson apologized and promised that the jeans would be fixed by that same afternoon. When the customer said she could not get back then, the salesperson offered to drive the jeans over to her home when she got off her shift, and stay to make sure they fit right! And she was as good as her word.

Key #3. The third key to Nordstrom's success is its total emphasis on the customer. Nordstrom believes in creating a memorable experience for its customers. To do this, Nordstrom stores feature more seating, larger fitting rooms, and wider aisles than its competitors. A tuxedo-clad pianist plays live music. In the shoe department, the chairs have arms and taller legs so that customers can concentrate on buying shoes rather than how to get out of the chair gracefully! It's this level of detail that earns customer accolades.

Create Legends. Employees are instructed to always make decisions in favor of the customer over the company: The store's primary rule is *use your good judgment in all situations.* Salespeople are never criticized for doing too much for the customer—only for doing too little.

Nowhere is this more evident than in "Heroics"—true tales of incredible customer service that are part and parcel of the Nordstrom corporate culture and mythology (see box at left).

HOW TO CREATE
CUSTOMER SERVICE CHANGE

Keeping the customer satisfied is the refrain sung by the leaders of a cross section of companies and industries including transportation, technology, communications, manufacturing, retail, and service. Savvy leaders have learned that keeping customers means knowing customers, and knowing customers means hearing and responding to them.

As an example of a change program, let's consider improving customer service. Your company can sail through the storms of change like a Lexus or a Nordstrom if you have the commitment from senior management to creating a winning customer service strategy. Without buy-in from the top of the organization, employees are unlikely to champion the program.

Just how do you go about creating such a program? Like any change, step by step. Here are 10 suggestions recommended by the Organizational Development Corp. in its *Re-Designing Customer Service Newsletter* for creating a winning customer service strategy in your company.

1 Establish Credibility. One of the best ways to effectively communicate a new mandate is to create a team whose members represent as many functional areas as possible and have company clout in the eyes of employees. Without this authority, "road blocks" may develop because other departments, managers, and frontline staff do not view the team as having the authority to make them change. It is important that employees understand that this change is supported throughout the organization, has full commitment from the top and that it involves them. It is up to the team to effectively communicate to employees and generate enthusiasm.

"The gulf between satisfied customers and completely satisfied customers can swallow a business."
—*Harvard Business Review*

Only when the program is fully championed will it have any hope of succeeding. To receive adequate attention, substantial priority and time must be devoted to the program.

2 **Prioritize Customer Service Issues.** One of the first tasks of the team is to identify *objectively and quantitatively* the issues that have the greatest impact on customer service. One effective method is to survey customers, either through anonymous questionnaires or focus groups. It is also useful to survey customers who have defected, to find out why they went elsewhere.

Review Customer Feedback At Three Levels

Before you collect customer data, you should have a plan to use it. A top executive group should use the results to allocate resources and decide on direction. Middle management groups should use the data to help support line functions. Groups of line people should look at the findings and report back up the hierarchy on what they need to improve performance.

Another source of information is feedback centers (customer complaint areas, information desks, receptionists, sales staff, etc.). Once the information has been collected, rank the responses numerically and according to revenue loss. This will help the team focus on solutions that will save or generate the most dollars for the program.

3 **Establish Realistic Goals.** After identifying the key customer service issues, it's time to agree which problems to solve first, and to set target completion dates. Issues can be ranked again—this time according to the level of activity required to solve them.

Attaching time lines to each issue is also necessary to track results. The A list may require multiple levels of approval, involve major technical support, take six months or more, etc. The B list might require input from other departments, but not require significant paperwork or investment. The C list might require minimal activity such as changing staff coverage, or reinforcing a policy that has fallen through the cracks. This is often a good place to start because you can demonstrate immediate results and get staff to "buy into" the program.

4 **Endorse The Program.** Once the team is clear about its goals and time lines it is time to "kickoff" the program at the corporate or department level. This is the time to introduce the team, share the vision, and communicate the intentions of the program and level of involvement.

5 **Raise Staff Awareness.** Meet with staff on a smaller scale and educate them as to what quality service means to the company. There are many exercises your staff can do to become more customer-oriented, from identifying all internal and external customers to creating their top 10 tips to improve customer service.

6 **Implement Continuous Quality Improvement Circles.** Input from frontline staff is critical to the success of a winning customer service strategy. To encourage participation, create employee-centered continuous improvement (quality) groups which address the customer, employee performance levels, and work processes.

7 **Develop Product And Service Quality Standards.** Staff and management together should establish standards of excellence followed by key performance indicators for employees. In this way employees know what is expected of them on a daily, weekly, and monthly basis and what is considered "excelling." Many supervisors find that negotiation with staff will result in higher productivity and levels of commitment to service.

8 **Benchmark.** It is important to "keep score" of performance levels and achievements by tracking key results on a company-wide level. It is best to establish several months of results so perfor-

"Quality in a service or product is not what you put into it. It is what the client or customer gets out of it."
—Peter Drucker

Make Benchmarking Fun

When you hear about a great idea another business is using, send out an "exploration party." Make it fun. For example, use the company van and rush everyone to the scene of good customer service. Encourage people to take notes and actually apply the lessons when they get back to the office or store. Invite employees to report good business experiences to their supervisors so your company can benefit. It's informal benchmarking, and it's a way to get everyone involved in continuous improvement.

—Paul Timm, *50 Powerful Ideas You Can Use to Keep Your Customers*

mance comparisons can be made, either by time or by group. One positive benefit of benchmarking is that many individuals begin to improve their performance levels when they know they are being tracked. It is important to publicize results on a regular basis to keep the momentum going.

9 Recognize And Reward. Initiating an employee incentive program can recognize, reinforce, and reward top performers, as well as remind staff of the importance of their jobs and the company's goals.

One reward is the bonus incentive which attaches dollar amounts to goals achieved. Employees like this because they are rewarded for their hard work and can earn extra money. Another type of plan is the creative incentive which can take the form of well-timed surprises or individually tailored perks, including free trips, days off, etc. A third recognition program is the Employee of the Month award which creates competition and public acknowledgment of individual achievements.

10 Promote Your Company's Quality Customer Service. Once your company can consistently reach the service and quality goals that have been established and you can be certain you have a proven track record, it is time to blow your horn a little. Publicity can be created through paid advertising, a direct mail program to customers, in-house visuals (T-shirts, banners, posters, billboards, mugs, etc.), and sales collateral. A catchy slogan (perhaps derived through an employee contest) can be part of a publicity campaign.

SUMMARY OF A SERVICE CHANGE PROGRAM

At this point you may think that you have "finished" what you set out to do. However, few companies ever reach the ultimate stage of customer satisfaction. Why? Because many variables are constantly changing. This makes creating and maintaining a customer-driven organization an ongoing process. However, if you stay focused on the customer, and keep improving how you serve them, you will realize significant results.

ACTION SUMMARY

Change is an inexorable fact of life. How we react to it is up to us. Positive or negative, Shift Happens. Here are 10 actionable ways to help you navigate the seas of change:

▶ Walk the talk. If you want others to bring about change, be willing to take the lead.

▶ Continually increase the number of individuals taking responsibility for their own changes.

▶ Embrace improvisation as the best path for both performance and change. Encourage lateral thinking, creativity, and imagination.

▶ Use team performance to drive change.

▶ Concentrate organizational designs on the work people do rather than the decision-making authority they have.

▶ Sell ideas by sharing results. Make everyone a part of the solution.

▶ Put people in the position to learn by doing, and provide the information and support they need just in time to perform.

▶ Treat mistakes as learning moments.

▶ Aim for success, not perfection.

▶ Confront your fears and allow yourself to be human.

Good luck in your journey!

Chapter 15

HOW TO IMPLEMENT CHANGE
A Linchpin Model

Rick Crandall

Rick Crandall, PhD, is a speaker, writer, and consultant, specializing in talks and workshops on marketing and sales, creativity, and change. He has spoken for *Inc.* magazine, the American Marketing Association, Autodesk, and the American Society for Training and Development. Dr. Crandall has presented well over 1,000 public seminars, given many keynote presentations, and worked with organizations from large law firms to the Air Force.

Dr. Crandall is the author of *Marketing Your Services: For People Who HATE to Sell* (1996), and editor of *10 Secrets of Marketing Success: How to Jump-Start Your Marketing* (1997). In addition, he serves as editor and marketing columnist for *Executive Edge* (a national management newsletter).

He is the founder and executive director of the Community Entrepreneurs Organization (since 1982). He is the recipient of an SBA Small Business Award, and is listed in various *Who's Whos*. With a PhD in Group Dynamics, Dr. Crandall taught business, research, or psychology full time at the University of Michigan, University of Illinois, and Texas Christian University in the 1970s.

Rick Crandall, PhD; Agent: Select Press, PO Box 37, Corte Madera, CA 94976-0037; phone (415) 924-1612; fax (415) 924-7179; e-mail SelectPr@aol.com.

Chapter 15

HOW TO IMPLEMENT CHANGE
A Linchpin Model

Rick Crandall

"The people who truly get things done are mono-
maniacs. They focus intensely on one thing at a time."
—Peter Drucker

The fable of the Gordian knot has been remembered through the ages because it has lasting
implications. Legend has it that people came from
all over the ancient world to try to untie the
intricate Gordian knot. It was said that whoever
undid the knot would become leader of all Asia.
People approached the problem from many directions, but all failed. Then Alexander the Great
severed the knot with one blow of his sword.
Perhaps he went on to rule the world because he
was the first to think "outside the box"! The
Gordian knot also represents solving a complex
problem with a sharp, focused approach.

As with a Gordian knot, change confronts us
with a complex tangle of factors that can be
approached in many ways.

TWO MODELS OF REALITY
The World Is Complex

One view sees the world as complicated—an intricate "Gordian knot" system with thousands of variables. In science, researchers operating from this assumption use a "multivariate" approach. They try to measure the impact of all the variables on each other simultaneously. They feel that if they can just include all possible causes, reciprocal effects, and two-way or three-way or n^{th}-way interactions, they'll then be able to explain 100% of any situation.

Certainly it's true that if you're trying to predict the success of a corporate change ini-

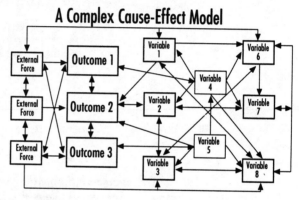

A Complex Cause-Effect Model

tiative, and you use five variables instead of two, or twenty instead of five, you're likely to be more successful in your predictions. You can probably name a dozen important variables that could affect the success of any change effort (e.g., the types of people in the organization, the competitive environment, the style of leadership, the interaction between different work groups, the interaction between leadership style and followers' needs, the interaction between the type of marketing used and the dynamics of the marketplace, the reactions of the competitors—the list goes on).

Look For Main Effects

The opposite approach is to look for simple, major "main" effects. Working from this philosophy, researchers attempting to explain the cause of an effect will start with a variable they believe will have big effects, rather than starting small and making gradual refinements.

For instance, if you were using this approach and wanted to change the behavior of people in an organization, you might start with an incentive pay system that allowed employees to double their salaries when they performed the way you wanted. You wouldn't test the importance of incentive pay by using small bonuses, where employees could increase their salaries no more than five percent.

```
Cause ———▶ Effect
```

A main-effects approach to the world is easy to understand and easy to communicate. A drawback is that it might ignore other important variables, particularly in cases where variables affect each other in unpredictable sequences (e.g., the biological/systems model of the world).

THE LINCHPIN MODEL OF CHANGE

It's a given that the world and your organization are complex. Depending on the time of day, the weather, and the mood of your people, the same action might have different results. Feedback loops can create all sorts of inadvertent results from your actions—and be hard to measure. Despite this complexity, I'm going to advocate what I call a "linchpin" model of change.

To get things done, it's most useful to look for simple, main effects. Or in the metaphor of the Gordian knot, it's easier to use the "sword" of a single focus to cut through the knot to create your changes rather than trying to trace each aspect of the knot and untie one thread at a time.

I call this a linchpin model because a linchpin is a key piece that holds important parts together. From the focused effort of changing the linchpin, you can make major changes in more complex structures.

Staying with the Gordian knot analogy, you might look at it as pulling on a single thread. While that wasn't sufficient to untie the Gordian knot, if you hammer one message over and over and don't allow yourself to be distracted, pulling on one thread will begin to unravel other issues which will cause other effects. While the effects are complex, your action was focused on one simple step.

MAIN EFFECTS → MAIN RESULTS

A Real Biological Systems Model

Here's an example for those who believe that life is too complex to achieve anything with simple, main effects. Let's take the case of diet. The human body is the ultimate in complex biological systems. If you start getting into its complexities, you quickly become overwhelmed. Everything can be related to everything. The amount of light that reaches the pineal gland may affect how you metabolize fat, which may interact with the time of day you eat, which may interact with the food you eat, with your mood, etc.

Calories consumed illustrate a simple main effect. If you go on a starvation diet and stop eating, it's not healthful, but you do lose weight. Many experts would tell you that you lose the wrong weight and when you gain it back it changes your body composition, which further complicates the results. Be that as it may, in World War II there was an experiment that makes my point.

Diet Or Fight!

There were very few conscientious objectors in World War II. It was a war that almost everybody supported. However, the Quaker faith does not believe in violence and war. There were a number of conscientious objectors from the ranks of the Quakers, men who served as medics and ambu-

"Focus means...setting a clear, realistic mission, and then working tirelessly to make sure everyone—from the chairman to the middle manager to the hourly employee—understands it."
—*Fortune* magazine

lance drivers and did other noncombat jobs.

One group of Quakers and other conscientious objectors in Minnesota were used in a Federal government study to see how to best rehabilitate people who had experienced starvation in concentration camps and other areas in Europe. First, they starved the volunteers until their body weights were as low as possible. Needless to say, the effects of starvation were profound. The volunteers became obsessed with food. For instance, the experimenters had to limit how much gum they could have, because some were chewing a pack of gum at a time just to get the extra calories. The volunteers would dream about food. Many changed their careers for the rest of their lives—they became chefs or took other food-related jobs.

The experimenters tested different ways to bring the starved people back to sound health. Some volunteers were fed high-carbohydrate diets, some high-protein diets, some lots of sugar, some vitamins and minerals, and so forth.

The Results: Just Feed Them

The results showed that it didn't matter what you fed starving people—what mattered was the total intake of calories. The fastest way to bring people back from starvation to a reasonable state of health was to give them as much food (calories) as they could eat, of whatever foods they liked. It didn't matter what the mix of vitamins, starches, fats, proteins, and so forth, was.

Here we have, in the most complex of all systems—the human body—a simple, main effect. If you take calories away, people lose weight and become obsessed with food. If you give them calories, they gain weight and return to health.

Cause	Effect
Calorie reduction	Weight loss; obsession with food
Calorie replacement	Weight gain; return to health

BENEFITS OF A LINCHPIN MAIN EFFECT

Using a complex model may always be more accurate for describing change in organizations *after the fact*. But to *create* change, it's more effective to communicate a simple message over and over in order to get your message out strongly and accurately to your audiences.

Another reason a simple linchpin approach to change works, is that it gives people something to believe in and something about which to be passionate. When you have to keep track of dozens of factors, it's hard to have much enthusiasm for any one of them.

The Attention Deficit

Most people use less than half of their intelligence when reading memos or listening to speeches or reading newsletters. Some people don't read anything, they just ask other people, "What was it all about?" Other people are distracted, thinking about their jobs, or their personal problems, or the opposite sex.

To put it bluntly, most people respond with the intelligence level of a small child to many of your "important" messages. This means that to get your message across effectively, you must be focused. Then you're going to have to repeat it over and over, so that your message has a chance to seep through their distractions.

"Now, listen carefully, you will make customers happy; you will make customers happy..."

The Credibility Deficit: Ready, Aim, Aim

Company change-programs often fail due to lack of interest. Management will announce plans

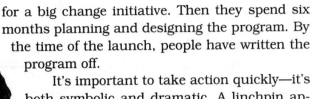

for a big change initiative. Then they spend six months planning and designing the program. By the time of the launch, people have written the program off.

It's important to take action quickly—it's both symbolic and dramatic. A linchpin approach makes this possible. I'm suggesting a "ready, fire, aim" experimental model of change, rather than a "ready, aim, aim, aim, aim" model.

In the parlance of the Old West, I'm looking for a quick draw with a six shooter, not a gentleman with a single-shot dueling pistol. In the "ready, fire, aim" approach, the results of your first shot give you information that allows you to adjust your aim so that your next bullets hit their target more accurately.

By saying that change is an experiment, you're not starting with an immaculate reengineering plan from "on high." An experimental label encourages input from the ranks to adjust your efforts as you all learn. It also encourages a culture of continuous change.

SPEED AS A CHANGE KEY

Speed is one simple example of how my linchpin theory applies to create multiple changes.

Speed Up Everything!

Let's take speed, much beloved by Tom Peters (and me), as a linchpin model application. If you want to make changes in your organization, speeding up processes makes sense. If you have quicker turns of inventory, deliver things faster, and develop products faster, you gain advantages in the marketplace—and you lower your costs. Speed can be a linchpin to keep the wheels rolling.

To get a speed initiative going, you'll need a champion—a necessary ingredient in all successful changes. The champion can simply advocate, "Let's make everything faster. Let's answer the phone on one ring instead of five rings. Let's have a policy to return all calls within an hour instead of a day. Let's use just-in-time. Let's cut product

> ## Just-In-Time
>
> Just-in-time (JIT) is a manufacturing strategy to reduce inventory costs by delivering parts to the assembly line from suppliers' trucks—just as they are needed.

development cycles. Let's collect information from customers faster. Let's collect our receivables faster, etc."

Speed is a simple message. And, there's so much waste and slack time in today's average organization that everyone knows there is room to get things done faster. For instance, an insurance company found that it took a month to process an application—two hours of actual work, and twenty days of waiting and paper-moving from one department to another!

An Example Of Speed

The insurance company, Life USA, makes everything revolve around speed. Life USA guarantees to make commission payments to agents within 24 hours, and responds to questions from them within 48 minutes. It issues policies to customers within 48 hours.

In order to support these speed promises, Life USA had to improve the flow of information within the organization—and get buy-in from the employees. To enlist the staff in the speed mission, they offer shared ownership. They implemented electronic processing of money transfers to pay commissions promptly. They also developed a better flow of documents with zero waiting time in order to process policies faster. Of course, there are other influences, but they've grown fast, recruited agents fast, and sold billions of dollars in policies with higher productivity per worker.

Other Speedy Examples

Life USA is not alone in being able to make big changes through speedy implementation. Northwestern National Insurance revamped their procedures so price quotes could be produced immediately on a laptop computer. This cut their costs and increased their success rate 50%. (Prospects would often use the lag time between their request for a quote and receiving it to shop around for a better deal.)

Any industry can benefit from speed. Doyle Wilson is the fastest home builder in Texas. Plus, his company won a Baldrige Award for quality. They average 124 days from permit to completion. This short cycle saves them money on carrying costs, allows them to "turn" inventory faster, and increases customer satisfaction.

Farnell Components is the European distribution hub of a large electronics company. They use speed to focus their business. They want workers to answer 99% of calls *before* the caller hears it ring, and 100% by two rings. They must ship 99% of components out the same day, etc. They link their top speed goals with bonuses for workers.

The Food and Drug Law Institute used to take four to six weeks to fulfill an order. After setting up a centralized service department, they cut turnaround time to 48 hours, a change that thrilled customers. In order to deliver better service, they cross-trained reps so employees could fill in for each other. After the fact, they said that all of their changes were obvious—they don't know why they didn't think of them sooner!

In a complex system, you need to have a linchpin that people can believe in and cling to in times of difficulty and doubt—in other words, in times of change!

> "The '90s will be a...nanosecond culture. There'll be only two kinds of managers: the quick and the dead."
> —David Vice,
> Northern Telecom
> Vice Chairman

Linchpin + Complexity

Despite my presentation of the world of change as multivariate versus main effects, reality is a complex shade of gray. When you have a single thread that you pull on, like speed, it tends to involve ever-increasing numbers of other variables in the organization—hence the term linchpin.

In order to answer the phone on the first ring, you might have to staff the phones better. In order to staff the phones better, you may have to cross-train people. In order to get back to people within an hour, you might have to standardize pro-

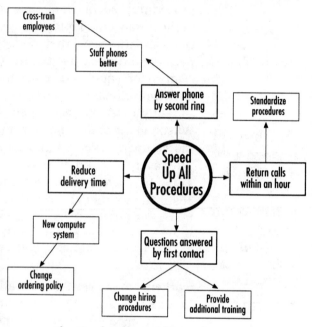

The Ripple Effects Of A Linchpin

cedures. In order to have customers' phone queries answered by their first contact, you might have to hire differently, provide additional training, etc. In order to deliver orders faster, you might have to change your computer system and change your ordering policy.

A single, major linchpin can cause the organizational chart to be turned upside down. Everything in the organization has to be changed, in order to support the linchpin feature. The single, linchpin issue causes complex changes throughout the organizational system.

A MARKETING ANALOGY

The power of a single key idea that permeates an entire business is also an important concept in the marketing field. It's called "positioning." The idea is to generate a simple message in the minds of the consumer that differentiates your product or service from those of everyone else. You want people to remember your product as the "toothpaste with fluoride" or "the toothpaste for people who can't brush after every meal" or "the cigarette for wanna-be cowboys."

Jack Trout (who coined the term "positioning") says that the first person or company in a category has the big advantage. For example, there were mainframe computers, minicomputers, and personal computers. When new vendors come into that market, they would try to carve out a new position (like mini/mainframe, or work station) in order to differentiate themselves from the other categories that were already occupied.

Moral: The easiest way to be the category leader? Start your own category!

To tie the marketing analogy directly to organizational change, you need a strong positioning statement that people can identify with. You need to market your change both within the organization and outside the organization to suppliers, customers, and other stakeholders. It's not a good marketing—or management—position to expound: "We're involved in a complex, interactive, multivariate change effort which, through interative effects, we expect to result in a stronger company that will serve you better."

It's much more powerful to have that linchpin or single major cause, and say, "We're going to serve you better by speeding up all of our procedures." This is a position that you can easily "sell" both inside and outside the company. Employees and customers remember it. It's clear, it's understandable, and it can have dramatic and rewarding results.

Pre-empt The Truth

If you have nothing different about yourself, you can "pre-empt the truth," like the beer company that fifty years ago talked about their bottles being washed in "live steam." At the time, everybody's bottles were washed in live steam, but nobody had capitalized on it in print. "Washed in live steam" became a position that was successful and defensible, and implied that everyone else's bottles were not as sterile.

A VALUES EXAMPLE

Values is a somewhat controversial area that provides an example of a linchpin model of change.

Much of the confusion about values in the business arena comes from the false assumption that values are synonymous with "goodness." Not all values involve goodness. Values can vary from something as vague as "beauty" to morality or even ruthlessness.

A big advantage of incorporating values into your organization's mission is that values can produce a vision to which customers and employees are attracted. Not everyone has to agree with your vision and values. The Fascist world domination vision of Adolf Hitler was powerful enough to almost destroy the world. It's an example of values and missions that aren't "good" at all.

When you have clear, simple values that everyone in the company understands, it becomes easy to identify gaps between what you believe and how you perform. Thus, real value statements can help companies or individuals "walk their talk."

When you truly believe in your values, they apply to both your personal and business life. They help you to integrate yourself, rather than be schizophrenically split, where you are ferocious in a dog-eat-dog business environment, but a kind contributor to the community at home.

Values Are A Growing Force

There is a broader, sociological reason why organizations that represent values with which employees can identify will be more successful. Workers coming out of the Depression were interested in job security. This fit with a corporate machine model, where people were interchangeable cogs. And it allowed many under-

Visionary Companies

Another label for companies with a clear mission that people can identify with is "visionary companies." A Stanford Business School study of long-term stock performance by Collins and Porras concluded that "visionary companies have outperformed the general market by 55 times."

trained, undereducated people to be employed at high-productivity, high-paying jobs in auto factories and assembly lines.

The Baby Boom generation do not have that Depression mentality. It isn't satisfying enough for them to fill a space in an assembly line and put a peg in a hole. They want jobs that are meaningful and fulfilling. Today's boomer employees, consumers, and their families are interested in identity issues—in the products they buy and use, and the companies from which they buy them.

In the services area, these values translate into what I like to call "bedside manner." Two lawyers might be equally skilled technically, but if one treats you impersonally and another is warm and friendly, it's almost a sure bet that you will choose to work with the latter. From a mechanistic organizational perspective, the two lawyers would be considered interchangeable, and an analyst might wonder why the first lawyer was more successful than the second.

A practical problem with values-inspired change is that most organizations are unable to focus on a narrow enough band of values to inspire or activate a program. If a committee creates the values statement of the company, it often comes out a generic mish-mash of "motherhood and apple pie." Everybody's for good service, fair treatment of employees, high quality, speed, efficiency, good profitability, product innovation, opportunities for employee advancement, good communication, a creative environment, and dozens of other "nice" values.

In support of my linchpin approach, practitioners find that when the list of values numbers more than five, focus is lost.

> "When aligned around shared values, and united in a common purpose, ordinary people accomplish extraordinary results."
> —Ken Blanchard and Michael O'Connor, *Managing by Values*

"Good" Values Position You

The Businesses for Social Responsibility group—headlined by Ben and Jerry's, The Body

Shop, Tom's of Maine, but including many other companies—have carved out new positions in the marketplace based on social "goodness" values (e.g., taking care of the environment, treating employees well, etc.).

All Companies Have Values

Old-line companies say that the only thing that counts in life is the bottom line; a company's only responsibility is to their stockholders, etc. Bill Gates, Jack Welch, and other gurus have stated that values are irrelevant to business. But Bill Gates is thinking of values as only a social goodness mandate, rather than the actual values that Microsoft obviously represents by their behavior. Microsoft tries to hire the smartest people, they work them very hard, they try to dominate every marketplace they're in, they're persistent, etc. Jack Welch, at GE, has similar values—such as to get out of any market where they can't be Number One or Number Two.

The old-line backlash against social-goodness values is stupid, because "goodness" has become a new marketing position for companies. Any company that can win support from employees, consumers, and other stakeholders will do far better on their bottom line. Other things being equal, people would rather buy a product that they felt was good for the environment than one that was bad. The best way to be successful is to meet other people's needs. One of those needs is to be associated with "good" companies, and thus, vicariously, feel that you're doing good.

Unfortunately, the "values" that underlie most bureaucratic organizations are: cover your ass, do only as much as you need to get by, and don't rock the boat.

Those organizations that are more likely to throw off bureaucratic culture use values like customer service or fun, and tools like worker

"Employees need values they can believe in. Without a reason to believe in the values and mission of an organization, profits and productivity will decline—and our Country's position will erode."
—Susan and Thomas Kuczmarski, *Values-Based Leadership*

"A sense of mission is the source of peak performance."
—Charles Garfield, *Peak Performers: The New Heroes of American Business*

empowerment and worker ownership. These values can help you to cut through the B.S. and focus everyone's energy on passionately delivering your services and products.

BIG BREAKS VERSUS SMALL STEPS

Just as I started by dividing the world into multivariate versus main-effect styles of thinking, we can divide approaches to change into two types.

You can't cross a 20-foot chasm in two 10-foot jumps.
—Old Irish saying

The first can be the "earthquake model." For instance, if you're going to merge two companies, do it! It's much better to downsize and take a big hit in your earnings one year than to keep the threat alive for years as you lay off people in waves. Perhaps this earthquake model is aligned with the main-effects model. People who see single, major effects may also prefer one revolutionary move.

The other approach is the incremental improvements of Kaizen (small, continuous changes). Logically, it may be that people who see life as complex and multivariate would prefer to tweak each variable in small, evolutionary steps.

TOWARDS INTEGRATION: A SINGLE FOCUS IN A COMPLEX WORLD

To get away from the simplistic black-and-white world, I'd like to suggest that the main-effects model actually works with an incremental change strategy as well. Focusing on one thing, like speed or values is a clear way to get started, a way that involves people. Then, depending on your situation, each of the steps that ripple outward from that key principle can either be small and incremental or create a tidal wave as one thing leads to another.

ACTION SUMMARY

"In a moment of decision, the best thing you can do is the right thing, the next best is the wrong thing, and the worst thing you can do is nothing."
—Theodore Roosevelt

This is the end of the chapter, and the book. The whitewaters of constant change around us can be distracting, but they also keep us moving forward to new places.

If you're involved in a change effort—formal or informal, business or personal—the best thing you can do is make your decisions based on the information you have, and take action. Your action will give you feedback which you can use to adjust your course. That's the way it happens in a complex world, even when you're guided by a focused, linchpin vision!

▶ Decide which view of the world you're most comfortable with: complex, multifactor, or main effects. What approaches to change will work best for your style?

▶ When communicating about change to others, deliver one clear simple message.

▶ Recognize that you have to "sell" changes to your employees, customers, and stakeholders. Develop a clear "positioning" statement. Will your audience respond best to changes driven by speed, customer service, values, or _____?

▶ For big, negative changes like downsizing, I recommend making them all at once. For organizational culture changes, I recommend incrementally introducing small steps that revolve around one main effect.

▶ Take action quickly to get momentum on your side. Use the results to guide your next "shot."

▶ A main-effects model of change can help you in making either big changes or incremental changes.

RESOURCES AND RECOMMENDING READING

Adizes, Ichak. *Corporate Lifecycles: How and Why Corporations Grow and Die and What to Do about It.* Paramus, NJ: Prentice Hall, 1988.

Argyris, Chris. *Knowledge for Action: A Guide to Overcoming Barriers to Organizational Change.* San Francisco, CA: Jossey-Bass, 1993.

Berry, Leonard. *On Great Service.* New York: Free Press, 1995.

Blanchard, Kenneth, and Michael O'Connor. *Managing By Values.* San Francisco: Berret Koehler, 1996.

Burrus, Daniel. *Technotrends.* New York: Harper Business, 1994.

Bridges, William. *Transitions: Making Sense of Life's Changes.* Reading, MA: Addison-Wesley, 1980.

Bridges, William. *Managing Transition: Making the Most of Change.* Reading, MA: Addison-Wesley, 1980.

Crosby, Philip. *Quality Is Still Free: Making Quality Certain in Uncertain Times.* New York: McGraw-Hill, 1995.

Drucker, Peter. *Managing for the Future.* New York: Penguin Group, 1992.

Covey, S.R. *The 7 Habits of Highly Effective People.* New York: Simon and Schuster, 1989.

Csikszentmihalyi, M. *Flow. The Psychology of Optimal Experience.* New York: Harper Perennial, 1990.

Daniels, William R. *Breakthrough Performance: Managing for Speed and Flexibility.* New York: AMACOM, 1995.

DeBono, E. *Six Thinking Hats.* Boston: Little, Brown, & Co., 1985.

DeBono, E. *Sur/Petition: Going Beyond Competition.* New York, Harper Business, 1993.

DuBrin, Andrew J. *10-Minute Guide to Effective Leadership.* New York: Simon & Schuster, 1997.

Gardner J. *Self Renewal: The Individual and the Innovative Society.* New York: W.W. Norton, 1984.

Glassman, E. *Creativity Handbook: Shift Paradigms and Harvest Creative Thinking at Work.* Chapel Hill, NC: The LCS Press, 1991.

Grossman, S.R., Rodgers, Bruce E., Moore, Beverly R. *Innovation, Inc. Unlocking Creativity in the Workplace.* Plano, TX: Wordware Publishers, 1988.

Hamel, Gary, and C.K. Prahalad. *Competing for the Future.* Boston: Harvard Business School Press, 1994.

Handy, Charles. *The Age of Paradox.* Boston: Harvard Business School Press, 1994.

Harrington-Mackin, Deborah. *Keeping the Team Going.* New York: AMACOM, 1996

Imai, Masaaki. *Kaizen: The Key to Japan's Competitive Success.* New York: McGraw-Hill, 1986.

Kotter, John P. *Leading Change.* Boston: Harvard Business School Press, *1996.*

Kuczmarski, Susan S. and Thomas D. Kuczmarski. *Values-Based Leadership.* Paramus, NJ: Prentice Hall, 1994.

LeBoeuf, M. *Imagineering: How to Profit from your Creative Powers.* New York: A Berkeley Book, 1980.

London, Manuel. *Change Agents: New Roles and Innovation Strategies for Human Resource Professionals.* San Francisco: Jossey-Bass, 1988.

Michalko, M. *Thinkertoys.* Berkeley, CA: Ten Speed Press, 1991.

Nelson, Bob. *1001 Ways to Reward Employees.* New York: Workman Publishing, 1995.

Peters, T. *The Pursuit of Wow.* New York: Vintage Books, 1994.

Potts, Tom, and Arnold Sykes. *Executive Talent: How to Identify & Develop the Best.* Homewood, IL: Business One Irwin, 1992.

Ray, M. *Creativity in Business.* New York: Doubleday, 1986.

Reichheld, Frederick R. with Thomas Teal. *The Loyalty Effect.* Boston: Harvard Business School Press, 1996.

Reynolds, Mary Robinson. *You Are a Success: 61 Proven Strategies for Developing Success.* Portland, OR: Heart Publications, 1991.

Schuster, John P. *Hum-Drum to Hot-Diggity: Creating Everyday Greatness in the World of Work.* Kansas City, MO: Steadfast Publications, 1993.

Scott, Cynthia D., and Dennis T. Jaffe. *Managing Change at Work.* Crisp Publications, 1989.

Scott, Cynthia D., and Dennis T. Jaffe. *Managing Personal Change.* Crisp Publications, 1989.

Spector, Robert. *The Nordstrom Way.* New York: Wiley, 1996.

Stack, Jack. *The Great Game of Business.* New York: Doubleday Currency, 1992.

Timm, Paul. *50 Powerful Ideas You Can Use to Keep Your Customers.* Hawthorn, NJ: Career Press.

Tompkins, James A. *The Genesis Enterprise: Creating Peak-toPeak Performance.* New York: McGraw-Hill, 1995.

Walton, Mary. *Deming Management at Work.* New York: Perigee Books, 1990.

Whitely, Richard, and Diane Hessan. *Customer-Centered Growth.* Reading, MA: Addison-Wesley, 1996.

INDEX